THE
WINE PRESS

AND

THE CELLAR

A MANUAL FOR
THE WINE-MAKER AND THE CELLAR-MAN

By EMMET HAWKINS RIXFORD

125TH-ANNIVERSARY EDITION
FOREWORD BY PAUL DRAPER

Robert Mondavi Institute
for Wine and Food Science
UCDAVIS

Robert Mondavi Institute for Wine and Food Science
University of California, Davis
One Shields Avenue
Davis, California 95616-5270
Web site: rmi.ucdavis.edu

ISBN-13: 978-0-9816345-0-0
Library of Congress Control Number: 2008928702

Originally published in San Francisco in 1883 by
Payot, Upham and Co.

125th-Anniversary Edition
Copyright © 2008
Regents of the University of California for the
Robert Mondavi Institute for Wine and Food Science
All rights reserved

No part of this publication may be reproduced, stored in a retrieval system, or transmitted, in any form or by any means, electronic, mechanical, photocopying, recording or otherwise, without written permission of the publisher.

Printed in the United States of America on acid-free archival paper.
Fong & Fong Printers and Lithographers, Sacramento, California
Lincoln & Allen Bindery, Portland, Oregon

The University of California does not discriminate in any of its policies, procedures or practices. The University is an affirmative action/equal opportunity employer.

Emmet Hawkins Rixford
February 2, 1841 – August 19, 1928
Portrait from Wellington C. Wolfe, *Men of California* (c. 1901).

FOREWORD

Born in Vermont in 1841, Emmet Hawkins Rixford came to San Francisco in 1869 to practice law; his avocation soon became winemaking. Drawing on American and European sources, he read all he could find on the subject. His organization of this material became *The Wine Press and the Cellar,* published in 1883. As Rixford notes in the preface, the book "is the result of research on the part of the author chiefly for his own benefit." In it, he hopes "that the beginner will always find a safe course pointed out to him . . . and that the experienced viniculturist will have brought to his mind many things forgotten."

Later that year (November 14, 1883), Rixford purchased forty acres of hillside land in Woodside, on the San Francisco Peninsula. There, he is said to have planted his vineyard to cabernet sauvignon, merlot, verdot and malbec—in the same proportions as had been planted at Châteaux Margaux, whose wines he particularly admired. He built a beautiful stone-and-redwood winery on the Woodside property and, by the 1890s, was making his first La Questa cabernets.

In 1915, the *American Wine Press* lauded Rixford the winemaker: "It is the work of just such men as Mr. Rixford that has done much to raise the standard of California vintages. The more there are of such men the higher will be the name and reputation of American wines as a whole." Leon Adams, dean of American wine writers, states in *The Wines of America* that Rixford "grew some of the most prized of all California Cabernets." In *American Wines*, published in 1941, Frank Schoonmaker and Tom Marvel write: "On most of the California wine lists of the early 1900's, the most expensive Cabernet listed was that produced by E. H. Rixford at the La Questa vineyard."

Rixford was an early advocate of making a single wine from a suitable site, rather than the typical California approach: plant every varietal imaginable; make many different wines. Reviews of his book were quite positive. Some of the most perceptive and appreciative comments came in a letter (published in the *San Francisco Merchant*) from one of California's most respected wine authorities, Professor E.W. Hilgard from the University of California, Berkeley. He praises Rixford's emphasis on terroir:

> You have certainly gathered into that unpretending volume a vast amount of just the kind of practical information so much needed by our wine-makers, now that it is getting to be understood that quality, and not only quantity, will hereafter determine the question of profit and loss. . . . The brevity and terseness of statement in your book will encourage numbers of vineyardists[,] who have heretofore trusted to luck for the result of their vintage, to systematize their work . . . corresponding to the natural condition of their locality and the character of its grape product. . . . Some of the best [California wines] have until recently been obtained by accident, rather than intelligent design, and could not be duplicated when wanted without the intervention of the dubious arts of the wine-doctor. Your little volume, in rendering accessible to all readers [an] easily intelligible summary of the whole subject of wine-making, leaves no excuse for the graver faults that have heretofore prevailed so extensively.

The Wine Press and the Cellar was the first book I read on winemaking. In the 1960s and 1970s, I was privileged to taste wines from great vintages of the top Bordeaux châteaux—the 1928s

---

La Questa
ONE OF THE
Finest Red Wines
IN THE WORLD

IS MADE from the same varieties of grapes as those which produce the famous Château Wines of the Médoc in France, grown in the owner's vineyard, at Woodside, San Mateo County, California.

The wine is all bottled at the vineyard, and sold in cases only.

PRODUCER
E. H. RIXFORD
Kohl Building   San Francisco, Cal.

Advertisement from George Wharton James, *The 1910 Trip of the Hotel Men's Mutual Benefit Association to California and the Pacific Coast* (1911).

1938

FOUNDED  IN 1883

WOODSIDE
CABERNET

PRODUCED & BOTTLED AT THE WINERY BY

LA QUESTA VINEYARD

WOODSIDE, REDWOOD CITY
CALIFORNIA

ALCOHOL 12% BY VOLUME

and '29s, the '45s, '47s and '49s, among others. Likewise, I had the far rarer opportunity to taste the Fountain Grove, Simi and Larkmead zinfandels from 1935, '37 and '39, the Inglenook cabernets from 1934 to 1939 and—most relevant—the 1936 and 1938 La Questa cabernets. In the 1970s, Esquin Imports of San Francisco offered half-bottles of the 1938 La Questa; several collectors still have it in their cellars. The opinions of those I have talked to coincide with mine: It is one of the finest California cabernets of any era. These wines convinced me that traditional techniques could not only produce great wine, but wine that is more complex, more interesting and finer than any relying on a modern, more technological approach.

So, how had these wines been made? What was the practical, day-to-day cellar work that guided their transformation from grapes to wine?

Rixford's book was the first—and, it seemed, only—publication in English containing a clear description of those practices. In essence, it lays out how the great Bordeaux and the finest California wines of the late nineteenth century had been made, and were still made until the mid-twentieth century.

These techniques, augmented by further and necessary detail from Raimond Boireau's work—so extensively cited by Rixford—became the basis of my own winemaking.

Often, explanations of how a process works are rendered obsolete by what science subsequently learns. The basic approach, however, developed experimentally over centuries of winemaking, remains sound. E.H. Rixford's book is historic among American wine publications and remains a practical introduction and guide today. It is a joy to see it published again in this beautiful edition, so carefully modeled on the original.

Paul Draper
Ridge Vineyards
Santa Cruz Mountains
April 2008

THE
WINE PRESS

AND

THE CELLAR.

A MANUAL FOR
THE WINE-MAKER AND THE CELLAR-MAN.

By E. H. RIXFORD.

San Francisco :	New York :
PAYOT, UPHAM & CO.	D. VAN NOSTRAND.

1883.

Entered according to Act of Congress, in the year 1883, by

E. H. RIXFORD,

In the Office of the Librarian of Congress, at Washington.

C. W. GORDON,
Steam Book and Job Printer,
San Francisco, Cal.

PREFACE.

IN 1876 the Mission grape sold in California for from $7.50 to $10 per ton, and foreign varieties for from $14 to $18 per ton, and consequently many vineyardists in districts remote from the market turned their hogs into the vineyard to gather the fruit. At this time farmers concluded that it would not pay to grow grapes, and the vines were rooted out of many vineyards, and the land devoted to the production of more profitable crops. In 1878, however, the prices were better, and the Mission grape brought from $12 to $14 per ton, and the foreign varieties from $22 to $26, and under a growing demand for California wines, the wine makers in the counties of Sonoma and Napa have paid during the past three seasons of 1880, 1881, and 1882, prices ranging from $16 to $22 per ton for Mission, and from $22 to $35 for other foreign varieties, and in some cases even as high as $40 per ton for wine grapes of the best varieties; the extremes in prices depending upon the activity of the competition in the different localities. Although in California we are accustomed to speak of the "Mission grape" and the "foreign varieties" in contradistinction, it may not be amiss to state for the benefit of other than California readers, that the "Mission" is undoubtedly a grape of European origin, and was cultivated by the Spanish priests at the missions existing in the country at the advent of the Americans, and hence the name. And notwithstanding the existence of our grape, *Vitis Californica*, the names "native" and "California grape" have been applied to the Mission, but the word "foreign" is never used in describing it.

The increase in the price of grapes has followed closely upon the increase in the demand for our wines, and the production has kept pace with the demand.

PREFACE.

The annual shipments of wine and brandy from California, commencing with 1875, according to the reports published from time to time, are as follows, in gallons:

Year.	Wine.	Brandy.
1875	1,031,507	42,318
1876	1,115,045	59,993
1877	1,462,792	138,992
1878	1,812,159	129,119
1879	2,155,944	163,892
1880	2,487,353	189,098
1881	2,845,365	209,677

The figures for 1882, as published, are larger than those for 1881, but the figures furnished by Mr. Stone, the statistician of the Merchants Exchange, give wine 2,721,428, brandy, 218,792; from which I am led to believe that those for 1881 are too large.

The total production of wine for 1878 has been stated to be from 6,000,000 to 7,000,000 gallons, for 1879, 7,790,000, for 1880, 10,000,000 to 12,000,000 gallons. Notwithstanding the increased acreage of our vineyards, the product in 1881 fell off one or two million gallons, and in the second annual report of the State Viticultural Commission, just published, the loss is estimated at one-third of the crop, making the product 9,000,000 gallons, or a little less. That of 1882 is about 10,000,000 gallons.

In 1880 we had about 60,000 acres of vineyards in the State, and according to Mr. Haraszthy's report as President of the Viticultural Commission, contained in the report of the commission last mentioned, the increase during the first two years after the first organization of the commission in 1880, amounts to 40,000 acres. Since the date of his report, April 19, 1882, the acreage must have been largely increased, and making a liberal allowance for errors, we must have at least 100,000 acres in vineyards in the State at the present time, which ought to produce, at a small estimate, 20,000,000 gallons of wine in five years from now, and in five years more, with the increased product from the greater age of the vines, and from those planted in the meantime, the yield ought to be doubled.

PREFACE.

Among those who are now planting vineyards are many who have had no experience in wine making; and in order that such may have the advantage of the experience of those of other countries who have spent their whole lives in perfecting the art, and have had the benefit of the knowledge derived from generations before them, the author has prepared the following work, in which he has attempted to lay before the reader an account of the methods followed in those portions of Europe, especially France, where the finest wines of the world are produced.

What is here given is the result of research on the part of the author chiefly for his own benefit; and in going over the literature of the subject of wine making, he failed to find a work in the English language which is adequate to the needs of the practical wine maker, or one who intends to become such. There are many good books in the French language, and, in fact, the principal works on the subject are to be found in that language. But the authors of many of them have hobbies, and the practice indicated in a certain connection by one often differs from that pointed out by another. It, therefore, became necessary to compare the writings of various authors, and where they differed in points of practice, to try and find out the reason therefor. This was not always an easy task; but the author confidently hopes that the beginner will always find a safe course pointed out to him in the following pages, and that the experienced viniculturist will have brought to his mind many things forgotten in the multitude of affairs, and the experimentalist, to whom we all are looking for further light, will here find many hints which may assist him in finding out what are the best methods under the conditions in which we find ourselves in the infancy of this absorbing industry.

What forcibly strikes one in reading the works of different authors on the subject of vinification is, that, notwithstanding the variations in the methods, there are but few *material* differences in the practices in different localities in making a given kind of wine. It is true that one method makes a red wine, a different one makes a white wine, that grapes of one degree of ripeness and the corresponding practice in vinification produces a sweet wine, and another a dry wine, but the author is convinced that the method and practice which will produce the best result in a given case in one locality will also produce the best result in any other.

If it is found that in the northern and central portions of France it is insisted that the casks be always kept full, and that in Spain they are left with a vacant space, it will also be found that this practice depends upon the alcoholic strength and robustness of the wine. When the grapes of the more northern regions are artificially matured till their saccharine strength approaches that of grapes of more southern climes, then the wine made from their must may safely be treated according to methods prevailing in the latter regions. If, on the other hand, the grapes of hot countries are gathered as soon as their must indicates a density of 20 to 24 per cent., the wine made from them would be absolutely ruined, if treated as the wine from overripe grapes, and it must be cared for as the weaker wines of the northern climes.

The essentials, then, of good wine making, which include the treatment in the cellar, are everywhere the same, and they only vary with the varieties of wine that are to be produced.

The general climate of California corresponds in many respects with that of the more southern wine-producing regions of Europe; and the percentage of sugar carried in the grapes grown in the southern and interior portions of our State is about the same as that of the musts of those regions. The musts produced in the central coast counties and the bay counties of the State, in average seasons, equal, if they do not exceed, in density the musts of the central and northern portions of France in their very best seasons.

The following tables will afford the figures necessary for a comparison between our wines and those of other countries, as to alcoholic strength and acidity. The first table is useful as illustrating an advance in wine making in this State. The earlier wine makers, guided by the experience derived from residence in the northern viticultural regions of Europe, or by the information from writers of those countries, allowed their grapes to arrive at an advanced state of maturity without considering the different conditions of climate. Musts, therefore, that were fit only for sweet wines, were treated according to dry wine methods, and no wonder they were found heady, used as table wines, with so high a percentage of alcohol.

The second table shows that we have learned to produce lighter wines, which means, not only that we are growing grapes that carry less sugar than the Mission, but chiefly that we do not allow the berries to become overripe, dried up, under the ardent rays of our constant sun.

The first figures are from a paper read by the late Major Snyder before the Napa Wine Growers' Association, and published in the *Rural Press*, August 3, 1871, Vol. IV, p. 66.

Color.	Name of Maker.	Year.	Vol. per cent. of Alcohol.
White	Craig	1867	Foreign grapes 14.4
"	"	1870	Mission 13.4
"	Dresel & Gundlach	1861	14.4
"	"	1870	13.3
"	"	1862	12.5
"	"	1867	13.6
"	J. R. Snyder	1865	Mission 12.5
"	"	1866	12.6
"	"	1867	13.3
"	"	1868	12.8
"	A. F. Haraszthy	1871	Foreign 11.5
"	"	1870	" 12.6
Red	Buena Vista Ass'n	1866	16.5
White	" "	1871	11.5
Red	" "	1871	12.6
White	H. Winkle	1869	Mission 13.2
"	"	1871	" 12.5
"	L. Goss	1871	Zinfandel 12.8

The following figures are from the Report of the Commissioner of Agriculture of the United States, for 1880, report of the Chemist. It will be observed that where the name is followed by a *, it is that of the Eastern dealer, and not that of the maker.

PREFACE.

DRY RED WINES.

Name.	Per cent. by vol. of alcohol.	Glucose.	Total acid as tartaric.	Maker.
Sonoma Mission, '79	10.03	None	.722	Gretsch & Mayer.*
" Zinfandel, 79	9.78	Trace	.693	" "
Mission	9.29	do	.917	B. Dreyfus & Co.
Zinfandel	11.35	do	.768	" "
Zinfandel, '78	10.30	do	.825	Dresel & Co.
Zinfandel, '78	11.08	do	.798	" "
Zinfandel	12.31	do	.814	Geo. Hamlin & Co.*
California Claret	10.56	do	.903	
Zinfandel	13.24	0.18	.726	

DRY WHITE WINES.

White Hock	17.37	0.09	.855	
White Hock	12.87	0.09	.767	
Muscatel	13.34	0.12	.767	
Sonoma Hock	12.05	0.13	.422	Perkins, Stern & Co*
Riesling	11.26	Trace	.846	Dresel & Co.
Hock	11.35	do	.785	" "
Dry Muscat	11.44	do	.619	Dreyfus & Co.
Zinfandel	11.26	do	.590	" "
Riesling	12.05	do	.696	" "
Gutedel	11.70	do	.756	" "
Hock	9.70	do	.723	" "
Sonoma Mission, '78	10.56	do	.619	Gretsch & Mayer.*
" Riesling. '77(?)	13.15	do	.695	" "
" " '79	13.15	do	.575	" "
" Mission, '79	10.38	do	.619	" "
" Gutedel, '79	11.87	do	.589	" "
Dry Muscat '74(?)	12.40	do	.816	" "
Zinfandel, '78	11.96	do	.761	" "
" '79	11.00	do	.740	" "

SWEET WINES.

PORT.

California Port	21.89	8.60	.790	
" "	20.89	5.78	.510	Kohler & Frohling.
" "	18.88	4.49	.755	Dreyfus & Co.

| | Per cent. by | | Total acid | |
Name.	vol. of alcohol.	Glucose.	as tartaric.	Maker.
California Port	19.87	5.88	.370	" "
" "	15.49	8.60	.486	Perkins, Stern & Co
"Sunny Slope"	15.12	11.57	.433	" "
Los Angeles	16.52	11.39	.508	Gretsch & Mayer.*

SHERRY.

California Sherry	17.96	.61	.532	
" "	16.15	2.45	.721	Dreyfus & Co.
" "	16.80	2.20	.573	" "

CHAMPAGNES.

"Grand Prize" med.dry	12.49	8.21	.821	Arpad Haraszthy.
"Eclipse," extra dry	11.87	6.51	.885	"

MISCELLANEOUS.

Gerke's White	14.74	2.21	.673	Henry Gerke.
Sweet Muscatel	18.58	25.37	.753	Perkins, Stern & Co
" "	22.36	11.59	.366	Dreyfus & Co,
" "	22.46	16.94	.331	" "
Los Angeles Muscatel	17.08	13.44	.533	Gretsch & Mayer.*
Angelica	11.79	12.48	.489	
"	13.90	13.25	.347	Perkins, Stern & Co
"	18.14	14.81	.430	Dreyfus & Co.
"	18.78	16.20	.466	Gretsch & Mayer.*
California Malaga	17.70	8.59	.659	Henry Gerke.

What is particularly striking in the figures last quoted, is the remarkably high percentage of acid, which far exceeds what we had hitherto supposed the acidity of our wines to be. Yet as a large proportion of the total acids was volatile, it may be that the wines had contracted acidity from improper methods of keeping.

From Prof. Hilgard's report of the work done in the viticultural laboratory of the College of Agriculture of the University of California, during the years 1881 and 1882, we extract Table V given in the appendix. The figures for the averages are our own. This report contains much valuable and interesting information regarding the work done in the laboratory, and gives many details of the analyses of these wines, which the limits of this volume will not permit us to give in full. And those who wish to see the results of the most complete analysis of California wines ever before made, are referred to the report itself.

It will be noticed that the average total acidity of the different wines mentioned in the table is much lower than that found by the chemist of the Department of Agriculture. The wines in this table were furnished by the producer in nearly every case, a few of them having been produced at the University, and were undoubtedly pure, and in a fair condition, as samples of badly kept wine would not likely be furnished by the maker for the purpose of analysis; and the condition of those analyzed by the chemist at Washington is, at least, doubtful.

From analyses by R. Fresenius and E. Borgman, tabulated in the *Journal of the Chemical Society*, London, for April, 1883, from *Zeits. Anal. Chem.*, XXII, 46–58, we extract the following figures, the alcoholic strength being reduced to volume per cent. as nearly as could be done from the per cent. by weight in volume without the specific gravity:

		Red Main.	White Main.	Hocks.	White French.	Red French.	Moselle.
Alcohol	Max.	11.76	12.54	12.77	12.17	11.52	10.77
	Min.	11.73	11.00	8.00	11.18	9.91	8.77
	Aver.	11 75	11.76	10.83	11.67	10.58	10.02
Acid	Max.	.62	.80	1.01	.71	.58	.95
	Min.	.54	.54	.48	.54	.48	.64
	Aver.	.58	.69	.66	.62	.54	.79

And from the analyses given in the work of Thudichum and Dupré, we deduce the following :

THIRTY-FIVE GERMAN WINES.

Vol. per cent. Alcohol { Maximum __ 14.45 / Minimum __ 9.15 / Average ___ 10.00 Acid as tartaric. { Maximum __ .823 / Minimum __ .416 / Average ___ .543

SIX FRENCH CLARETS.

Alcohol { Maximum __ 12.38 / Minimum __ 10.42 / Average ___ 10.95 Acid { Maximum __ .645 / Minimum __ .548 / Average ___ .593

FOUR BURGUNDIES.

Alcohol $\begin{cases} \text{Maximum}\_\_14.97 \\ \text{Minimum}\_\_11.54 \\ \text{Average}\_\_\_12.78 \end{cases}$ Acid $\begin{cases} \text{Maximum}\_\_ \ .668 \\ \text{Minimum}\_\_ \ .495 \\ \text{Average}\_\_\_ \ \cdot562 \end{cases}$

ELEVEN SHERRIES.

Alcohol $\begin{cases} \text{Maximum}\_\_22.75 \\ \text{Minimum}\_\_17.03 \\ \text{Average}\_\_\_20.93 \end{cases}$ Acid $\begin{cases} \text{Maximum}\_\_ \ .626 \\ \text{Minimum}\_\_ \ .372 \\ \text{Average}\_\_\_ \ .476 \end{cases}$

SIX SO-CALLED NATURAL SHERRIES.

Alcohol $\begin{cases} \text{Maximum}\_\_18.87 \\ \text{Minimum}\_\_16.60 \\ \text{Average}\_\_\_17.37 \end{cases}$ Acid $\begin{cases} \text{Maximum}\_\_ \ .510 \\ \text{Minimum}\_\_ \ .397 \\ \text{Average}\_\_\_ \ .454 \end{cases}$

ELEVEN PORT WINES.

Alcohol $\begin{cases} \text{Maximum}\_\_23.34 \\ \text{Minimum}\_\_18.04 \\ \text{Average}\_\_\_21.50 \end{cases}$ Acid $\begin{cases} \text{Maximum}\_\_ \ .510 \\ \text{Minimum}\_\_ \ .398 \\ \text{Average}\_\_\_ \ .424 \end{cases}$

TEN HUNGARIAN WINES.

Alcohol $\begin{cases} \text{Maximum}\_\_14.55 \\ \text{Minimum}\_\_11.55 \\ \text{Average}\_\_\_12.85 \end{cases}$ Acid $\begin{cases} \text{Maximum}\_\_ \ .716 \\ \text{Minimum}\_\_ \ .570 \\ \text{Average}\_\_\_ \ .637 \end{cases}$

The analyses of many other wines are given, and many other details which would be of little use to the practical man, belonging rather to the domain of the chemistry of wines.

There is a vast field open to the wine maker of this State, for we have differences of soil and climate suitable for the production of a wonderful variety of wines. But every man must decide for himself what kind of wine his soil and situation are best adapted to produce, and his aim then should be to produce the best of that kind.

Thanks to the work of the State Viticultural Commission, we are beginning to learn what varieties of grapes are best suited to the different districts of the State. It is true that only a beginning has been made, and the actual work of experimenting in this direction can only be carried on by the practical viticulturists themselves. It is for the Commission to bring order out of chaos, and furnish for the information of the public the results of the labors of the experimenters in the field.

Through the endeavors of the Commission, and especially of its chief executive Viticultural officer, Mr. Charles A. Wetmore, who has an extended knowledge of the different varieties of grapes grown in the State, and where they are produced, the viticulturists are beginning to compare notes, and an exchange of knowledge is now going on, which without the Commission would be impossible.

It is not within the scope of this work to enter into the details of vine planting, or to point out what particular varieties of grapes should be planted in the different sections, and probably the time to produce a work which would convey definite and satisfactory information on the latter subjcct has not yet arrived. As fast as reliable information is acquired, it will undoubtedly be made known by the Commission, and every intended vine grower should carefully study its reports, as well as to keep himself familiar with the discussions of the local viticultural societies, and those of the general conventions.

If every grower in the State will only devote a portion of his ground to the cultivation of the choicest varieties of grapes, making sure that he knows what he is cultivating, will use the best methods of vinification, preserve each kind of wine by itself, or keep a careful record of his blends, and will age and rear the different products according to the best and most intelligent methods, the writer confidently expects that favored spots will be found in time which will produce wines that will compare favorably with the fine wines of Europe; and we may even venture to hope that some lucky individual will find that he is possessed of a vineyard that will make his name famous as the producer of a grand wine equal to the most renowned wines of the world.

The writers lays claim to but very little originality in the the following pages. What the intended wine maker wants is not new, untried theories, but the results of the experience of others who have already labored in the field, in order that he may not spend his time in inventing methods which, later he learns, have already been tried by the laborers before him.

In this connection, the author makes his acknowledgments to the following authors and their productions, as well as to others mentioned in the body of the work. And if, in some cases, he has failed to give credit where it is due, it is because the information remains, but the source is forgotten.

A. Du Breuil, Les Vignobles et les Arbres et Fruits à Cidre, Paris, 1875.

Dr. Jules Guyot, Culture de la Vigne et Vinification, Paris, 1861.

Henri Machard, Traité Pratique sur les Vins, Bensançon, 1874.

Raimond Boireau, Culture de la Vigne, Traitement des Vins, Vinification, Distillation, etc., 2 vols., Bordeaux, 1876.

A. Haraszthy, Grape Culture, Wines, and Wine Making, New York, 1862, including translations of Johann Carl Leuchs on Wine Making, and Dr. L. Gall, Improvement in Wine Making.

L. Pasteur, on Fermentation, Annales de Chimie, 3 Series, Vol. LVIII, p. 330.

Joseph Boussingault, Sur la Fermentation des Fruits á Noyau Annales de Chimie, 4 Series, Vol. VIII, p. 210.

M. Boussingault, Expériences pour constater la perte en sucre dans le sucrage du moût de du marc de raisin. Annales de Chimie, 5 Series, Vol. VII, p. 433.

Andre Pellicot, Le Vigneron Provençal, Montpellier, 1866.

Henry Vizitelli, Facts about Sherry, London, 1876; Facts about Port and Madeira, London, 1880.

J. L. W. Thudichum and August Dupre, Origin, Nature, and Varieties of Wine, London, 1872.

N. Basset, Guide Théorique et Pratique du Frabricant d' Alcool et du Distillateur.

J. J. Griffin, Chemical Testing of Wines and Liquors, London.

L. F. Dubief, Traité Complet Théorique et Pratique de Vinification ou Art de Faire du Vin, 4 Ed., Paris.

P. Schutzenberger, On Fermentation, International Scientific Series, New York, 1876.

E. J. Maumene, Traité Théorique et Pratique du Travail des Vins, Paris, 1874.

M. W. Maigne, Nouveau Manuel Complet du Sommelier et du Marchand de Vins (Manuels-Roret), Paris, 1874.

DON PEDRO VERDAD, From Vineyard to Decanter, a Book about Sherry, London, 1876.

GEN. E. D. KEYES, Letter to Major J. R. Snyder, on Sherry making, published in San Francisco *Daily Evening Bulletin*, May 29, 1877.

PROF. E. W. HILGARD, Report of work done in the Viticultural Laboratory under the charge of F. W. Morse, University of California, College of Agriculture; Report of 1882, State Printer, Sacramento, 1883.

August, 1883.

CONTENTS.

PREFACE.

Prices of grapes in California from 1876 to 1882, the Mission grape, v; annual shipments of wine and brandy from California, annual production of wine, acreage of vines, probable future production of wine, vi; objects of this book, want of works on the subject in English, method of vinification varies with kind of wine rather than with locality or climate, vii; climate of California and density of must similar to those of southern Europe, viii; comparison between California and European wines, viii–xiii; State Viticultural Commission, xiii; advice to grape growers, xiv; acknowledgments by the author, list of authorities, xv.

CHAPTER I.
GATHERING THE GRAPES — MATURITY.

Utensils for picking, number of pickers necessary, when to commence, 1; when to gather, successive gathering, 2; sorting the grapes, requisite degree of maturity, 3; signs of ripeness, gathering before complete maturity, 4; gathering after complete maturity, ripeness according to required strength, 5.

CHAPTER II.
MUST.

Composition, grape sugar, 6; must scale, 7; testing for sugar, 8; correcting for temperature, 10; sugar and alcohol, alcohol in wine, 11.

CHAPTER III.
SUGARING AND WATERING MUST.

Sugaring, 13; nothing gained by adding sugar, 15; cost of glucose wine, 16; experiment with glucose, the use of glucose condemned, 17; watering, 18.

CHAPTER IV.
STEMMING AND CRUSHING.

Diversity of opinion on stemming, effect of stemming, proper practice, 20; to estimate tannin, stemmers, 21; how to remove the stems, crushing, methods of crushing, 22; aerating the must, crushers, 23; rapidity of operation, special practice, 24.

xviii *CONTENTS.*

CHAPTER V.
FERMENTATION — ITS CAUSES.

Several different kinds of fermentation, alcoholic fermentation, the yeast plant, 25; functions of yeast, normal conditions of the life of yeast, 26; action of various chemical and physical agents, 28; viscous or mannitic fermentation, lactic fermentation, 29; acetic fermentation, 30; origin of ferments, 31; ALCOHOLIC FERMENTATION IN WINE MAKING: vinous or alcoholic fermentation, sugar, 32; alcohol by weight and by volume, 33; fermentation, its products, per cent. sugar to per cent. alcohol, different authors, 34; limits of sugar and spirit, 36; temperature, 37; fermenting houses, 38.

CHAPTER VI.
RED WINE.

Coloring matter, fermenting tanks or vats, filling the tanks, 39; open vats, closed vats, 40; the best practice, 41; hermetically sealed tanks, practice in the Médoc, stirring the pomace in the vat, 42; when to draw from the vat, 43; the objections to long vatting, in making fine wines, 44; how to know when to draw from the vat, method of drawing from the vat and filling the casks, 45; wine presses, 46; pressing and press wine, special practice for fine wines, TREATMENT OF RED WINES: insensible fermentation, 47; ulling or filling up, 48; summary of the rules for the treatment of new red wines, 50; treatment of old red wines, 51; summary of rules for the care of old red wines, 53.

CHAPTER VII.
WHITE WINE.

Made from both red and white grapes, differences between red and white wine, hygienic effect of red and white wine, 54; process of making, the barrels, filling the barrels during fermentation, 55; pressing and filling, different kinds of white wine, dry white wines, mellow white wines, 56, sweet white wines, grand white wines, 57; treatment of white wines, to keep sweet, 58; dry white wines, mellow white wines, 59; summary of rules, racking, 60.

CHAPTER VIII.
CASKS.

Different woods, oak wood, storing casks, 61; new casks, 62; old casks, rinsing chain, visitor to examine the inside of a cask, 63; empty casks, washing, sulphuring casks, condition to be examined, 64; flatness in the cask, acidity, mouldy casks, 65; rottenness, brandy casks, caution as to sulphuring, cask borers, 66; size of casks, 67.

CONTENTS.

CHAPTER IX.
SULPHURING. ARRESTING FERMENTATION.

Sulphuring casks, must and wine, sulphurous oxide or sulphur dioxide, the sulphurer or sulphur burner, 69; sulphur matches or bands, to sulphur a cask, 70; to sulphur wine, sulphuring should be avoided in certain cases, 71; arresting fermentation, unfermented must, prepared in two ways, 72; clarification and care of unfermented must, sulphur flavor, 73; other substances to arrest fermentation, burning alcohol, aqueous solution of sulphurous acid, bisulphite of lime, 74; salicylic acid, 75.

CHAPTER X.
AGING. — EFFECTS OF VARIOUS INFLUENCES.

General considerations, how new wine differs from old, development of bouquet and flavor, old wine, characteristics of, 76; color, aroma, flavor, influences which develop, also destroy, influence of the air, 77; variations of temperature, influence of heat, 78; aging by heat, 79; preserving wine by heat, 80; influence of cold, treatment of frozen wine, 81; influence of light, aging by sunlight, effect of motion of voyages, wines suitable for shipment, 82; shipping new wine, 83; other motions, aging by fining, aging generally, 84; wines which gain the most by aging processes, 85.

CHAPTER XI.
GENERAL TREATMENT — CELLARS.

Unfortified or table wines, deposits, lees, etc., 86; to prevent degeneration, CELLARS: temperature, 87; dampness, ventilation, evaporation, 88; other precautions, supports for casks and tuns, 89.

CHAPTER XII.
RACKING.

Object of, time for, conditions indispensable for a good racking, 91; new red wines, 92; old red wines, new white wines, first racking, subsequent rackings, 93; care to be observed, other precautions, 94; different methods of racking, implements for tipping the cask, 95; racking without contact with the air, pumps and siphons, 97.

CHAPTER XIII.
CLARIFICATION — FINING.

Objects of fining, different substances employed, gelatinous substances, 99; gelatine, its preparation, isinglass, fish glue, or ichthyocol, 100; albuminous substances, blood, milk, white of eggs, 101; clarifying powders, gum arabic, addition of salt, addition of alcohol, addition of tannin, preparation, 102; method of operation, implements for stirring, 103.

CONTENTS.

CHAPTER XIV.
SWEET WINES — FORTIFIED WINES.

Generally, to increase sugar in must, without fermentation, care required, 105; clarification, boiling must, left on the lees, 106; sweet muscat, pressing, marc of sweet wines, amount of alcohol to be added, density, furmint wine, 107, straw wine, PORT WINE in the Upper Douro: the must, lagars, etc., 108, treading, fermentation, Vizitelli's description, 109; lodges or storehouses, mixing, port loses color in wood, alcoholic strength and loss by evaporation, 112; MADEIRA: making, casks, treatment, heating house, heating, 113; solera system, ullage, alcohol, 114; SHERRY: climate, vintage, crushing, gypsum, 115; pressing, 116; plastering, fermenting, adding spirit, 117; bodegas or storehouses, changes in the wine, fino, oloroso, basto, flowers, 118; sweet wine, vino dulce, color wine, vino de color, arrope, 119; mature wine, THE SOLERA SYSTEM: establishing a solera, 120; standard soleras and their foundation, 121; blending for shipment, 122; formulas, fining, 124.

CHAPTER XV.
DEFECTS AND DISEASES.

Divided into two classes, general considerations, 125; NATURAL DEFECTS: earthy flavor, its causes, 126; how prevented, treatment, 127; wild taste and grassy flavor, greenness, causes, 128; prevention, treatment, 129; roughness, causes, not a fault, disappears in time, how avoided, 130; how removed, bitterness, causes, how prevented, treatment, taste of the stems, 131; sourness, causes, how prevented, treatment, 132: alcoholic weakness, how avoided, treatment, 133; want of color, causes, how guarded against, treatment, dull, bluish, lead-colored wine and flavor of the lees, causes, 134; treatment, 135; putrid decomposition, causes, 136; how avoided, treatment, different defects together, ACQUIRED DEFECTS AND DISEASES: flat wines, flowers, causes, 137; prevention, 138; treatment, 139; sourness, acidity, pricked wine, causes, what wine liable to, 140; how prevented, treatment, 141; experiment before treatment, 142; Machard's treatment, other methods, 144; cask flavor, barrel flavor, causes, 145; treatment, 146; mouldy flavor, causes, prevention and treatment, foreign flavors, 147; ropiness, causes, treatment, ropy wines in bottles, and other treatment, 148; acrity, treatment, bitterness, 149; treatment, two kinds according to Maumené, 150; fermentation, taste of the lees, yeasty flavor, 151; how prevented, treatment, degeneration, putrid fermentation, duration of different wines, 152; treatment, 153.

CHAPTER XVI.
WINE IN BOTTLES.

When ready for bottling, how long to remain in wood, 154; how prepared for bottling, the most favorable time for bottling, 155; bottles, 156; filling

CONTENTS. xxi

the bottles, 157; corks, 158; corking machines, 159; preparation of the corks, driving in corks, 160; sealing corks, sealing wax, applying the same, coloring same, 161; capsules, capsuling, piling bottles, 162; racks and bins for bottles, 164; treatment of wine in bottles, fermentation in bottles, 165; deposits and turbidity, 166; bitterness and acrity, ropiness, degeneration and putridity, 167; decantation, 168; operation, instrument, 169.

CHAPTER XVII.
CUTTING OR MIXING WINES.

Most French wines mixed, when necessary, effect of, 171; wines of same nature should be used, fine wines, 173; ordinary wines, must be allowed sufficient time, large quantities, new and old wine, green wines, 174; white and red wines, diseased wines, mixing grapes, precaution, 175.

CHAPTER XVIII.
WINE LEES, MARC, AND PIQUETTE.

Pomace and lees often placed in the still, WINE LEES: the lees should be cared for, quantity of wine in lees, constituents of dry lees, analysis, vary, 176; treatment of lees, 177; extraction of wine from the lees, 178; fining the wine from the lees, 179; red wine from lees, white wine from lees, pressing the sediment, 180; use of dry lees, MARC OR POMACE—PIQUETTE: unfermented marc of white wine or of red wine not entirely fermented, fermented marc of red wine, washing the marc, Pezeyre's method, 183.

CHAPTER XIX.
THE COMPOSITION OF WINE.

Generally, 185; table of substances recognized, 186; alcohol, estimate of, 187; ethers, sugar, estimate of, 190; mannite, mucilage and mellowness, 191; pectose, pectin, fatty matter, glycerin, coloring matter, aldehydes, 192; acids, tartaric, malic, citric, pectic, tannic, carbonic, 193; acetic, lactic, valeric, succinic, total acids, the bouquet, artificial bouquet, 194; Maumené's experiment, 195; different substances employed, iris, 196; strawberry, gillyflower or stockgilly, 197; vine flowers, mignonette, nutmeg, bitter almonds and fruit pits, sassafras, 198; other aromas, effects, 199.

CHAPTER XX.
GENERAL CHAPTER—MISCELLANEOUS.

Proportion of juice to marc, 200; proportion of wine to grapes, 201; wooden and metal utensils, 202; cleanliness, 203; different cellar utensils, 204, 205; USEFUL RULES: to ascertain the weight of a given number of gallons of a liquid, for reducing must, for sugaring must, 206; for fortifying and reducing wines, to reduce with water, 207; to reduce with weaker or fortify with stronger wine or alcohol, PLASTERING, 208; common practice in Spain and southern France, objects, chemical effects, 209; effects on health, 210; plastering sherry, quantity used, 212; by adding water, sherry flavor, 213.

APPENDIX.

Sugar tables: Table I, Balling's degrees (per cent. sugar), corresponding degrees Baumé, and specific gravity at $63\frac{1}{2}°$ F., 215; Table II, Baumé's degrees, corresponding degrees Balling (per cent. sugar), and specific gravity at $63\frac{1}{2}°$ F. 216; Table III, Baumé's degrees and corresponding per cent. sugar, at 60° F. 217; Alcohol table, Table IV, showing per cent. by volume for every one-tenth per cent. from 0.1 to 30 per cent., corresponding per cent. by weight, and specific gravity, 218-19; Table V, showing amount of alcohol and acid in different California wines, 220-23.

LIST OF ILLUSTRATIONS.

Fig.		Page.
1.	HYDROMETER	8
2.	HYDROMETER JAR	9
3.	WOODEN STEMMER	21
4.	CRUSHER	23
5.	FERMENTING VAT	41
6.	WINE PRESSES	46
7. 8.	} ULLING POTS	49
9. 10.	} Z FUNNELS	49
11. 12.	RINSING CHAIN VISITOR FOR EXAMINING THE INSIDE OF A CASK	63
13. 14.	SULPHURER MAUMENE'S SULPHURER	69
15.	CASK AND SUPPORT	89
16. 17.	JACK FOR TIPPING A CASK FORK FOR TIPPING A CASK	95
18. 19.	} IMPLEMENTS FOR TIPPING A CASK	96
20. 21. 22.	A METHOD OF RACKING } SIPHONS	97
23.	ROTARY FORCE PUMP	98
24. 25. 26.	} IMPLEMENTS FOR STIRRING	103
27. 28. 29.	BOTTLE WASHER } BOTTLE DRAINERS	156
30.	RESERVOIRS FOR FILLING BOTTLES	157
31.	BUNG SCREW	158
32.	CORKING MACHINES	159
33.	CORKING MACHINES AND NEEDLES	160
34. 35.	PINCERS FOR REMOVING WAX CAPSULER	162
36.	PILING BOTTLES	163
37. 38.	} BOTTLE RACKS	164
39.	BURROW'S SLIDER BIN	165
40. 41. 42.	DECANTING BASKET CORKSCREWS DECANTING INSTRUMENT	169

ERRATA.

On page 216, Table II, read 63½° F, instead of 93½° F.

On page 218, Table IV, opposite 13.6 by volume, read 11.00 per cent. by weight, instead of 10.10.

On page 219, Table IV, opposite 17.03 by weight, read 20.9 by volume, instead of 20.7; and opposite 23.4 by volume, read .97251 specific gravity, instead of .96251.

On page 222 read Tienturier instead of Tenturier.

THE WINE PRESS AND THE CELLAR.

CHAPTER I.

GATHERING THE GRAPES—MATURITY.

The first step in wine making proper, is the gathering of the grapes, or "picking," as it is usually termed in California.

Utensils for Picking.—Knives, scissors, and pruning shears are used to cut the stems, and every one will adopt the tool that he finds most convenient in practice; but if the berries are inclined to drop off, scissors or pruning shears are preferable. Some authors give minute descriptions of receptacles of various sizes and forms in which to gather the grapes, but the practice in that respect usually followed in this State will be found the most convenient. The grapes here are generally picked directly into boxes holding about fifty pounds. The box is provided with an oblong hole at each end near the top, or three or four holes bored with an inch auger, by which the picker can easily move it from vine to vine, and one man can carry it with both hands to the wagon. These boxes are piled on the wagon without emptying, transported to the wine house, and brought back empty, to be filled again.

Number of Pickers necessary—When to Commence.—There ought to be a sufficient number of men employed in picking to fill at least one fermenting vat in a day, in making red wine. If, however, circumstances render this impossible, it would be well to pile up the grapes on a good clean floor, under cover, till sufficient are gathered to fill the tank, and then crush them, and fill the tank in one day. (See *Red Wine*.) Picking ought to commence as soon as the grapes are of a fair average ripeness, beginning with the earliest and ending with the latest variety. In the chapter on musts, we shall endeavor to indicate the requisite maturity of the grapes, and it will there appear that they may become too ripe by remaining too long on the vine, so that it is very important that a sufficient number of pickers should be employed to finish the gathering as promptly as possible, and before too much sugar is developed. (See *Musts*.)

When to Gather.—It is of little importance at what time of the day the grapes are picked, whether in the cool of the morning or the heat of mid-day, or whether the dew is on or off, as long as they are ripe. In some countries, however, and in what are known as bad years, the grapes do not arrive at complete maturity, and therefore great care is taken to gather them only in dry weather, and after the dew has disappeared. (See *Fermentation—Temperature*.) If they are picked during the heat of the day, fermentation will commence sooner than if picked in the cool of the morning; and for this reason, in making white wine from colored grapes, care should be taken to pick and press them when cool, if it is desired that the wine should be free from color; for if the slightest fermentation sets in before pressing, as it is apt to do if the grapes are warm, some of the coloring matter is pretty sure to be extracted from the skins and will discolor the wine.

Successive Gathering.—It is sometimes recommended that the grapes should be gathered as they ripen, by going over a vineyard two or three times, and picking off not only the bunches that are ripe, leaving the green ones, but even picking off separately three or four grapes from each bunch where it is not evenly ripened, and this is the practice that is followed to-day in making the great white wines of France and Germany; but it certainly will not be adopted in this State while labor is as dear, and wine is as cheap as it is at present. Instead, that practice will be followed which is recommended by those writers who advise that the grapes of each variety be left on the vines till they are all fairly ripe, and that they be gathered clean at one picking. Where, however, different varieties are planted in the same vineyard, which ripen at different periods, those only should be picked at the same time which ripen together. Gather the early ones first, and the later ones successively as they ripen, but pick clean. The same rule also applies to grapes of the same variety, but grown on different soils and in different situations, as it is well known that the same variety of vine will ripen its grapes on high land and poor soil, earlier than on low land and rich soil.

Sorting the Grapes.—It will frequently happen, however, that there are some bunches of green grapes, and they should always be thrown aside, if picked with the others. Sometimes, also, there is what is called a second crop, which ripens so much later than the main one that two gatherings are necessary. In that case it would be injurious to the grapes of the earlier crop to leave them on the vine till the complete maturity of those of the second. Careful wine makers, therefore, will find it to their advantage, either to leave the green grapes upon the vines for a second picking, or, if all are picked together, to throw the green ones into a separate receptacle, or to sort them out from the ripe ones before crushing. Those who wish to take extra care will even have the unripe, rotten, and dried berries clipped from the bunches with scissors. These extra precautions are those which are observed in making the great wines of Europe; but they are not suggested here in the expectation that they will be generally followed by the wine makers of California, but rather for the purpose of indicating the best practices to those who may find out that on account of the varieties they cultivate, and of the situation and soil of their vineyards, they too can produce such wines by using the same care.

Requisite Degree of Maturity.—It is insisted by all intelligent writers on the subject, that, with possible exceptions, which will be mentioned, the grapes should not be gathered till they have arrived at a state of complete maturity. Without this, wines from the finest varieties of grapes would not possess that beauty of color, that delicious flavor, that fragrant bouquet, and that alcoholic strength which they possess in so eminent a degree. And if it is so necessary that the grapes of fine varieties should be thoroughly ripe, it is quite as important that those of the poorer varieties should be equally so. For these latter are generally wanting in sugar, and consequently their wines are feeble in strength, and as the sugar increases directly with the degree of maturity of the grape, so the quantity of alcohol in their wines increases accordingly, and thus by ripeness they make up for their natural defects.

Signs of Ripeness.—Complete maturity of the grape is indicated by the concurrence of the following signs:

1. The stem of the bunch changes from green to brown.
2. The bunch becomes pendant.
3. The berry has lost its firmness; the skin has become thin and translucent.
4. The berries are easily separated from the stem.
5. The juice of the grape has acquired an agreeable flavor; has become sweet, thick, and glutinous.
6. The seeds have become void of glutinous substances.

These are the signs given by several French authors, and are here taken from Prof. Du Breuil, who says, nevertheless, that, under some circumstances the grapes should be gathered before arriving at the state of maturity indicated by these signs, and under other conditions should be gathered even later. He says:

Gathering before Complete Maturity.—1. In certain localities north of the viticultural region the grape hardly ever arrives at the degree of maturity just indicated. Yet the crop must be gathered, or otherwise it would rot on the vines. Under these circumstances, the only thing that can be done is to leave the grapes on the vine as long as they derive any benefit from it.

2. Grapes intended to make sparkling wine should also be gathered before the moment of absolute maturity.

3. In the southern part of France, white grapes intended for the making of dry wines, ought to be picked before reaching the last degree of maturity. Otherwise, in that hot climate, the quantity of sugar in the grape would increase to such an extent that it would be impossible to make a dry wine. This is the practice in making the dry white wines of Lunel, of Coudrieux, of the Hermitage, and of Saint Peray.

4. For all the ordinary red wines of the region inhabited by the olive, if the gathering of the grapes is delayed till the last degree of ripeness, the must will contain more sugar than can be transformed into alcohol by fermentation. The result will be that these wines will undergo a sort of continuous fermentation, which will make its appearance whenever they are moved, and which will soon change into acetic fermentation. The only way to cure this tendency and to render the wines capable of shipment, is to strongly fortify them by the addition of spirits.

To prevent this difficulty in the first place, the grapes should be gathered before complete maturity.

Some very respectable authors, whose experience has been confined to the colder wine making regions, tell us that in all cases the grapes should be allowed to remain on the vine as long as they gain in sugar, and that in order to correct the excess that they would thus in many cases acquire, they recommend that the must be reduced by water. (See *Watering Musts*.)

Gathering after Complete Maturity.—To make sweet wines, the grapes should remain on the vine until they have developed the greatest possible quantity of sugar. For this purpose the grapes are not only allowed to shrivel before gathering, but also artificial means are resorted to, such as twisting the stem, or drying them on straw after picking, and even applying heat to them in various ways. (See *Sweet Wines*.)

Ripeness according to Required Strength.—If the wine maker will first determine how strong in alcohol he wishes his wines to be, he may anticipate the result approximately by testing from time to time the amount of sugar contained in the grapes, and by gathering them at the period when the sugar in the juice shows that, fermented, it will produce the desired percentage of spirit. This testing is easily performed by the use of the must-scale or the saccharometer; and for information on this subject, the reader is referred to the chapter on musts.

CHAPTER II.

MUST.

Must is the name applied to the juice of the grape before fermentation.

Composition.—A good, average must, contains in 100 parts by weight, the following ingredients, and in the proportions as indicated, by weight, according to Dr. Guyot; but the amount of sugar would be considered too small in California:

Pure water, - - - -	78
Grape sugar (glucose) - - -	20
Free acids (tartaric, tannic, etc.), -	00.25
Salts, or organic acids (bitartrate), - -	1.50
Mineral salts, - - - -	0.20
Nitrogenous, fermentive matter, ⎫	
Essential oils, ⎬ -	.05
Mucilaginous and starchy substances, ⎭	

These constituents vary, however, according to variety of grape, degree of maturity, soil, climate, etc.; and some of them may rise in amount to double the average quantity given, or may even, under some circumstances, descend to the one-fourth of it. Although all these ingredients doubtless have important effects upon the quality of the wine produced by fermentation, the acid giving zest and freshness of taste, and the other minor ingredients, smoothness or harshness, as the case may be, yet the principal one that we have to deal with is the sugar, and it is the only one that the practical wine maker will give much attention to, although in those countries where the grape in some seasons does not ripen, the amount of acid is an important element to be taken into consideration in testing the specific gravity of the must. (See *Composition of Wines*, for further details.)

Grape Sugar, or glucose, as it is known in chemical language, as already remarked, is the most important element entering into the composition of must, and upon its quantity depends directly the amount of alcohol contained in the wine. The intelligent wine maker, then, who wishes to know what will be the alcoholic strength of the wine produced by the must which he is about to subject to the action of fermentation, will test the must to ascertain what percentage of sugar it contains. This is very easily done by the use of an instrument prepared for the purpose.

Must Scale.—A certain quantity of sugar being heavier than the same volume of water—pure cane sugar weighing about one and six-tenths to one of water—it follows that the more sugar there is added to a given quantity of water the heavier it becomes, and the more it will bear up anything floating on it; or, as it is generally stated, the less of the liquid will be displaced by the floating body. On this principle, the specific gravity of liquids, or their weight as compared with water, is ascertained. The instrument employed is known by the general name of areometer, but it is now more commonly called a hydrometer, and various specific names are given to it according to the uses for which it is intended. When constructed for testing the strength of sugar syrups it is called a syrup-scale, saccharometer, *pèse-sirop*, etc., and those especially for testing musts are called must-scales, *pèse-moût*, etc. These latter are constructed on the theory that the liquid contains only cane sugar and water—the difference in specific gravity between cane sugar and grape sugar being disregarded— and that its density depends on the quantity of sugar; and although the density of must is somewhat affected by other solid matters than sugar contained in it, yet these instruments, whether syrup-scales or must-scales proper, will give results sufficiently accurate for the purposes of the wine maker, a small allowance being made for the other solids, as hereafter mentioned. There are three instruments which are the most generally used in this country: Oechsle's must-scale, Balling's saccharometer or syrup-scale, and Baumé's syrup-scale, or *pèse-sirop*. The degrees of Oechsle's instrument indicate specific gravity in the manner mentioned under Table I; Balling's indicates percentages of sugar directly; and Baumé's degrees are arbitrary. (See Tables II and

III.) There are other instruments used in France—the gleucoœnometer, reading upwards for spirit and down for sugar on the same stem, corresponding in degrees to Baumé's—and the gleucometer, which indicates at once the percentage of alcohol which the wine will contain after fermentation. Baumé's and Balling's instruments are better suited for use in California, where the musts often show a specific gravity higher than is indicated by Oechsle's scale, which frequently is graduated only up to 80 deg., or 19.75 per cent. of sugar. They are all made on the same general plan, and are usually constructed of glass. The instrument consists of a tube about the size of a pipe-stem, terminating below in a bulb or expansion, weighted at the bottom so that it will stand upright and float when placed in a liquid. The scale is marked on the stem, commencing at the top and numbering downward. The first mark is zero, and shows how far the hydrometer sinks in pure water. (Fig. 1.) As hydrometers are not always accurate, it is safer before using one to have it tested by a chemist or a gauger, as but few others have the necessary skill or the instruments requisite for that purpose. If, however, an instrument which has been tested is accessible, another one can be easily compared with that by ascertaining if both sink to the same point in the same sugar solutions.

Fig. 1.

Hydrometer.

TESTING FOR SUGAR.

Any person, provided with one of the hydrometers mentioned, can easily ascertain the percentage of sugar contained in any must with tolerable accuracy, providing the grapes from which it is pressed are ripe; for if they are green, and contain an undue amount of acid, the density will be materially affected by that. There is no occasion, however, for making wine from green grapes in this State.

Fig. 2.

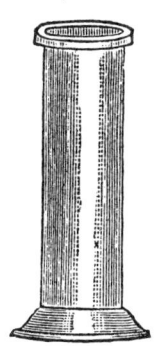

Hydrometer-Jar.

In addition to the hydrometer, it is necessary to be provided with a thermometer with which to ascertain the temperature of the must. Besides the hydrometer and the thermometer, the only other article necessary is a glass tube closed at the bottom and provided with a foot, so that it will stand upright, called the hydrometer-jar. (Fig. 2.) This jar should have a diameter a little greater than that of the bulb of the hydrometer, and must be of such a height that the latter instrument will stand upright and float freely in it, when filled with a liquid. In the absence of the hydrometer-jar, an empty fruit jar, or a tall tin cup or can will answer its purpose. In performing the operation, see that all the articles used are perfectly clean, more particularly the hydrometer, for anything that would slightly affect its weight would render the result of the test useless. Having taken this precaution, press the juice from a small quantity of grapes and strain it through a cloth, and pour sufficient into the hydrometer-jar, that when the hydrometer is plunged into it, it will just bring the level of the liquid to the upper edge of the vessel, or to such a height that the figure on the stem can easily be read. Now place the thermometer in the must and ascertain its temperature, for the instruments are intended to be used at a certain degree of heat, although three or four degrees variation either way will not materially affect the result. Baumé's instrument, as originally constructed, was graduated for a temperature of 10° Reamur, which corresponds with $54\frac{1}{2}°$ F.; but as constructed now-a-days, is generally graduated for a temperature of 58° or 60° F.; and Balling's and Oechsle's for a temperature of $63\frac{1}{2}°$ F. Some of Balling's instruments sold in the market are graduated for 62° F. If it is found that the temperature is above or below the degree indicated, it may be lowered by cooling, or raised by warming, till about the right temperature is reached. Then the hydrometer, being clean, should be taken by the stem at the top and gradually lowered into the must until it floats. Press it down slightly with the finger and let it come to equilibrium, being careful that there is not a drop of water on the stem above the surface of the liquid, nor a bubble of air below. On looking at the stem where it meets the surface, it will be seen that the liquid there curves upwards around the instrument, and that the top of this curve marks one degree higher than the general surface. If the reading is taken from the point marked by the top of the curve (the figures reading downwards), add one degree, or in other words, ascertain the mark on the stem corresponding to the general surface of the liquid. If Balling's scale is used, the number at this mark shows the percentage of sugar which the must contains; if Baumé's is used, consult Table II or III, and opposite this number will be found the corresponding per cent. of sugar. If Oechsle's scale is used, find from Table I or II the specific gravity and the corresponding sugar per cent. Under Table I instructions will be found for reading Oechsle's scale. If Baumé's instrument is used, and a table is not at hand, multiply the observed figure by 1.8, and the product will be nearly the per cent. of sugar.

Correction for Temperature.—It is known that a sugar solution or a must expands as the temperature increases, and contracts as it diminishes; and nice experiments have been performed to show the amount of dilatation and contraction at different temperatures, and the consequent variation in the specific gravity of the liquid, but there is considerable difference in the results of the researches of different authors, and it would seem that further experiments are necessary; but a rule may be deduced which may be used instead of changing the temperature of the must to make it correspond with that for which the instrument is graduated, and although not strictly correct, is sufficient for our purpose; and that is to add one-half per cent. to the sugar per cent. indicated by the hydrometer for every 15° F. above the standard temperature, and subtract ½ per cent. for every 15° below. For instance, if Baumé's instrument shows 22½ per cent. of sugar at 75° F., the actual strength is 23 per cent., and it would mark that at 60°. If the same instrument shows 23½ per cent. at 45° F., the real strength is 23 per cent. In using Balling's scale graduated at 63½° F., the 15° in our example would make 78½° for the first supposed case, and 48½° for the second.

In most cases the variation in temperature will be so little that it may be disregarded; but if the test is made soon after the grapes have been exposed to a hot sun, the must may show a temperature of 90° or 95°F., and it would indicate one per cent. less than its real sugar strength. But the temperature would go below the freezing point of water before the must would mark one per cent. too much.

As the must contains a small quantity of acids and extractive matter which affect its density, some authors recommend that from one-tenth to one-fifteenth of the figures indicating the density by Baumé should be deducted, calling the remainder sugar, and this is about equivalent to deducting one for every twelve per cent. of sugar. But if the grapes are ripe and the must is strained, for all practical purposes all of the solid matter may be called sugar, considering that we make a pretty liberal allowance of sugar for one per cent. of alcohol. Fresh must should always be taken for the purpose of testing for sugar, for as alcohol is much lighter than water, if fermentation has commenced, it will be impossible to ascertain the amount of sugar by means of the hydrometer.

Sugar and Alcohol.—It will be shown in the chapter on fermenation that, in actual practice, it takes about two per cent. of sugar, as indicated by the hydrometer, to produce one per cent. by volume of alcohol; therefore, divide the percentage of sugar contained in the must, as shown by the hydrometer, by two, and the quotient is approximately the per cent. of alcohol which will be contained in the wine after complete fermentation.

Alcohol in Wine.—A good, saleable dry wine ought to contain from eleven to twelve or thirteen per cent. of alcohol; and to produce such a wine the must should indicate from 22 to 26 per cent. of sugar by the hydrometer. A wine which is soon to be consumed at home does not require that degree of strength necessary for shipment abroad and for keeping, and may contain only ten per cent. of alcohol, and even less, and be found a very palatable drink, and less "heady" than that of a higher degree of spirit. And a wine may contain as much as 14 per cent. of spirit, and be very acceptable to the wine merchant for mixing with weaker wines.

A must which does not contain more than 24 per cent. of sugar per hydrometer, if properly managed, will complete its fermentation, and if it does not contain less than 22 per cent., will make a good, sound, shipping wine, which will keep in almost any climate. Mr. Crabb, a well known wine maker of Oakville, in this State, writes me that such a must will ferment dry in six days, but that if it contains more than 24 per cent. of sugar, fermentation is likely to be arrested by the amount of alcohol, when it amounts to 12 per cent. This gentleman is an intelligent viniculturist and a practical man, and it would be safe to follow his advice. Mr. Arpad Haraszthy, who is noted in this connection, in his lecture on fermentation before the convention of winegrowers, held at San Francisco in September, 1882, indicated 22 per cent. as a proper degree of sugar in the must; and it is reported that the wine makers of Los Angeles county, in fixing the prices of grapes in 1882, adopted 23 per cent. as the standard. Undoubtedly the fermentation will be finished sooner, and will be less troublesome, if the must contains sugar within the limits of 22 and 24 per cent., than if allowed to go beyond. (See *Maturity*.) If it should go to 26 per cent. and beyond, the chances are that the fermentation will be incomplete, and that a portion of the sugar will remain in the wine, which will cause it to ferment when exposed to changes of temperature; it may become *milk sour*, and there will be danger of rapid deterioration. From which it follows that, except for making sweet wines, the grapes should be gathered before they develop much more than 24 per cent. of sugar. Supposing, however, that picking commences as soon as the must shows 22 per cent., sufficient force should be employed to finish before it goes beyond the limit indicated. For the writer has seen grapes gathered at the beginning of the season and made into wine which showed 11 per cent. of alcohol, when the wine made from grapes of the same vineyard, gathered too late, either on account of lack of pickers or of fermenting tanks, contained 14.5 per cent., and was still sweet.

CHAPTER III.

SUGARING AND WATERING MUST.

Sugaring.—As early as 1776, Macquer, in France, found that by adding sugar to the must of green grapes, he could make wine; and since his time many authors, notably Chaptal, Gall, and Petiot, have recommended the addition of sugar to the must of bad years when the grapes did not ripen; and had the practice been limited to the addition of sufficient sugar of good quality to a must which was deficient in that respect, but little harm would have been done. The next step, however, was to take the must of partly ripe grapes which contained an undue quantity of acid, and reduce it by the addition of water till the acid corresponded in quantity to that contained in a must of ripe grapes, and then to add sufficient sugar to bring it up again to the necessary degree of sweetness. This may be permissible in those countries where in some years the grapes do not ripen, and in order to make a drinkable wine, water to reduce the acid, and sugar to give sweetness, must be added. But this did not satisfy the greed of the artificial wine makers; they found, so they say, that they could press the juice from the grapes, ferment it by itself, then add to the marc water and sugar enough to bring it back to its original quantity and sugar strength, draw off the artificial juice slightly colored by the skins, and repeat the operation, and so make three and four times the quantity of wine that could otherwise be made, and *all good wine*.

It was thought that wine making in Europe would be revolutionized, and untold wealth would pour into the coffers of the wine makers. It was found, however, that cane sugar was too expensive, but artificial glucose could be made from grain and potatoes at a very small cost, and by reason of its cheapness its use was forthwith recommended; and to such an extent was the matter carried, that one would suppose that in order to make good wine, it was only necessary to soak a few grape skins in a quantity of sweetened water and let it ferment!

The practice, however, to the extent mentioned, did not commend itself to sensible men, and wine making did not become revolutionized. Yet it was to some extent adopted, and the effect upon the wines of Burgundy is shown by Dubrunfaut in his work on *Sucrage de Moûts*. He says that starch-sugar (glucose) factories were established in Burgundy, and from 1825 to 1845, this material was used to strengthen the musts. But complaints arose in France and elsewhere against Burgundy wines; they had a new flavor, and unexpected changes in many respects had come over them. A congress of wine makers was held at Dijon in 1845, at which the abandonment of the use of glucose was decreed upon the report of a committee of merchants and proprietors of Beaune, which was in effect as follows: that the long extolled and generally practiced system of sugaring, and against which a reaction set in some years ago, ought to be completely abandoned, as being fatal (*funeste*) to Burgundy. He considers, however, as do some others who condemn the use of glucose, that the use of refined cane sugar is unobjectionable if used in small quantities and merely to fortify the must when it needs it. There are many authors, however, who speak highly of the wines produced by the addition of sugar and water to the skins after the juice has been drawn off, but it does not seem reasonable that a good wine can be made in that manner. If a good must contained only water, sugar, and acids, then there would be reason for believing that the wine so made would be good. But it is well known that many other ingredients enter into the composition of the juice of the grape which, in some unknown manner, have a very important influence upon the wine made from it. Attempts have been made to produce an artificial must, which is carrying the process but little farther than it is carried by some of the writers on the subject; but Mr. Boireau says that what is produced resembles cider rather than wine. He gives the following composition as approaching very nearly a must for common white wine:

    Refined Sugar, - - - - 25 kilog.
    Tincture of tannin, - - - - 20 gr.

Crystals of tartaric acid,   -   -   500 gr.
Gum arabic,   -   -   -   -   -   1 kilog.
Vine leaves and fresh twigs chopped,   -   5 kilog.
Distilled or filtered water,   -   -   -   1 hectol.

The author last quoted is a practical man, and his opinion is valuable. He says, when the fermentation of this artificial must is most active, it has analogies with ordinary white wine, but it costs much more than the natural wine; and when its fermentation is complete, it has not a bad taste, and there is nothing hurtful in its composition, but that it has not the *taste of white wine;* and the only time when it has any analogy to white wine is during the tumultuous fermentation as already mentioned. Many attempts have been made to vary the formula, but without important results. Tolerably agreeable drinks are obtained, *but they are not wine*. M. Boussingault gives his experience in sugaring and watering must; and the wine produced lacked acid, color, astringency, and was very inferior to the wine first made from the pure juice; it lacked the fixed substances and aromatic principles. He says that some would prefer it to cider, but that it only differed from *piquette* in having a greater degree of alcohol.

To give even a summary of what has been written upon this subject would occupy a volume, but the results arrived at by the more intelligent modern writers and experimenters may be summed up as follows:

1. That good wine can be made only from the pure juice of the grape.

2. That in case the grapes do not ripen sufficiently to make a drinkable wine, water may be added to reduce the acid, and then sugar enough to bring it up to the average sugar strength; but in no case should any but the refined cane sugar be used; artificial glucose, never.

Nothing gained by adding Sugar.—Aside from the question of quality, it may not be amiss to add a few remarks for the benefit of intended wine makers who may have been led to believe, by mistaken authors, that the profits of wine making may be increased by adding sugar and water, and thereby augmenting the quantity. Assuming that it is permissible to use only refined sugar, it can easily be shown that it is as cheap, if not cheaper, to make wine from grapes than from sugar, as long as grapes can be bought for $30 per ton.

A gallon of dry wine of average specific gravity, containing 10 per cent. by weight, or 12.4 by volume, of alcohol, weighs about $8\frac{1}{4}$ pounds, and contains about .825 of a pound of pure alcohol. To produce a pound of alcohol requires about $2\frac{1}{4}$ lbs. of pure grape sugar, or 2.138 lbs. of pure cane sugar, in practice, according to the chapter on fermentation; so that to produce the .825 lbs. of alcohol in one gallon of wine, requires about 1.80 lbs. of pure cane sugar. But refined crystalized sugar is not pure sugar (anhydrous), as it contains about 10 per cent. of water; so, to make our 1.8 of pure sugar, requires 2 lbs. of ordinary refined sugar. At 10 cents per pound, which would be cheap for this market, it would cost 20 cents to make the must for a gallon of wine.

Supposing that a ton of grapes costs $30, and produces 150 gallons of wine, each gallon would cost 20 cents. So that there is nothing to be gained by adding sugar at 10 cents a pound, even if a ton of grapes costs $30 a ton, for the same facts would apply to every pound of sugar added to a must, as well as in the case supposed, where all the sugar was supplied.

Cost of Glucose Wine.—Supposing that artificial glucose contains 80 per cent. of pure (anhydrous) sugar, it would require $2\frac{1}{8}$ lbs. to make our gallon of wine; and if it could be laid down here at 5 cents a pound, the gallon of wine would cost nearly 12 cents, and this would be equivalent to paying $18 a ton for grapes.

When we take into consideration that every pound of glucose and water added to a must will diminish the price of every gallon of wine produced, it is probable that but little, if anything, could be gained even by the use of this article; for the product will not bring the price of an honest wine, and in the long run will destroy the reputation of our wines, and reflect injury upon every wine maker in the State.

Experiment with Glucose.—Mr. Crabb, of Oakville, gave his experience with glucose in a paper read before the St. Helena Vinicultural Club, in July, 1882, as follows: I took three packages of equal size, one containing pure grape juice, the two others containing each equal parts of the same juice and glucose water, all showing 23 per cent. sugar by Balling's saccharometer. The pure juice was dry in 15 days (the room being cold). One package of the mixture was dry in 30 days; the other continued in fermentation 60 days, both emitting a rank offensive odor during the process, arising from the amount of chalk and sulphuric acid required in its (glucose) manufacture. Racking at this time appeared to remove the greater part of the offensive odor, and in 30 days the wine was clear and bright enough to pass for a two-years'-old wine. I now thought it contained a very superior fining principle, and if a small enough quantity would answer the purpose, it might be a valuable acquisition. But this was its most favorable period; it had reached its zenith, and while the pure juice was now beginning to develop its vinous properties, the mixture commenced to deteriorate, becoming flat and insipid, as any grape juice would by being one-half water, and the sulphuric acid and chalk (sulphate of lime) developing a disagreeable after-taste. Notwithstanding that I have racked it again and fined it to a perfect condition, there is not the least improvement, and I believe as it becomes more dry with age, that the bitter, nauseous after-taste will become more and more pronounced, so that one glass of it will leave such a lasting impression on the palate as to never want any more; whereas, the package of pure juice is now vinous, sprightly, refreshing and inviting.

The use of Glucose condemned.—On the 16th day of July, 1881, the St. Helena Vinicultural Association adopted resolutions condemning in the strongest terms the use of glucose in the making of wine and brandy, and promising to expose all parties importing or receiving the substance by publishing their names, and pledging the Society to use all honorable means to prevent the adulteration of the product of our vineyards. The resolutions passed unanimously, and were published in the different newspapers. One man in the district, notwithstanding the warning, did cause to be shipped to him a quantity of glucose, and the President and Secretary of the Society published in several different newspapers, in December, 1881, over their own signatures, and in the name of the Association, a notice reciting the resolutions, and stating that a person (giving his name) "imported eighty barrels of grape sugar, made from corn, commonly called glucose, and used the same, or the greater part of it, in the manufacture of wine during the last vintage."

We believe that this was an exceptional case, and that its use in this State has been exceedingly rare.

Watering.—Another question which has been a good deal discussed is, whether it is better to pick the grapes as soon as they develop sufficient sugar, or leave them on the vine till they develop an excess, and then reduce the must with water. Dr. Guyot having laid it down as a fundamental principle in wine making in France, that the grapes should be left on the vine as late as possible, and until they have reached the highest point of maturity, except, *perhaps*, in some of the most extreme southern portions, he is consistent in counseling the addition of water to the must. But the only reason given by him for it is that it is consonant with *his principle* previously stated. Du Breuil is also of the same opinion. Both are men of high authority, but it does not appear that either of them ever made wine in a warm climate, where the grapes would develop so much sugar as to require the addition of water, if left upon the vine as late as possible. We have, on the other hand, the testimony of Boireau, who, speaking on the subject, says that it is probable that the theoricians who are in favor of the practice have never made wine of *must too rich in sugar and of water*. He says, it is true that the quantity is increased, and fermentation is complete, but that the wine so made is only fit for the still, will not keep and readily turns sour. The Greeks have followed this practice from time immemorial in the Archipelago, where he tasted their wine so made in 1865, and which they can keep with difficulty for one year, in spite of the addition of a large quantity of rosin, which they introduce during fermentation. And yet, these wines are not weak, having an average of 10½ to 11 per cent. of alcohol. He says that but few grapes give musts too rich in sugar, if they are gathered as soon as ripe; for even in viticultural countries situated farthest south, as the south of France, Spain, Italy, Greece, and Africa, the grape *just ripe* gives a must which does not exceed 14° Baumé, unless left on the vine until part of the water of vegetation has evaporated.

Having alluded to both sides of the question, it would seem to be a fair inference from the foregoing that the safest course would be, in a hot climate, to gather the grapes as soon as fairly ripe. This may easily be done, where each grape grower makes his own wine, and has immediate supervision of the picking, and has sufficient men to finish it with promptness. But in the case of large manufacturers who buy their grapes and cannot supervise or order the gathering in the numerous vineyards whose crops they purchase, it may sometimes be necessary, when the grapes come in over-ripe, and it is not desirable to make sweet wine, to add a small quantity of water to insure prompt and complete fermentation. When the necessity arises, great caution should be used, and the necessity should be avoided when possible.

CHAPTER IV.

STEMMING AND CRUSHING.

Diversity of Opinion on Stemming.—There is no subject connected with wine-making upon which there is a greater difference of opinion than that of stemming. And it would seem that the diversity of practice is not always caused by the different conditions and exigencies of location, variety of grapes, etc.; but among the different wine-makers in the same locality, some remove the stems, and others do not; from which Dr. Guyot infers that the practice cannot be classed among the essential principles governing vinification, but is a mere matter of detail, and that stemming may be practiced or omitted without materially affecting the wine. But Machard, a writer of the Jura, lays it down imperiously as one of the very essentials of good wine-making that the grapes should be fermented with the stems, and calls stemming a pernicious practice.

Effect of Stemming.—All agree, however, that the stems, during fermentation, if not removed, yield tannin to the wine, and thereby give it astringency. It is also said to increase fermentation, by furnishing to the must additional germs of fermentation adhering to the stems, and perhaps acting also in a mechanical way, by presenting many salient points, and exposing a greater surface to the action of the ferment.* They also add a certain amount of acid to the wine, if green. It is evident that they increase the labor of pressing, by adding to the mass of marc.

Proper Practice.—If, therefore, by reason of the variety of grapes cultivated, or the soil, or situation, your wine is too soft, lacks life and astringency, ferment with all or a portion of the stems; but if your wine is rough, too astringent, it will be found beneficial to stem the grapes. If your grapes lack the fermentive principle, and fermentation is slow and incomplete, leave the

---

*Pasteur, in his Studies on Beer, says that the reason has not yet been discovered, but that he has no doubt that it may be attributed, principally, to the fact that the interstices between the grapes, and the spaces which the bunch leaves throughout, considerably increase the volume of air placed at the service of the germs of ferment.

STEMMING AND CRUSHING.

grapes on the stem; and in the same way the fermentation will be assisted, if the grapes are over-ripe.

When the grapes are fermented with the stems, care must be taken that they do not remain too long in the vat, or the wine may acquire a bitter, disagreeable flavor, called by the French *goût de râpe*, or stem flavor, which is caused by the bitter principle contained therein, and which is dissolved out by maceration.

To Estimate Tannin.—A certain amount of tannin is necessary to the proper clearing of the wine, which is brought about by the tannin combining with albuminous matters, and they are then precipitated, and the wine may be drawn off, leaving them at the bottom of the cask. It is on the application of this well-known principle that Maumené gives a very simple method of ascertaining whether the grapes should be stemmed or not. He says: First make a small quantity of wine without the stems, and add tannin, or, what is better, a decoction made by boiling a quantity of stems, and if sensible precipitation is produced, it is better to ferment with the stems, for tannin is wanting; but if the precipitation is not formed, the grapes should be stemmed.

Stemmers.—This is usually effected in California by the use of the common hand stemmer, though some large establishments are using a stemmer run by steam or horse-power. The common stemmer consists of an oblong shallow box or frame, six or eight feet long by two wide, or any convenient size, and about six inches deep, with a coarse wire netting or grating stretched across the bottom. This grating is usually made of heavy galvanized-iron wire, with ¾ inch or

Fig. 3.

Wooden Stemmer.

inch meshes. Instead of having the grating extend the whole length, a portion at one end may be floored with wood, upon which a box of grapes can be placed without injuring the grating. The only objection to this stemmer is that the grape juice comes in contact with the metal of the grating, and it is a well-known fact that nearly, if not all, of the baser metals are corroded by the acids; it would be better to replace the wire with a wooden grating, as in France (fig. 3).

How to Remove the Stems.—The grapes are dumped from the boxes directly into the stemmer, and the workman seizes as many as he can easily manage with both hands, and rubs and rolls them to and fro upon the wire grating, and the berries, as they are rubbed off, fall through the meshes, and the stems remain in the hand. The few grapes that may remain are removed by raising the mass of stems and forcibly throwing them two or three times upon the grating. Sometimes the stems, with the few grapes clinging to them, are turned over to another workman, who, with a hay fork, tosses them about upon another grating till all the berries are removed. The stemmer ought to be situated over the hopper of the crusher, so that the grapes will fall directly into it, as they are separated from the stems.

Crushing.—It is generally considered essential to crush the grapes whether stemmed or not, although in some special cases, to be hereafter noted, crushing is omitted.

Methods of Crushing.—It is well known that in Europe the grapes are usually crushed by being trodden with the feet of men, usually barefooted, but sometimes in wooden shoes, and many of the best writers of to-day are of the opinion that the wine is better when the grapes have been well trodden with the bare feet, for by thoroughly rubbing the skins and pounding them into a pulp without breaking the seeds, they think that more color and aroma are developed than can be obtained by simply crushing them, as in a machine, and afterwards fermenting. Although the practice of treading is the more common one in Europe, yet there are exceptions, and in some places the crushing is done by rollers and with satisfactory results. In California we are accustomed to regard the treading of grapes as an antiquated practice, and a relic of a past age, and it is almost universally discarded, being practiced only occasionally and by Europeans, who have not yet wholly fallen into our methods of practice. Those who are fastidious in this matter may rest assured, that if they will drink California wine, they run but very small risk of imbibing a liquid which a man has had his feet in.

Aerating the Must.—There seems to be some confusion on this subject, for some claim that the must is better exposed to the air, and prepared for fermentation, by treading. This may be true of *treading in the vat* during fermentation, but simply treading the grapes to crush them does not aerate the must as much as crushing with rollers, for in the latter case the juice falls through a considerable distance in a finely divided form, which thoroughly exposes it to the air.

Crushers.—The machine generally employed consists of two rollers made of wood, iron, or other suitable material, 6 or 8, or even more, inches in diameter, geared together so that they revolve in opposite directions and towards each other, and so that the grapes will be drawn between them from above. The rollers run near each other, but do not touch, so that the grapes will be crushed, and the seeds remain unbroken. It is operated by one man turning a crank, either attached to one of the rollers or to a pinion. Figure 4 represents such a crusher, except that in the figure the rollers are openwork, instead of solid, as they should be. It is surmounted by a hopper which allows the grapes to fall between the rollers as they revolve, and the whole apparatus should be so placed that the pomace may fall into the fermenting vats, or be easily conveyed to them or to the press, accordingly as it is to be made into red or white wine.

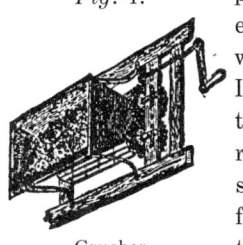

Fig. 4.

Crusher.

Some stemmers have corrugated instead of plain rollers, but there is no advantage in this, and unless they are very nicely adjusted to the motion of the cog wheels, they may break the seeds, which is always considered injurious to the wine.

Rapidity of Operation.—Five men—one to handle the boxes of grapes, two to stem, standing on opposite sides of the stemmer, one to operate the crusher, and one to take the stems and remove the remaining grapes and to make himself generally useful—can stem and crush with these hand machines twenty tons of grapes per day, enough to make three thousand gallons of wine. And the work can be done much more rapidly by the use of the stemmer and crusher combined, which is to some extent used in the largest establishments.

Special Practice.—Boireau says that it has been observed that of the Médoc wines, those made without crushing the grapes have less color than those made from grapes of the same crop which have been crushed, but that they have a more refined and delicate taste (*plus fins de goût*), and that consequently many of the proprietors of the *grands crûs* of the Médoc in those years which are favorable to the maturity of the grape do not crush; they only do it in inferior years, when the grapes have not become sufficiently ripe, and when they fear that the wine may not have a suitable color. And in another place he tells us that in those grand wines which are intended to be bottled, a superabundance of tannin and its consequent roughness may be avoided by complete stemming, fermenting the whole berries, and by drawing from the fermenting vat at just the right time.

CHAPTER V.

FERMENTATION — ITS CAUSES.

It is with some hesitancy that I attempt to give a brief summary of the results of scientific investigation into this subject, for fear of going beyond the legitimate limits of a practical work, as this book is intended preëminently for practical men. But as the work would be incomplete without it, and as a knowledge of the general phenomena of fermentation, and of the diferent influences to which it is subject, are of vast importance to those who will intelligently apply their principles, I give the following as but a brief *resumé*, and will put it as plainly as the subject will permit. Most of the ideas given below are extracted from Schutzenberger's work on fermentation.

There are several different kinds of Fermentation, as (1) vinous, alcoholic or spirituous fermentation; (2) mucous or viscous fermentation; (3) lactic fermentation; (4) ammoniacal fermentation; (5) butyric fermentation; (6) putrifaction; and (7) acetic fermentation, or fermentation by oxidation, and others.

Alcoholic Fermentation is that which sugar undergoes under the influence of the ferment or yeast; and it is now agreed that this ferment consists principally of an aggregation of living organisms, or an assemblage of microscopic cells.

The Yeast Plant.—Our author gives them the name of *saccharomyces cerevisiæ*, following those who consider it to be a species of fungus, and states that it is now very generally admitted that ferments are fungi, although by some they have been considered animal in their nature. These cells are round or oval, and are from .00031 to .00035 of an inch in their greatest diameter. "They are formed of a thin and elastic membrane of colorless celluose, and of a protoplasm, also colorless, sometimes homogeneous, sometimes composed of small granulations." The cells are separate or united two by two. When they are deposited in a fermentable liquid, as a sugar solution or a must, small prominences are seen to arise at one or rarely two points, the interior of which is filled with protoplasm from the mother cell; these prominences grow until they have attained the size of the original cell, when the base contracts, forming a kind of neck, and immediately they separate from the mother cell, and under favorable conditions one cell produces several generations, but by degrees it loses all its protoplasm, which at last unites in granules swimming in superabundant cellular juice. The cell ceases to produce, and dies; the membrane is ruptured, and the granular contents are diffused in the liquid. In the manufacture of beer the fermentation is of two kinds: surface fermentation and sedimentary fermentation, depending upon a high or a low degree of heat. The surface *saccharomyces* develop more rapidly than the others, are larger, and they bud so rapidly that the cells which issue from each other do not separate, but remain attached, forming ramified chains of from six to twelve or more buds. The bubbles of rising gas have a greater hold on these chaplets than on single cells, which causes the newly formed yeast to rise to the surface during active fermentation. These organisms or fungi produce spores which are sown on the surface of fruits, and get into the juice by crushing, when they commence their reproduction by budding. So that the basis or cause of the phenomena which we call fermentation is the growth and reproduction of yeast or ferment, which is made up principally of the minute organisms just described.

Functions of Yeast.—Yeast is a living organism, belonging to the family of *fungi*, genus *Saccharomyces*, destitute of mycelium, capable of reproduction, like all the elementary fungi, by buds and spores. Its composition singularly resembles that of other vegetable tissues, and especially the plants of the same family. It does not differ essentially from other elementary cells, unprovided with chlorophyll.

Normal Conditions of the Life of Yeast.—The conditions which our author calls normal in the life-history of yeast, are those in which it develops itself and increases with the greatest activity and energy. They are of two orders, physical and chemical.

FERMENTATION. 27

With respect to *physical conditions*, it is only necessary to notice the temperature. That most favorable to the nutrition of yeast, and that which is found advantageous to other cellular vegetable organisms, is between 25° C. and 35° C. (77° and 95° F.) Above and below these limits, the vital manifestations do not cease until we descend below 9° C. (48.2° F.), or rise above 60° C. (140° F.), the temperature at which albuminoid principles begin to coagulate.

With regard to the *chemical conditions*, our author says that the most favorable medium is that which contains the most appropriate nutritive elements. And as yeast contains water, mineral salts, especially potassium, magnesium, and calcium phosphates, therefore water and the alkaline and alkaline-earthy phosphates will be necessary. We find, besides, a great proportion of nitrogenous substances, either albuminous or otherwise; and therefore the food of yeast must contain nitrogen. It is supposed, however, that the cells are not directly nourished by albuminoids in the juices of fruits, the wort of beer, or yeast water, but by analogous compounds contained in them, which have the property of passing by osmose through the membranes; for the albuminoids themselves, it is said, cannot pass through. Pasteur has shown by his experiments, that mineral salts are absolutely necessary to the development and nutrition of the yeast cell; and Mayer follows him with details as follows: Preparations of iron, in small quantities, seem to have no influence; in larger proportions, they are injurious. Potassium phosphate is indispensable, and the absence of lime has little effect. Magnesium, on the contrary, appeared to be very useful, if not indispensable. The combinations of sodium present no material effects.

Sugar is one of the most important elements in the nourishment of the yeast cells, and Pasteur has shown that, in alcoholic fermentation, a part of the sugar is fixed in the yeast, in the state of cellulose or some analogous body, for, when the fermentation is completed, it is found that more yeast is present than at the commencement. Water is necessary, and the yeast cell manifests its activity, develops and is nourished within the limits of 40 and

80 per cent. of water, though yeast, dried with precaution, may regain its power when moistened. And the fact that a solution containing over 35 per cent. of sugar will not ferment, is explained on the theory that such a solution takes from the cells by osmose a sufficient quantity of water to lower their hydration below 40 per cent. The cells of the *Saccharomyces cerevisiæ*, introduced into a liquid medium, absorb oxygen with great rapidity, and develop a corresponding quantity of carbon dioxide. This constitutes respiration, comparable to that of animals. By careful experiments it has been shown that yeast breathes when placed in contact with dissolved oxygen, and the respiration is more active than that of fishes, and it plays as important a part in the life of those minute vegetable cells as in the higher forms of vegetable and animal life. Oxygen is furnished by atmospheric air, and fermentation is more rapid when a large surface of the liquid is exposed, and then the budding is more active.

Action of various Chemical and Physical Agents.—"It has long been known that certain chemical compounds, especially those which coagulate albuminous substances, and disorganize the tissues, or which, by their presence in sufficient quantities, are incompatible with life, are opposed to fermentation; such are the acids and alkalies in suitable proportions, silver nitrate, chlorine, iodine, the soluble iron, copper, and lead salts, tannin, phenol, creosote, chloroform, essence of mustard, alcohol when its strength is above 20 per cent., hydrocyanic and oxalic acids, even in very small quantities.

"An excess of neutral alkaline salts or sugar acts in the same manner, by diminishing in the interior of the cell the minimum quantity of water, which is necessary to the manifestation of its vital activity.

"The red mercury oxide, calomel, manganese peroxide, the alkaline sulphites and sulphates, the essences of turpentine and of lemon, etc., also interfere with, and destroy alcoholic fermentation.

"Phosphoric and arsenious acids are, on the contrary, inactive."

Experiments have shown that sparks of electricity passing

through yeast do not modify its power of changing cane sugar into glucose, nor its activity as an alcoholic ferment. Fermentation is slower in the dark, and also in a vacuum. Flour of sulphur did not sensibly affect fermentation, but the carbonic acid evolved contained sulphuretted hydrogen. Sulphurous acid, however, arrests fermentation. Yeast is always acid, but an addition of an excess of different acids arrests the decomposition of sugar. If one hundred times the amount of acid contained in the yeast is added, fermentation does not take place.

M. Dumas has shown the action of various salts on yeast, but the subject has little if any interest for the wine maker.

Viscous or Mannitic Fermentation is also excited, according to Pasteur, by special ferment acting on glucose, transforming it into a kind of gum or dextrin, mannite, and carbon dioxide. This ferment is also formed of small globules united as in a necklace, whose diameter varies from .000047 to .000055 of an inch. These globules, sown in a saccharine liquid containing nutritive nitrogenous matter and mineral substances, always give rise to viscous fermentation. One hundred parts of cane sugar give: mannite, 51.09; gum, 45.48; and carbon dioxide, 6.18. The liquids which are most apt to produce viscous fermentation can also undergo lactic and butyric fermentation, but in this case the organized forms of life which are developed in the liquid are of a different nature. The conditions of action necessary to these gummy and mannitic ferments are the same as those which suit alcoholic ferment. The most favorable temperature is 30° C. (86° F.) This fermentation is what gives rise to the disease of wines, called by the French *la graisse*, or ropiness. White wine is more subject to it than red, and it is generally due to the want of tannin. (See *Ropiness*.)

Lactic Fermentation is the transformation which certain sugars, as sugar of milk and grape sugar, undergo, and by which they are changed into lactic acid. This takes place in the souring of milk. The most favorable temperature for it seems to be about 95° F. This also depends on a special ferment. Sugar solutions are also capable of *butyric fermentation* and *putrefaction*, and we generally see viscous, lactic, and butyric fermentation appear in succession.

Acetic Fermentation is to the wine maker and wine dealer, after alcoholic fermentation, the most important.

Fermentable matter and ferment are also concerned in it, but oxygen also is necessary.

It has long been known that the alcohol contained in fermented liquids, such as wine, beer, etc., will disappear under certain circumstances, and give place to vinegar or acetic acid, and that the air, or rather its oxygen, plays a part in this reaction.

To the chemist the reaction is simple, and is formulated thus:

$$\underset{\text{Alcohol.}}{C_2 H_6 O} + O_2 = \underset{\text{Water.}}{H_2 O} + \underset{\text{Acetic Acid.}}{C_2 H_4 O_2},$$

or the oxidation may take place by two reactions, with the production of an intermediate product, aldehyde:

$$\underset{\text{Alcohol.}}{C_2 H_6 O} + O = H_2 O + \underset{\text{Aldehyde.}}{C_2 H_4 O},$$

$$\underset{\text{Aldedyde.}}{C_2 H_4 O} + O = \underset{\text{Acetic Acid.}}{C_2 H_4 O_2}$$

According to Pasteur, the oxidation of alcohol is the consequence of the action of a ferment or cryptogam, *Mycoderma aceti*, and it makes its appearance on the surface of liquids, while in acetic fermentation, in the form of a continuous membrane, mother of vinegar, either wrinkled or smooth, which is generally formed of very minute elongated cells, whose greater diameter varies from .000059 to .000118 of an inch; these cells are united in chains, or in the form of curved rods. Multiplication seems to be effected by the transverse division of the fully developed cells. The conditions of nutrition are similar to those suitable to the alcoholic ferment, the hydro-carbon matter being supplied by dilute alcohol. It may, however, be supplemented by the acetic acid itself; for if the process is left too long to itself, the vinegar loses its strength by being consumed. The most favorable temperature is between 76° and 82° F.

Antiseptic agents, which arrest the development of beer yeast, act in the same manner on the *Mycoderma aceti*. Sulphurous acid is especially active in this manner; hence the use of the sulphur match in sulphuring wine casks.

There is another ferment, *Mycoderma vini*, or flowers of wine, which is found in wine and other alcoholic liquids exposed to the air when fermentation is over or has become languid, which resembles in many respects the acetic ferment. It has the power of producing alcoholic fermentation, and is supposed by some to be derived from the *Saccharomyces*. Like the *Mycoderma aceti*, it is developed on the surface of fermented alcoholic liquors, in the form of smooth or wrinkled films or membranes, but thicker and more compact. It grows with great rapidity, and it has been calculated that one cell would, in forty-eight hours, produce about 35,378 cells. These cells are of various forms, ovoid, ellipsoidal, and cylindrical, with rounded extremities. The ovoid cells have their greater diameter about .000236, and their smaller one, .000157 of an inch. The cylinders have their diameters .00047 × .000118 in. The nutritive principles are the same as those of the mother of vinegar: alcohol, salts and nitrogenous compounds. It also appears capable of utilizing for nutrition the secondary products of alcoholic fermentation, such as succinic acid and glycerine. Its development is most active between 61° and 86° F. (See *Sherry*.)

Origin of Ferments.—In order to produce the different kinds of fermentation, the necessary ferment must be added, unless it is already contained in the fermentable matter or in the air. In the manufacture of beer and bread, yeast must be used; the other kinds of fermentation, except alcoholic, can generally be produced by the ferments or their spores furnished by the atmosphere; but Pasteur, in the course of his investigations, never produced alcoholic fermentation from spores found in the air. But the germs of the *Saccharomyces cerevisiæ* and of *Mycoderma vini* seem to be found only on the surface of fruits, and their stems.†

---

†Ferment cells, however, occur in considerable numbers in the neighborhood of places where alcoholic fermentation is carried on, and the germs, perhaps, may be found in the atmosphere near a vineyard, and in those cases the ferments and their germs may be borne about to some extent by the wind.

32 FERMENTATION.

These different germs, however, are all found in the must of grapes, and in wine, and are ready to develop whenever favorable conditions offer themselves, and produce diseases in the wine. It is found that these germs are killed by raising the temperature of the liquid to 140° F., and hence the process of heating wines to preserve them (*which see*).

Leaving the germ theory of fermentation, we will pass to what is of more practical importance.

ALCOHOLIC FERMENTATION IN WINE MAKING.

Vinous or Alcoholic Fermentation transforms the juice of the grape into wine, and, as already shown, is caused by the yeast or ferment, which finds its way into the must; and by this fermentation the sugar of the grape is changed principally into alcohol, and carbon dioxide, or carbonic acid gas. And in order to show the relations between the sugar and the alcohol produced, it is necessary to say something about the chemical constituents of each.

Sugar.—In general terms, cane sugar may be expressed by the chemical formula, $C_{12} H_{22} O_{11}$, or, in other words, one molecule contains 12 atoms of carbon, 22 of hydrogen, and 11 of oxygen.

And the general term glucose, or grape sugar, may be expressed by the formula $C_6 H_{12} O_6$, or one molecule contains 6 atoms of carbon, 12 of hydrogen, and 11 of oxygen.

If, instead of using the word atoms, we use the word pounds, the chemical formula may be made clear to the unscientific. Taking the formula for cane sugar, already given, it simply means that 342 pounds contain the following ingredients, in the following proportions:

			lbs.		lbs.
12 parts	carbon,	each weighing	12,	- - -	144
22 "	hydrogen,	"	1,	- - -	22
11 "	oxygen,	"	16,	- - -	176
					342

FERMENTATION.

And the formula for glucose means that 180 pounds contain:

		lbs.		lbs.
6 parts of	carbon, @	12,	- - - - - - -	72
12 "	hydrogen, "	1,	- - - - - - -	12
6 "	oxygen, "	16,	- - - - - - -	96
				180

And the formula for water means that 18 pounds contain:

		lbs.		lbs.
2 parts of hydrogen,	@	1,	- - - - - -	2
1 part " oxygen,	"	16,	- - - - - -	16
				18

In fermentation, it is glucose which is immediately transformed, although cane sugar ferments also; but, before doing so, it becomes changed or inverted into glucose, and one molecule takes up a molecule of water, and produces two of glucose, thus:

Cane Sugar.　　Water.　　Glucose.
$$C_{12}H_{22}O_{11} + H_2O = 2\,C_6H_{12}O_6$$
$$342 \quad + \quad 18 = 2 \times 180 = 360.$$

Or, in the production of alcohol, 100 lbs. of pure cane sugar are equal to 105.26 lbs. of pure grape sugar.

The general formula for alcohol is C_2H_6O, and for carbonic acid CO_2.

Alcohol by Weight and by Volume. — The quantity of alcohol contained in a given mixture of alcohol and water may be expressed as per cent. by weight, or per cent. by volume. The first method is usually used by chemists, and the second in commerce. If we have 100 lbs. of a mixture of alcohol and water of which 10 lbs. are alcohol and 90 lbs. water, it contains 10 per cent. of alcohol by *weight*. If, however, we have 100 gallons of a mixture in which there are 10 gallons of alcohol and 90 gallons of water, we say that it contains 10 per cent. by *volume* of alcohol. This will serve to illustrate the meaning of the terms per cent. by volume and by weight, although it is well known that, owing to shrinkage, 10 gallons of alcohol and 90 gallons of water do not produce quite 100 gallons of mixture.

Whenever merchants and wine makers use the term per cent. of alcohol, they mean per cent. by volume or measure; and whenever the expression is used in this work, it is used in that sense, unless otherwise expressed.

Fermentation — Its Products. — Per cent. Sugar to per cent. Alcohol. — In theory, glucose, during the process of fermentation, is entirely changed into alcohol and carbonic acid; the two substances produced containing the same elements as glucose, and no others. If there was no loss of sugar, or degeneration, as it is called, the reaction would be exactly expressed as follows:

$$\underset{\text{Glucose.}}{C_6 H_{12} O_6} = \underset{\text{Alcohol.}}{2\ C_2 H_6 O} + \underset{\text{Carbonic Acid.}}{2\ CO_2}$$
$$180 \quad = \quad 92 \quad + \quad 88$$

And the old authorities said, if 180 parts of glucose produce 92 of alcohol, 100 will produce 51.1111, thus:

180 : 92 : : 100 : x = 51.1111, leaving the balance to be accounted for by carbonic acid 48.8889
―――――
100

And again, if it takes 100 parts of glucose to produce 51.1111 alcohol, how much does it take to produce 1 per cent. by weight?

51.1111 : 1 : : 100 : x = 1.9565.

These figures are now true only of that part of the sugar which is transformed into alcohol and carbon dioxide.

Different Authors. — Pasteur has shown that a portion of the glucose was changed into succinic acid and glycerine, and as the result of one of the experiments which he gives, out of a large number, it appears that 100 parts of glucose produce about 48.46 of alcohol, and it would require 2.063 to produce 1 per cent. of alcohol by weight, and 1.65 to produce 1 per cent. by volume.

But this eminent chemist's experiments were conducted in the laboratory, and under the most favorable circumstances, so that no loss by evaporation could occur—conditions under which fermentation on a large scale is never carried on.

Dr. Guyot states that it takes about 1.5 per cent. of grape

FERMENTATION.

sugar to produce 1 per cent. of alcohol, which is even less than is required according to Pasteur, and is manifestly too little. And the statement has been made, that a must containing 20 per cent. of sugar will produce 13 per cent. of alcohol, which is impossible.

J. J. Griffin quotes Pasteur, and estimating the average loss to be $4\frac{1}{2}$ per cent. of the sugar, deduces the figures .4881 as the per cent. by weight of alcohol produced by 1 per cent. of grape sugar. Dubief says that it takes 1.7 per cent. of cane sugar to produce 1 per cent. of alcohol by volume. Mr. Joseph Boussingault gives his experiments on musts fermented in small vessels under conditions similar to those under which fermentation is carried on in wine making on a large scale; and the result of his researches is that the product in alcohol is about 90 per cent. of what the chemical theory calls for: say, .46 by weight for 1 of sugar, or 1.7+glucose for 1 per cent. of alcohol by volume. Mr. M. Boussingault gives it as the result of his experiment, that it takes 1.8 per cent. of sugar to produce 1 per cent. of alcohol.

So that it is pretty safe to say that it takes on an average about 1.8 of sugar to make 1 of alcohol, making some allowance for loss by evaporation, etc.

As has already been stated in the chapter on Musts, 1 per cent. for every 12 should be deducted from the percentage of sugar shown by the hydrometer for other matters than sugar.

If, therefore, we have a must which shows 24° by the saccharometer, we will deduct two, and call the remainder 22, sugar. Although it is not strictly correct to say that 22 divided by 1.8 will give the per cent. of alcohol which may be expected after fermentation, owing to the well known variation between per cent. by weight and by volume, as the figures increase, yet it is sufficient for all practical purposes.

Let us then divide 22, the supposed sugar in the must, by 1.8, the amount required to produce 1 per cent. of alcohol, and we obtain 12 and a fraction. Now the total indication by the saccharometer was 24 per cent.; if we divide this by two we get the same result in round numbers.

Hence the rule: one-half of the figure indicating the total per cent. by the saccharometer (hydrometer) is approximately the per cent. of alcohol to be expected in the wine.

Owing to the fact that the loss by evaporation and degeneration may vary greatly in different cases, this will be only a rough estimate, but it will prove as satisfactory as any method that can be adopted, and it corresponds very closely with the statement made by N. Basset, that in actual practice, a must of 20 per cent. gives only 7.88 per cent. of alcohol by weight, which corresponds with 10 per cent. by volume, nearly; and it is the rule given by Petiot and Dr. Gall for a natural must.

It seems, however, from what follows below, that this is only true of a normal must, but that a different rule applies to one of a very high degree of sugar.

Limits of Sugar and Spirit.—It is said that when a solution or a must contains over 35 per cent. of sugar, it will not ferment; nor will a wine or other alcoholic mixture which contains 20 per cent. of spirit ferment. Boireau says that the maximum of alcohol which a wine can attain by the fermentation of the richest must is between 15 and 16 per cent., and those wines which show a higher degree have been fortified. He says that the highest degree of spirit ever observed by him in a natural red wine was 15.4 per cent., when it was a year old; from that time the strength diminished, but the wine always remained sweet.

There is, however, a remarkable case given, and which seems to be well authenticated, of an Australian wine which contained naturally, by fermentation, 32.4° of British proof spirit, which is equal to about 18.21 per cent. And Vizitelli states that Mr. Ellis, of the firm of Graham & Co., asserts that perfectly fermented Alto Douro wine will develop 32° proof spirit, or 18 per cent. of alcohol, and when made exclusively from the Bastardo grape, as much as 34°, or about 19 per cent. of spirit. And Mr. Vizitelli adds that he is satisfied from what he saw at Jeres, that sherry wines which have had merely 1 or 2 per cent of spirit added to them will in the course of time indicate 34°. To produce these results would seem to require more than 35 per cent.

of sugar, according to our rule; but while it is approximately correct to say that 2 per cent. of sugar produces 1 per cent. of alcohol as long as we are dealing with a must of 24 or 25 per cent. and under, it may not be true of a must of 30 to 35 per cent., for the other solid matters probably do not increase in proportion to the sugar. Therefore, to reconcile this high degree of alcohol with the statement that a must containing over 35 per cent. of sugar will not ferment, we must use Pasteur's figures, and then we will find that by them 35 per cent. of sugar is capable of producing over 20 per cent. of alcohol.

Temperature.—The temperature most favorable to fermentation—that is, at which it commences most promptly, and goes on the most rapidly—is between 77° and 95° F., and it does not cease until the temperature descends below 49°, or rises above 140.° If the temperature is favorable, fermentation ought to commence in ten or twelve hours from the time the pomace is put into the vat, or the juice into the barrel. In countries where the weather is cold at the wine-making season, it is necessary that the grapes should be gathered in the heat of the day, or fermentation will be long in commencing; and if the weather continues unfavorable, so that the grapes do not become warmed by the sun, it is even necessary to heat a portion of the must artificially, and pour it into the vats or casks, or to raise the temperature of the fermenting house.

Mr. Maumené also recommends that the vats be surrounded with mats of loose straw, four or five inches thick, to be kept in place by a covering of linen cloth; and in this way the temperature produced by the fermentation may be maintained in cool weather, without resorting to fires in the fermenting house.

It is not necessary, however, that the temperature of the surrounding atmosphere should be as high as that indicated as most favorable to fermentation; for it commences readily in a temperature of about 70°, and the liquid will soon rise to 85° or 95°, by the heat developed during the process; and unless the surrounding temperature descends below 65°, this heat will be maintained, and the fermentation will not be checked. Dr.

Guyot says, however, that, to make fine wines, it should be maintained at 68°, at least; and that, in other cases, it should not be allowed to fall below 60°.

Fermenting Houses.—It is important not only that fermentation should commence promptly, but that it should be maintained regularly; and although a great amount of heat is developed by fermentation, yet the must is liable to cool during the night and cold days, unless the vats and casks are protected from the change of temperature, whereby the fermentation may be checked, to the injury of the wine. The natural conclusion is that the must ought to be fermented in closed places. In California, however, it is not necessary to construct the fermenting house with the same care required in colder climates, where it is deemed desirable to furnish them with double windows and doors. It cannot be denied that good wine is made in this State, in places where the vats remain out of doors, shaded only by trees; but the practice is not to be encouraged, for the fermentation will be checked if the temperature of the surrounding atmosphere goes to 60° and below. In constructing a fermenting house, it ought to be so arranged, when practicable, as to be on a lower level than that of the stemmer and crusher, and higher than the cellar; for then the pomace and must can be run immediately into the vats and casks, and, after the first fermentation, the wine can be drawn off through a hose into the casks in the cellar, thereby saving time and labor.

CHAPTER VI.

RED WINE.

Red wines are made from colored grapes, and the color is extracted from the skins during fermentation. The coloring matter is blue, but is changed to red by the action of the acids in the must. (See *Coloring Matter—Oenocyanine.*) In order to develop this color, the grapes are fermented, skins and juice together, and the press is only brought into requisition after the first fermentation is completed.

Fermenting Tanks or Vats.—The tanks or vats in which red wine is fermented, in France are generally made of oak, sometimes of masonry, but in this State redwood has been almost universally adopted, and I am not aware of any serious inconveniences from its use. It is advisable before using them the first time, to steam them for several hours, or thoroughly soak them to extract the coloring matter of the wood.

The capacity depends upon the quantity of wine to be made in a season, varying from 1000 gallons to 2500 gallons and more, and a sufficient number should be provided that when wine making has commenced, it can be carried on without interruption till the crop is worked up. The number of workmen must be considered as well as the amount of grapes, and everything ought to be so arranged that the fermentation will be finished in the first tank filled, by the time the last one is full, so that the first can be emptied and filled again, and then the second, and so on. A hole must be bored in each vat two or three inches from the bottom by which to draw the wine through a faucet. And some kind of a strainer must be put over this hole inside to keep back the marc—a piece of perforated tin, a grating of small sticks, or a bundle of straw or vine-cuttings kept in place by a stone.

Filling the Tanks.—In order that the whole mass in one tank may be equally fermented, it should receive its full complement of grapes in one day. By putting in part of the grapes one day and part another, not only will some of them complete their fermentation before the others, but the addition of fresh grapes to the fermenting mass will interrupt the fermentation, and prove injurious to the wine. The vats must not be filled to their full capacity, for during violent fermentation the marc, consisting of skins and seeds, or those with the stems, rises to the top, brought up by the bubbles of carbonic acid which are constantly rising, and a portion of the boiling and foaming mass may be carried over the top, and much wine thereby be lost. They should only be filled to within a foot or a foot and a-half of the top, and a little experience will show the proper practice. Guyot says that they should only be filled to five-sixths of their capacity at most. Another reason for not filling the tank is that a layer of carbonic acid gas will occupy the space left vacant by the pomace, and prevent the contact of the air and the consequent souring of the wine, by the changing of a portion of the alcohol into acetic acid—vinegar.

Red wine is fermented in open vats, vats loosely covered, or in vats hermetically sealed, and good wine is made in each way.

In Open Vats, other conditions being equally favorable, fermentation commences more promptly and is sooner ended, owing to the free access of the air, a certain amount of oxygen, as already shown, being necessary to fermentation. Although fermentation will continue away from the air when once started, it will be slow. The objections to open vats are, that although there is a layer of carbonic acid resting above the must, yet it is liable to be disturbed and become mixed with the air, and if the fermentation is long continued, a portion of the wine may become sour. Those who employ open tanks should also avail themselves of those conditions under which the wine will complete its fermentation in a few days, and should draw off promptly.

Closed Vats.—By using closed vats fermentation will be longer in commencing, and will proceed more slowly, but as already intimated, the wine can with safety be left longer in them than in open tanks. When it is necessary to develop much color, it

RED WINE.

would be advisable to use covered tanks, for the longer the wine is left in contact with the skins, the darker it becomes. The covering should be close enough to prevent the immediate contact of the open air, and yet allow the escape of gas—of close boards, but not luted, unless provided with a safety valve.

The Best Practice, however, in all cases, whether the vats are closed or not, is to have a false head resting directly upon the pomace, and which will keep the latter submerged during the whole

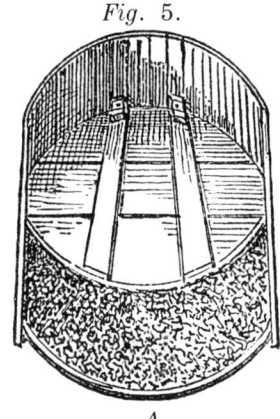

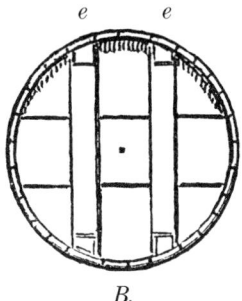

Fig. 5.

A.   B.

process of fermentation. In this way good color will be developed, and the marc will be kept from the air, and the danger of souring will be avoided. In figure 5, *A* represents a fermenting vat with the front half removed, showing the false head in place.

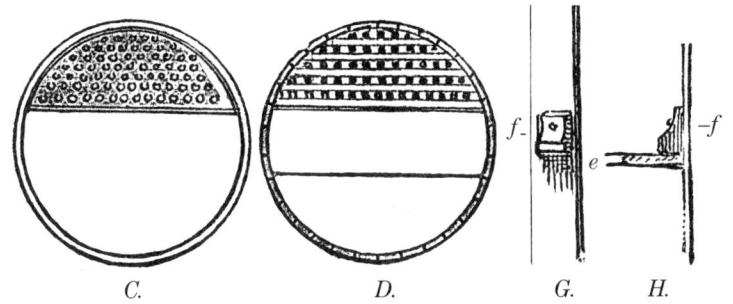

C.   D.   G.   H.

This head is made of several pieces which can be laid one by one upon the pomace, and may be perforated with auger holes as represented in *C*, or may be a wooden grating, *D*. These pieces or sections together constitute the head *B*, and are kept in place by two cross pieces, *e e*, which are held down by blocks bolted or pinned to the inside of the tank. *G* is a stave with a block, *f*, attached, and *H* the same, showing the cross piece, *e*, slipped under it. When the tank is filled to the required height, the false head is put in, resting on the pomace, the ends of the cross pieces are slipped under the blocks, and everything is ready. As soon as the fermentation becomes violent, the whole will be submerged in the bubbling wine.

Hermetically Sealed Tanks.—Closely covered tanks must be provided with a safety valve or pipe for the discharge of carbonic acid gas, leading and discharging into a vessel of water, which completely prevents contact with the air. Under pressure the fermentation is much slower, and is not so complete. Yet great advantages are claimed for this method by some writers who maintain that by keeping the cover cool with wet straw or cloth, or by using a safety tube in the form of a worm passing through a condenser on the top of the vat, the vapors are condensed and fall back into the liquid, preventing loss of alcohol, and increasing the aroma, and that the wine acquires a superior fineness and velvety smoothness under the pressure of the gas. Boireau says that this latter quality is caused by the complete dissolution of the mucilaginous matters; and Pasteur has shown that more glycerine is produced when the fermentation is slow, which may contribute to the mellowness and smoothness.

Practice in the Medoc.—Mr. Boireau says that the greater part of the grand red wines of the Médoc, the prime St. Emilion, and the prime Graves, are fermented in closed vats; though a certain number of the viniculturists still follow the old custom, and make their wine in open vats.

Stirring the Pomace in the Vats.—In Burgundy, and in some other parts of France, it is considered necessary to give the mass a thorough stirring (*foulage*) during the active fermentation, in order that all parts may be equally exposed to the action of the ferment, and also that a good color may be developed; and for this purpose men enter into the vats and thoroughly mix the pomace and stir it about with their naked bodies and limbs, a practice not only disgusting in the extreme, but dangerous for the men, who are exposed to the poisonous effects of carbonic acid. It is by no means a general practice, and is of doubtful utility, even if it should be done by other agents than the naked human body.

It is evident that two opposing forces are at work when the must is stirred during fermentation. By the aeration fermentation would naturally be increased; but Dr. Guyot shows that stirring actually diminishes its activity, and he advocates the practice in order that the fermentation be not too tumultuous. The temperature of the surrounding atmosphere being lower than that of the fermenting mass, aeration by stirring must, by lowering the temperature, diminish the activity of the fermentation. Mr. Haraszthy, in his lecture before the Convention of Viniculturists in 1882, recommended that the mass be stirred when the fermentation commences to lag, on the theory that by thus mixing again the yeast with the liquid, so exposing it again completely to the action of the ferment, fermentation would start again with renewed vigor. It can easily be stirred with poles provided with shoulders or short cross pieces.

It has already been stated that the must is sufficiently aerated by crushing the grapes with rollers, and where the vats are provided with a false head to keep the pomace submerged, the wine will have sufficient color without the stirring; and it would seem that the wine would clear sooner if the lees were not stirred into it near the end of fermentation. *Where the vats are not covered, and the grapes are not stemmed and not kept submerged*, a crust or cap is formed on the top of the fermenting mass, which sours and rots if long exposed to the air, and the mixing of this with the liquid has a most deleterious effect upon the wine.

When to Draw from the Vats.—When the first or active fermentation in the vats is completed, the new wine must be drawn off into pipes, and thus be separated from the marc, consisting of skins, seeds, and sometimes stems, and also from the heavy lees which has settled in the vats, and it is important to know the proper time to do this.

The duration of active fermentation depends upon several causes and conditions as already indicated, such as heat, the amount of sugar contained in the must, whether the vats are covered or open, the immersion of the marc, and whether the grapes are stemmed, etc. It may be completed in four or five days, or it may continue for fifteen or twenty days. In case of musts poor in sugar it may rarely terminate in twenty-four hours. In some parts of France the grapes are allowed to macerate for weeks and even months (for they cannot ferment actively for that length of time), and what might be good wine, thus is often spoiled.

The Objections to Long Vatting are that the marc will absorb an undue amount of alcohol, as is shown when it is submitted to to distillation in brandy making, for marcs which have remained long in the vats with the wine yield more spirits, and, of course, the wine is deprived of so much strength. This objection, however, would have but little force where the grapes are stemmed. Another and more serious objection is, that by a long exposure to the air which is apt to take place when the vats are not closely covered, some of the alcohol will be changed to vinegar, and the wine will rapidly degenerate, and become sour. Long contact with the seeds, skins and stems also produces a foreign taste in the wine known to the French as *goût de râpe*, stem flavor; and it is obvious that if the marc is allowed to remain in the liquid till it macerates and rots, it will acquire a still more disagreeable aroma and flavor. It is also said that some varieties of grapes which will not produce a wine with a bouquet, when allowed to remain long in the tank, will develop it in a vatting of short duration. The only advantage to be gained by leaving a wine in the vat after the active fermentation is finished, is in the way of color. When it is desirable—if it ever is—to produce a dark-colored wine at the expense of other good qualites, it may be left in the vat to *soak*. Such wines have their use, and that is to mix with those which lack color, but it is much better to mix in a quantity of grapes which naturally produce good color.

In making Fine Wines, a dark color is not looked for nor desired, but rather a bright and lively red; and they should be allowed to remain in the vat only long enough to convert the greater part of the sugar into alcohol.

How to Know when to Draw from the Vat.—It is said in general terms that the wine should be drawn from the vat when the active fermentation is finished. This is known by the taste of the wine by those long familiar with the vinous flavor which takes the place of the sweet taste of the sugar; it is also recognized by the cessation of the production of carbonic acid and the consequent bubbling, the falling of the temperature, the settling down of the marc, and by the clearing of the liquid. If the must or new wine shows from 0° to 1° by Baumé's hydrometer, or from 0° to 2° by Balling's saccharometer, nearly all the sugar will have been converted into alcohol; I say nearly all, for all the sugar is not converted till long after the wine is drawn from the vat. Boireau says that the fermentation is yet incomplete when the hydrometer marks several degrees of density, and the liquid is warm, sweetish, and muddy. He says, moreover, that care should be taken that active fermentation has entirely ceased before putting the wine in pipes, for if it is still sweetish and fermenting, it will remain sweet a long time, and ferments will often remain in suspension, which will render the wine difficult to clear, and liable to ferment and become sour.

Method of Drawing from Vats and filling Casks.—If the pipes are on the same level with the vat, or higher, the new wine is run from the vat through a faucet into buckets and carried in them to the casks and poured into these through a funnel, or is run into a large receptacle or tub placed immediately under the faucet and pumped into the casks by means of a force pump. But the more expeditious way is to have the casks ranged on a level lower than the bottom of the fermenting tank, and then to run the wine directly into them through a hose attached to the faucet. Of course, careful men must be in attendance to watch the operation, and close the faucet as soon as the cask is filled, and immediately transfer the hose to an empty one, so that the wine may not run over and waste.

Where the wine is drawn from more than one vat, it should

be equally distributed through all the casks, so that the quality may be as nearly uniform as possible. If the press wine is to be mixed with the vat wine, the casks should only be filled to three-fourths or four-fifths of their capacity, in order to leave room for the former.

Wine Presses.—Wine presses are constructed in several different forms, and the force is applied by means of a simple lever, consisting of a long timber weighted at the end and rigged with a rope and pulley to raise and lower it, or by means of a large screw. Hydraulic presses are also used in large establishments. It is not necessary here to give a detailed description of a press of either kind, for the prospective wine maker will examine the different ones and see them in action, and choose according to his means and necessities. Fig. 6 represents screw presses. A very simple one, however, and which can be made by any carpenter, consists of a box two or three feet square, and a foot or more high. This box, however, is made up of sections, each of which is five or six inches high; and they should be constructed of strong two-inch timber, well mortised together, and perforated with small holes through which the wine may ooze out. The height, and consequently the capacity of the box or receptacle will depend upon the number of sections used. A broad board constitutes the bottom of the press and should be larger than the receptacle itself, and be provided with a rim open in the middle of the lower side, and having a shallow spout for the wine to run through. This bottom is firmly placed so as to incline slightly forward, the sections are placed on it, one on the other, till the box is of the desired height, then the marc

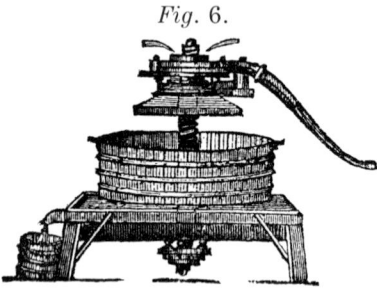

Fig. 6.

Wine Presses.

from the vat is filled in and a head or follower fitted to the inside of the box is placed on the marc, and pressure is applied with a lever. This lever is a strong piece of timber with its fulcrum end placed in a mortise in a large tree, or adjusted in any other suitable manner, allowing free play to the other end to which is attached the rope and pulley to facilitate its movement.

Pressing and Press Wine.—In the manufacture of all but fine wines, it is the usual practice to mix the press wine with the wine from the vat. And as the wine remaining in the pomace is about one-fourth of the whole, it will be equally distributed among all the casks by filling with it the vacancy left in them. If a light pressure is first applied, the wine of the first pressing will differ but little from the vat wine. After this, however, the marc should be spaded and stirred and pressure applied again, and the process repeated till the wine no longer flows. During the last pressing it is necessary to apply so much force that a great amount of coloring matter is pressed from the skins, and tannin from the seeds, and also from the stems when not removed, and the advantage of color may be more than counterbalanced by the excess of tannin. There may be danger of giving the wine too much astringency by mixing the last pressings.

Special Practice for Fine Wines.—Mr. Boireau indicates the practice in making common wines, as follows, as a warning to those who can make fine wines. He says that the wine which the marc contains is removed by pressing it almost to dryness, and that the wine thus obtained is very muddy, very harsh, and sometimes sour, particularly when the upper part of the crust has not been removed, where open vats are used and the marc not submerged. The greater part of the proprietors of the ordinary growths have the deplorable habit of mixing the press wine, without clearing it, with the limpid part drawn from the vat. He says that it should be kept separate, or otherwise the better part of the wine will be made muddy and difficult to clear.

TREATMENT OF RED WINE.

Insensible Fermentation.—After the wine has undergone its active fermentation, has been drawn from the vat and been filled into casks, the latter should be at once stored in a suitable place above ground of even, moderate temperature, or in an underground cellar whose temperature is not much below 60° F. The new wine still contains some sugar, and a slow fermentation goes on, bubbles of gas are given off, and sediment falls to the bottom. This is called the secondary or insensible fermentation, and when this is finished and no more gas arises, the wine has become clear. A good deal of the carbonic acid that rises in bubbles is not produced by the insensible fermentation, but has become dissolved in the wine during the active fermentation, and is gradually given off with the new gas produced. While the gas is produced in the cask, it must not be closely bunged, but the bung-holes should be loosely covered with a vine leaf, a block, an inverted bung, or a bag of sand, so that the gas may escape. Various patent bungs have been devised with the same object.

The wine should be tasted at each filling of the cask during this period to ascertain whether the insensible fermentation has entirely ceased, which may be known from the fact that it has lost the peculiar pungent flavor of the carbonic acid. As soon as this fermentation is ended, the casks should be tightly bunged with conical bungs, which can be easily removed during the period when it is necessary to fill up frequently.

Ulling or Filling Up.—Owing to the escape of gas and to evaporation, vacant spaces are rapidly formed in the casks which must be filled with the same kind of wine as that contained in them. It is well to keep a certain amount of the wine of each vintage in smaller vessels, to be used for this purpose, such as barrels, kegs, demijohns, and bottles, according to the extent of the vintage. If one vessel is partly emptied, the remaining wine should be put into a smaller one. It is absolutely necessary that all of the casks be kept full or the wine will spoil. (See exceptions under *Sweet Wine*.) For this purpose, during the first week they should be filled every day or two, then two or three times the next week, and later, once a week, once in two weeks, and finally once a month. This is governed a good deal by the rapidity of the evaporation, which depends upon the cellar or place of storage. This operation is performed by means of any vessel with which the wine can easily be poured into the bung hole; the convenient utensil, however, is a vessel in the form of a small watering pot with a

Fig. 7.   *Fig.* 8.

Ulling Pots.

long spout, with which the bung can easily be reached. (Figs. 7 and 8.) A good substitute is an ordinary tin funnel with a flexible rubber tube attached to the small opening. Where the casks are piled up in the cellar so that the bungs cannot otherwise be reached, a funnel called the Z funnel (fig. 9) is used, which is provided with a long spout or tube turning at right angles to the upper part, and whose tip turns down, and which can easily be passed between the casks to the bung. If, however, the bung cannot be reached, a small hole is bored in the upper part of the head of the cask, and the wine put in with a Z funnel whose tube turns at right angles but does not turn down at the tip (fig. 10.) The vent is opened in the highest part of the bulge, and wine is poured into the funnel whose tip is in the end hole till it rises to the vent, which is then closed, and the funnel is removed and the hole closed.

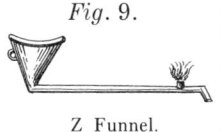

Fig. 9.

Z Funnel.

Fig. 10.

Z Funnel.

As some wine is liable to be lost in ulling a cask whose bung is out of sight, to avoid this, an instrument in the form of a watering pot, similar to figs. 7 and 8, has been devised, but whose top is entirely covered, the wine being poured into it through a tube which is closed with a cork when in use. The vent is near the tip of the spout on the under side, so that the wine will run as long as the cask is not full, but will stop as soon as the vent is covered by the wine rising in the cask. It is convenient to have a stopcock on the spout.

Many of these implements are provided with a socket to hold a candle.

Summary of the Rules for the Treatment of New Red Wines.

1. Put the casks, well bunged, in a cellar or other well closed place, and keep them constantly full, by frequently and regularly filling them with wine of the same kind.

2. Rack the wine as soon as the insensible fermentation has ceased and the wine has become limpid, *i. e.*, about December; rack again before the vernal equinox; towards the summer solstice; and also near the autumnal equinox. Racking should always be done, if possible, during cool weather. (See *Racking*.)

3. To prevent secondary fermenations, draw off the wine whenever by tasting you recognize by the flavor that it is commencing to work.

If the wines are bright, avoid fining, and so preserve their fruity flavor; but if they remain muddy after the second racking, fine them after the third drawing off with the whites of eggs, and leave them the shortest possible time on the finings.

Mr. Boireau says that by such treatment wines will be obtained limpid and free from secondary fermentations, and that grand wines will so preserve their fruity flavor; while if they are allowed to work again after the cessation of the insensible fermentation, they will lose their fruity flavor and mellowness, and become too dry. In order to avoid this dryness produced by secondary fermentations, which will considerably diminish the value of the wines, and especially of grand wines, some wine makers place the casks with the bung on one side after the June racking; this practice should not be followed, for the elevation of the temperature at that season is liable to set them fermenting.

The idea is in all cases to avoid mixing the lees with the wine, and if young wines are to be shipped before the arrival of the period of the first racking, they should nevertheless be carefully drawn off, if they have already become clear, for to mingle again the lees with wine, predisposes it to secondary fermentations, and renders it difficult to clarify.

Treatment of Old Red Wines.—Wines after the fourth racking are treated as old wines. When they have acquired a clean taste, are limpid and no longer ferment, the casks should be carefully filled and tightly bunged, and they should be stored in a suitable place, with the bung turned to one side. The bung being thus constantly wet swells and exactly fills the hole, the wine keeps better, there is less loss by evaporation, and constant filling up is avoided.

If it happens that by bad treatment the wines are not clear and behave badly, they should receive the necessary treatment, and be clarified before permanently put away with the bung at the side.

In cellars and other well closed places, old red wine, clean tasting, bright and quiet, stored in good, well hooped casks, need only two rackings per year, one in March and the other in September, unless for some reason it loses its limpidity by entering again into fermentation, which will be discovered by tasting from time to time. In that case, it should immediately be drawn off without regard to the date of the former racking, and then fined.

Care should be taken not to leave ullage in the cask of old wine, by frequent samplings and tastings. And when it occurs, in order to avoid its effects, the wine may immediately be drawn into a smaller cask, and this is necessary more frequently in airy storehouses where the evaporation is greater than in cellars.

Boireau says that if these rules are carefully observed the wines will improve, and develop all the qualities which by their nature they are susceptible of acquiring. The greater or less degree of fineness which they acquire by aging under proper conditions results principally from two causes: The first is the deposit of coloring matter and divers salts which the new wine contains in dissolution, and which become insoluble by entering into new combinations, and which in their turn are removed at each racking, with the lees; the second cause is the transformation of the tannin, which gives the wine a certain degree of roughness, into gallic acid, and its extraction in the insoluble combinations which it forms with the different principles contained in the wine and with the finings which are introduced. It follows that old wine loses part of its color and soluble salts, and a great part of the tannin which it originally contained. Its taste is more delicate, its flavor, which was masked by these different matters, comes out better, its bouquet commences to develop, and its mellowness is more pronounced.

These remarks are more particularly applicable to grand wines, for in many of the ordinary ones the fruity flavor which they have when new is lost before the end of the first year, because the mucilages and pectine, which give them their mellowness, are either precipitated with the lees or are destroyed by insensible fermentation. In general these wines lack firmness, body and tannin, and many of them show a strong tendency to lose their color.

The time necessary for wines to remain in wood in order to acquire the highest degree of perfection which they can acquire in casks, depends upon the quality of the wine; wines of strength and body require more time than feeble ones.

Our author says that, on the average, the poorest wines of the Médoc become bright about the end of two years, and if they are kept longer, they lose their mellowness. But on the other hand, the firm and full-bodied wines of the same localities require to remain in wood a year longer to arrive at perfect maturity. Certain wines strongly charged with tannin, coming from certain localities, and those made from the *verdot* grape, are long in developing, but they keep so much the longer.

When they have attained their entire development and the separation of the lees is complete, they must be bottled, for they will lose their qualities if left in casks. In bottles they arrive at perfection; they acquire bouquet while they preserve their mellowness, but in casks, they finally lose their fruity flavor and velvety smoothness, and become dry.

And he gives the following

Summary of Rules for the Care of Old Red Wines.

1. They should be kept in places perfectly closed, and before turning the bung to one side, we should be satisfied that they are perfectly bright, quiet, and well behaved.

2. They should be drawn from the lees twice a year; the casks should be kept full; and they should be kept from secondary fermentations by watching and opportune racking.

3. Keep down the loss by evaporation by all means possible, and keep them in close cellars, in strong, well hooped casks, and avoid ullage.

4. Bottle them before they lose their fruity flavor, and as soon as they cease to deposit.

Thus will they acquire all the qualities of which by their nature they are susceptible.

But if they are kept in places to which the air has free access, the evaporation will be great; and if the casks are left with ullage caused by too frequent sampling, or too infrequent racking, they will work, become dry, lose their mellowness, and become slightly affected by acetic acid, produced by contact with the air.

CHAPTER VII.

WHITE WINE.

Made from both Red and White Grapes.—As the color of grapes resides entirely in the skins, with the exception of a few varieties such as the *Tienturiers* and the American variety *Lenoir*, which have colored juice, with these exceptions, white wine may be made from both white and colored grapes.

Differences between Red and White Wine.—Instead of putting the pomace into fermenting vats, it is taken immediately to the press, and the juice is fermented by itself, free from stems, skins, and seeds, and is therefore not only free from the coloring matter contained in the skins, but also from the numerous matters that are contained in red wine, extracted from the pomace during fermentation. It is true that white wine may be made from white grapes by the process that is employed in making red wine from colored grapes, but then it ceases to be what is commonly called white wine, and possesses all the characteristics of red wine except its color, which of itself has little effect upon the wine, except to change its appearance; for when white wine has been colored by the addition of a small quantity of very dark wine, it remains white wine still in all its other characteristics, and the difference is readily detected by experts.

Hygienic effects of Red and of White Wine.— Dr. Guyot says that white wines generally are diffusible stimulants of the nervous system; if they are light, they act rapidly upon the human organism, and excite all its functions. But they escape as readily by the skin and excretory organs, and their effect is of short duration. Red wines, on the other hand, are tonic and persistent stimulants of the nerves, muscles, and digestive organs; their action is slower and more prolonged; they do not increase perspiration or the excretions, and their action generally is astringent, persistent, and concentrated.

Process of Making.—As the must comes from the press it is either immediately run into casks, or is first put into a vat to settle. In the latter case it is allowed to stand in the settling vat from twelve to twenty-four hours, and a large portion of the yeasty parts settle to the bottom, a thick scum rises to the surface, and the must becomes partially cleared. The scum is then skimmed from the top, and the liquid is drawn off into casks, leaving the heavy lees. By this means a great part of the fermentive matter is immediately removed, and the wine does not ferment as thoroughly nor as rapidly as it otherwise would, and retains a portion of its sugar and its sweetness longer. In the Champagne districts the musts for sparkling wines are thus treated. If the weather is very warm, it may not be practicable to do this, because fermentation will set in before the must has time to settle. If, however, it is desired to make a dry wine, the must is not put into a settling vat, but is run from the press directly into the casks.

The Barrels in which white wine is fermented and stored are generally of small size, of a capacity of from 30 to 150 gallons, or say 50 or 60 gallons on an average, and it is considered in France that it preserves its good qualities in casks of moderate size better than in large ones. It is to be understood, however, that it is considered advisable in most parts of France that white wine should retain a portion of its sweetness and be mellow rather than dry; but if it is desirable to make a dry wine, larger casks may be used for fermenting and storing. (But see *Summary of Rules*, below, and *Casks*.)

Filling the Barrels during Fermentation.—A question upon which there is some difference of opinion, is whether the casks should be immediately filled to their full capacity and kept filled up during the first fermentation, so that the scum and foam will be thrown out of the bung, or whether a vacant space shall be left in each barrel, so that all the matter thrown up by the fermentation shall remain. The objections to allowing the wine to *boil over* are that much good wine is thereby lost, and the outside of the barrels and the floor of the fermenting house or cellar becomes foul. When the active fermentation ceases, whatever has been thrown up in the form of a dirty scum will settle to the bottom with the rest of the lees, and is no more injurious than the latter. If, however, the foam is allowed to run over by keeping the barrels full, a portion of the yeasty parts will be thrown out, fermentation will not go on as tumultuously nor be as complete, and the wine will longer retain a portion of its sweetness. So that the practice in this behalf, as in most others where there is a diversity of practices in making white wine, depends upon whether it is desired to make a very dry wine, or one that retains a portion of its sugar. But in the Champagne districts, although they allow the marc to settle, they do not allow it to run over in fermenting.

Pressing and Filling.—The pomace is pressed in the same manner as the marc of red wine, in two or three different pressings. The usual practice is to fill the barrels with an equal amount of must from each pressing, so that the contents of all shall be uniform in quality. If it is known beforehand how much wine can be made from a given quantity of grapes, the requisite number of barrels will be provided for each lot, and the must of each pressing will be equally distributed in all. (See *General Chapter*.)

Different kinds of White Wine.—Boireau divides white wines into three classes: dry, mellow, and sweet, whose characteristics depend essentially upon the density of their musts.

In Dry White Wines fermentation is complete, and all the sugar that is appreciable by the taste or the hydrometer, except the small amount changed into other substances, is transformed into alcohol and carbonic acid. The grapes are gathered as soon as ripe, and are not allowed to shrivel. The density of the must rarely exceeds 13° Baumé.

Mellow White Wines are those which preserve a small quantity of sugar after the tumultuous fermentation has ceased, and which gives them mellowness and unctuosity. To produce these wines, it is necessary to increase the density of the must, which is accomplished in the Gironde by leaving the grapes upon the vines until they shrivel and turn brown (white grapes are used), and they are gathered by several successive pickings. The density of the must is from 12° to 15° Baumé. These wines occupy the place between dry wines and sweet wines.

White Sweet Wines (vins de liqueur) are those which preserve a considerable portion of their sugar, which renders them very sweet. And in order that they may retain their sweetness in aging, the must should mark 15° to 20° Baumé.

The Grand White Wines of France and Germany do not require any different treatment from that already described, except that the greatest care is exercised in assorting the grapes and allowing them to arrive at the period of greatest maturity, and, of course, they are made from the choicest varieties.

In describing the condition in which the grapes are when gathered, the French use the word *pourris*, which is usually translated *rotten*. But Boireau says that it must not be supposed that the grapes are spoiled (*gâtés*) because they are *pourris*; the condition which is sought is a sort of natural dessication effected by the heat of the sun, which evaporates a part of the water of vegetation and concentrates the saccharine matter, as well as the savory and aromatic principle, and bakes the grape, as it were. If the weather remains dry, the grapes remain for a fortnight perfectly ripe without any deterioration of the skin, but little by little it changes from yellow or golden to brown, loses its consistency and *rots*, or rather cracks and gives way. It is then that dessication commences; the rays of the sun penetrate the thin pellicle and volatilize the water of vegetation. In order to better accomplish this result a portion of the leaves are removed from the vine when the grapes are nearly ripe. Those grapes only are picked which are sufficiently shriveled; if only a part of the cluster is ripe, a few grapes are removed at a picking. The vines are usually gone over in this manner three times. At Barsac and Sauternes the white wines are known by three different names, indicating in their order their strength and sweetness: The first, or sweetest, are called *têtes;* the second, *centres;* and the third, *queues;* or head wines, middle wines, and tail wines. If the must does not indicate more than 12°, 13°, or 14° Baumé, the wine cannot be expected to preserve its sweetness and mellowness in aging. If it is desired to make the sweet head wines, having the inimitable flavor (*goût de roti*) which they get from the great maturity of the grapes, the density must be allowed to increase till Baumé's instrument marks 18° to 20°. Wines from must of 16° Baumé will preserve their sweetness for a long time, but as they develop a large amount of alcohol, it is preferable that they be sweeter, and that the must mark 18° to 20°. As these wines do not develop more than 15 to 16 per cent. of alcohol by fermentation, they will not bear transportation through tropical climates with safety, and it is necessary to add spirit enough to raise the strength to 18 per cent. If, however, they are carefully managed, and kept in a cool cellar, they will remain sweet.

Treatment of White Wines.—During the active fermentation they should be left in a moderately warm place of even temperature, and until the foaming has ceased. Then, they may be stored in a cooler place if desirable, or may be left where they are. But then the bungs should be loosely closed with a chip or anything that will allow the escape of gas, and the casks must be filled up every two or three days. When the gas has ceased, they should be bunged tight, and filled up once or twice a week, according to the rapidity of evaporation, until the first racking. (*See below.*)

To keep Sweet.—If it is desired that the wine should preserve a portion of its sweetness and remain mellow, care should be taken not to disturb it after it has commenced depositing, for thereby the sediment and ferment will be again mingled with the wine and its fermentation rendered more active, all its sugar may be transformed, and the wine become dry. Fermentation may be checked at any period by sulphuring, as is described under the proper head (see *Sulphuring and Unfermented Must*), and so the wines may be made dry or sweet at will; but if the sweet ones contain less than 15 per cent. of alcohol they will ferment. By sulphuring they may be kept sweet from one vintage to another, even if the musts have not a high degree of sugar; but they must be constantly kept under the influence of sulphurous acid and protected from the air. But the frequent sulphuring and racking which they must necessarily undergo gives them an odor and a flavor of sulphur; and if they are not watched they ferment.

The care to be given to white wines after the first racking depends upon their character.

In the Case of Dry Wines, whose sugar has all been transformed, the same attentions are to be bestowed as in the case of new red wines, and the rules laid down are referred to. (See *Red Wine*.)

Mellow White Wines, that is, those which retain a portion of their sweetness after the tumultuous fermentation, particularly if they do not carry 15 per cent. of alcohol, require the greatest amount of care in order to preserve their mellowness in aging; for if left to themselves they will again enter into fermentation, and become dry. Such wines should be preserved against all ulterior fermentations, and should be made perfectly bright and freed from ferments, but this should be done with as little fining or filtration as possible, which diminishes their mellowness.

It may be well to note that the less alcohol that mellow wines have, the more susceptible they are to fermentation, and the consequent loss of their mellowness.

Those which have 15 per cent. and have kept their mellowness after the first fermentation, do not lose it as readily as those of a less degree. If they have less than 15 per cent. of spirit and are sweet, to retain their sweetness, they must be completely clarified to free them from ferments; and in some cases it is necessary not only to rack them, but at the same time to sulphur them, and fine them with gelatine after adding tannin.

Such wines, not having naturally terminated their fermentation, which was arrested by sulphurous acid, reiterated rackings, the extraction of ferments, and the lowering of the temperature—have a natural tendency to ferment; and the arrested fermentation readily recommences if the wine is left to itself, if vigilance is relaxed, if the temperature increases, or if subjected to the movement of transportation.

WHITE WINE.

On the contrary, in those which have acquired the largest amount of alcohol possible by fermentation (between 15 and 16 per cent.), no new spirit is formed at the expense of the sugar, except in case of loss of strength by evaporation or other enfeebling cause.

Summary of Rules for the treatment of mellow white wines, according to Boireau:

1. They should be stored in perfectly closed places, in strong, well hooped casks.

2. The casks should always be kept tightly bunged, and constantly full, by frequent and regular ullings, with bright wine of the same quality, and having the same temperature.

3. They should become bright, be protected against secondary fermentations, and freed from the yeast which they contain by rackings during the first year, according as their lees are deposited. Fining should not be resorted to except when they cannot be cleared by racking at the proper time (rigorously protected from contact with the air) into a cask sulphured with a double square of a sulphur match.

4. When they have been three or four years in wood, if they are not then bottled, they should be racked and transferred to tuns where they receive the same care; the tuns should be first tempered with wines of the same class.

5. They must be constantly watched and frequently tasted to assure one's self that they do not enter into fermentation; if they do, they must be racked at once.

Racking.—When they remain calm after the insensible fermentation is terminated, whether they are old or young, they should be racked three times each year; first, at the sprouting of the vine in the spring, in March, before the equinox; secondly, at the flowering of the vine in June, before the summer solstice; and thirdly, at the ripening of the grape in September, before the autumnal equinox. (See *Racking*.)

CHAPTER VIII.

CASKS.

Casks are almost universally made of oak, though other material has been tried, but generally to be abandoned in favor of the first named. Large, covered tanks of redwood are used to some extent in California for storing red wine, being first well steamed to extract the coloring matter of the wood, but they are not considered desirable, and had better be replaced by oak casks.

Oak Wood.—In France very nice distinctions used to be made as to the kind and nationality of the wood used, the shook from the north, Dantzig, Lubeck, Memel, Riga, and Stettin, taking the first rank, that from America the second, and that known as Bosnian, from the southern provinces of Austria and the north of Turkey in Europe, the third, and that of France the fourth. That from America is the most pliable, but is liable to be found worm-eaten.

All kinds of oak wood contain in different proportions fourteen different principles, several of which are dissolved by wine, and among the most important of which are tannin, gallic acid, a bitter extractive, mucilage, vegetable albumen, and several of pronounced smell and taste. The Bosnian oak contains the most tannin and soluble matter, and is suitable for highly colored wines. But now-a-days there is not so much stress laid upon the quality of the wood as formerly. Their extracts serve often to correct some of the defects of the wine, and many of them are neutralized by the ingredients of the latter. By the introduction of their tannin and albumen the clarification of wine is facilitated; but none but new wine whose insensible fermentation is not yet completed should be put into new casks, for they cause older wines to lose their transparency, and give them a woody flavor which may last a long time. Therefore, temper your new casks with new wine.

Storing Casks.—Casks should be kept in a closed place, not so dry as to cause much shrinkage, nor so damp as to cause mould. In California during the summer, there is no danger from the latter, but the former should be guarded against. In winter, the reverse is the rule. Where casks are to be kept a long time empty, they should be sulphured and tightly bunged, and the sulphuring should be repeated every six months. But they must be carefully washed before putting wine into them. They are less liable to be attacked by the borer if stored in a dark place.

New Casks.—Before putting wine into a new cask, it is ordinarily sufficient to give it a thorough washing with boiling water. Pour in one or two gallons of hot water, bung it up, and roll it and shake it about till it is thoroughly rinsed, letting it rest awhile on each end, and not only will this sufficiently cleanse the cask, but will show if there are any leaks. When the water is nearly cold, let it run out, and thoroughly rinse with cold water, and turn down the bung-hole and leave till well drained.

Mr. Maigne recommends that a couple of pounds of salt be dissolved in the first water, and that the second washing be made with a decoction of peach leaves. Often the casks are soaked for a day with cold water, then washed with lime water, prepared by adding four pounds of lime to two gallons of boiling water for a 100-gallon cask. After thorough agitation, it is washed with cold water. Sometimes, too, the cask is washed with a gallon or so of boiling wine, but it is an unnecessary waste.

Mr. Boireau says that when it is necessary to put old or very delicate wines into new casks, the greater part of the soluble matters can be extracted in the following manner: Pour in about two gallons of boiling lye made from ashes or potash, or other alkaline substance, such as slacked lime or pulverized chalk, etc., for they will dissolve out more of those soluble matters than pure water. After thoroughly agitating the cask, pour out the lye, and repeat the process; afterwards rinse with boiling water, and run it out before cold; then wash with cold water acidulated with one-tenth part of sulphuric acid, which enfeebles the solubility of these matters; finally, rinse with cold water and drain.

These latter operations may be avoided by first washing with hot water, and then filling the casks with common wine of the color of that intended to be put into them, and leaving them for about two weeks.

And before filling them with a grand red wine, it will be well to moisten the inner walls of the cask with a glass or so of good, old brandy.

Old Casks, or those which have been in use, should be well washed as soon as emptied, and the washings should be repeated with clean water until it runs out perfectly clear. Oftentimes the cask will have more or less lees adhering to its inner walls, which cannot be removed by an ordinary washing, but it will be necessary to make use of the *rinsing chain*. This chain is about six feet long, consisting of links made of square iron whose corners will more readily detach the lees. One end is attached to a long conical bung to keep it from falling into the cask, and the other is armed with a square block of iron of a size to easily go into the bung-hole (fig. 11). After pouring in two or three gallons of boiling water, leave the cask for a while so that the lees may become softened, then introduce the chain by the bung-hole, and close it with the bung at the other end of the instrument. Thoroughly roll and agitate the cask till the chain and its iron block have removed the lees so that they will run out with the water. Repeat the operation with clean water as often as necessary, and rinse till the water runs out limpid, and let the cask drain.

Fig. 11. 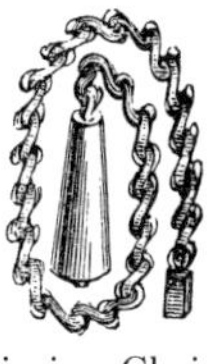
Rinsing Chain.

Fig. 12.

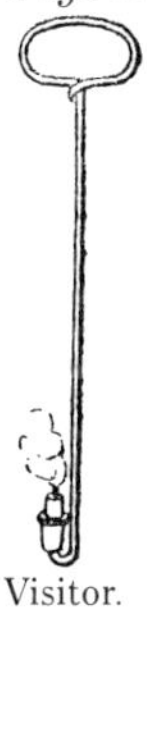

To Examine the Inside of a Cask, an instrument called a *visitor* is used. This is simply a piece of heavy wire bent into a loop or handle at the upper end, with the lower end turned up and bent around into the form of a small ring into which a candle can be inserted (fig. 12). Put a piece of a candle into this candlestick or socket, light it, and lower it into the cask through the bung, and the interior can be inspected.

Visitor.

Empty Casks should not be allowed to remain long without Washing; as soon as the lees are removed, they should be rinsed as already mentioned, and they should not be put to drain in the sun, for the heat will transform the alcohol remaining into vinegar in a few hours.

Sulphuring Casks.—If the cask is to be kept empty for some time, after it has been washed and then drained for a few minutes, it should be sulphured by burning in it a piece of sulphur match about an inch square, and it should then be left to drain dry. After twenty-four hours, burn in it three or four inches of the match, and bung it up with the gas in it. Store it in a suitable place as described for new casks, and sulphur it every three months. (See *Sulphuring*.)

Condition to be Examined.—In using an old cask, as well as a new one, the first thing to ascertain is if it leaks. If the hoops are loose, they should be driven; then pour in two or three pails of water, and stand the cask alternately on each end, and if it is found to leak, soak it till it is tight. If the leaks cannot be stopped by driving the hoops and by soaking, it must be repaired.

The next thing to ascertain is, if the cask has become sour, mouldy, or has been otherwise injuriously affected, as it is liable to be if put away without being carefully washed and cared for. This can be ascertained by examining with the *visitor*, or by smelling. If, when the candle or a piece of lighted sulphur match is lowered into the cask, it ceases to burn, the cask probably contains a noxious gas, which must be expelled. This may be done by blowing in the bung-hole with a hand-bellows till the air is changed, or by standing the cask on its lower end with the hole in the upper head open, and the open bung turned towards the wind. If, however, it is in the condition which the French call *eventé*, which corresponds with that diseased condition of wine called by the same name and which we call flatness, the gas being carbonic acid, and heavier than air, will run out of its own accord if the open bung is turned down and the cask left for a while in that position.

Flatness in the Cask, as we will call it for want of a better term, Boireau says, consists in the disengagement of carbonic acid gas which is produced in the interior, and is generally found in casks which have been bunged up without washing, and which gives them an odor of stagnant lees with slight acidity, and will extinguish the sulphur match. After the bad air has been expelled the cask should be well washed with the use of the chain. A cask which has contained wine that has become flat should receive the same treatment. If a large tun is to be treated, the foul air should be expelled, and a man should not enter till a light will burn in it. (See *the disease, Flatness.*)

Acidity will be found in the cask if it is left for several days uncared for; the alcohol contained in the wine remaining on the inside of the cask acidifies in contact with the oxygen of the air, and is soon changed into acetic acid, and the change is much more rapid in a high temperature. Instead of being simply flat, the cask is now really sour, and smells of vinegar. The treatment consists in either removing or neutralizing the acid. The first can be done by steam. Turn the bung-hole down, and conduct a jet of steam into the cask either through the faucet-hole or the bung; the water condensed from the steam charged with acid runs out at the bung-hole, and the process must be continued till the water no longer has an acid flavor.

Where it is not convenient to use steam, rinse the cask by using the chain, and scald it out with hot lye made from wood ashes or potash, or with quicklime dissolved in hot water. Give it several rinsings with the alkaline solution without allowing it to cool, and, if possible, fill it with cold water and let it soak three or four days, and rinse as usual. If the water is allowed to remain longer in the cask it may become stagnant.

Mouldy Casks.—Casks may become mouldy inside when left in a damp place, if the bungs are left out, or if they are leaky through defective staves or hoops, sometimes even when they have been sulphured, and much more if they have not been. This condition is recognized by a mouldy smell. The surest way to treat a mouldy cask is to take out the head, and give it a thorough scrubbing with a stiff broom and water. If after removing the mould the staves resume the color of wine-stained wood, it is proof that the wood has not been affected, and the head may be replaced, and the cask rinsed in the usual way. If, however, after removing the mould, the wood is found to be of a brown color, it is more or less rotten.

Rottenness is due to the same causes as mouldiness, and when the inside of a cask is decayed, it is no longer fit for wine. If, however, the mouldy cask is brown only in spots, they should be entirely scraped off, and then it may be used. But it is best not to put good wine into such casks, for there is danger of spoiling it.

Brandy Casks, when emptied, should simply be bunged up, without washing, as the alcohol remaining will have a preservative effect. They should not be kept in a place which is too damp.

Do not Sulphur Old Brandy or Whisky Casks which have recently been emptied or in which any alcohol remains, or you may cause a disastrous explosion. In preparing new casks for the reception of brandy, they should be washed and left to drain for twenty-four hours and until they are dry, and if they are to be kept some time, throw in a glass or two of brandy, bung tightly, and roll and shake till the inside is moistened with the liquor. If they are to be used at once, they ought to be first soaked with water for three or four days to remove the woody taste.

Boireau says that common wines may be put into brandy barrels, or even oil barrels which have not become rancid (olive oil barrels, I presume), but that fine wines should never be put into them. He also adds that wine should not be put into casks which have been used for rum, kirsch, vinegar, absinthe, vermouth, or any other liquor having a strong odor, traces of which will be preserved in the pores of the wood, even after the staves have been scraped.

Cask Borers.—There is a beetle which is very destructive of casks in California, which Mr. J. J. Rivers, curator of the museum of the University, describes as *Sinoxlylon dective* of the family of

Bostrichidae. In a paper read before the Anthrozoic Club, and reported in the *Rural Press*, Vol. XX, p. 153, 1880, he states that at the request of Mr. Schram, of Napa county, he experimented with the insect in order to ascertain a remedy for the ruin caused by it. He says that "Its primary mischief is caused by the habit of the parent insect boring a hole three or more inches for the purpose of depositing eggs. As casks are usually much less than three inches in thickness, the beetle taps the liquid contents, and loss accrues by leakage. The remedy I first thought of was to select some species of wood suitable for cask making that would be unpalatable to this insect. My endeavors in that way have resulted in failure for the reason that this beetle appears to have no particular dislike to oak, chesnut, pine, whitewood, and several of the eucalypti. The next step was to saturate the outside of the cask with a strong solution of alum water applied hot, and when dry, a coat of linseed oil, this latter to prevent the alum from being washed out, as it would be in time. This proved a success, for all the examples treated with the solution were untouched, while the unprepared were riddled by the borer." The insect is more destructive to casks stored in light places; it is therefore better to keep them in the dark.

The Size of the Casks is a matter of a good deal of importance. For shipping, the ordinary pipe or puncheon holding from 150 to 200 gallons is of a convenient size for handling, but for storing it is better to use as large a vessel as possible, and where the quantity stored is large, tuns of from 1000 to 3000 gallons or more in size are far preferable. In the first place, it is a well known fact that wine made at the same time, of grapes of like varieties, from the same vineyard, and under the same apparent conditions, turns out quite differently in different casks, and the contents of one cask may far excel in quality that of another. In order to insure uniformity in a large quantity of wine, it is necessary to store it in large receptacles.

Another, and perhaps still more important consideration, is that there is much less loss by evaporation when the wine is stored in large casks. The evaporation in a small barrel will be almost as great as in a cask three or four times the size, and to keep the small one full will require about the same amount of wine at each ulling, which must be performed nearly as often. There are two reasons for this: first, because the staves of small casks are thinner, and secondly, because in them a greater surface of wine is exposed to evaporation, according to the volume, than in the case of the larger vessel.

Guyot says, however, that the larger the receptacles, other conditions being equal, the more rapid the development of the wines, and the sooner they go through the periods of their life, and arrive at decrepitude. He says that the greater part of wines, especially light wines and white wines, cannot endure a long sojourn in tuns, vats, and cisterns. They go through the phases of their life with a rapidity fatal to their good qualities; nevertheless, this fact may be utilized to hasten the epoch when wine may be used or put upon the market; also to produce dry wines, to vinify sweet ones, and to age those of good body. If, therefore, his theory is well founded—and we know that fermentation once established is more active, if the mass is great—the intelligent man will act in this behalf as circumstances require. It would seem, however, that a large mass would be less affected by sudden changes of temperature, and therefore, better protected from their consequent ill effects.

And Boireau recommends that white wines be stored in tuns, when mature, as already mentioned. (See *Aging*.)

CHAPTER IX.

SULPHURING—ARRESTING FERMENTATION.

Casks are sulphured for the purpose of destroying the activity of the ferments contained in the lees which may remain in them, and thereby to prevent their moulding or souring, and must and wine are sulphured to prevent or to check fermentation, and white wine also to keep it from turning yellow.

Sulphurous Oxide, or Sulphur Dioxide, is produced by burning sulpur. It is a colorless gas, of a suffocating odor, and is composed of equal weights of sulphur and oxygen, or, one part of the former and two of the latter, SO_2, and with water becomes sulphurous acid. It arrests fermentation in two ways: first, it absorbs oxygen with avidity, and thereby removes what may be in the must or wine, or in the cask, thus taking away one of the conditions necessary to the life and activity of the ferment. (See *Fermentation*.) In the second place, by the absorption of oxygen, sulphuric acid is formed from the sulphurous acid, in a highly concentrated state, which is destructive of the life of the ferment.

The Sulphurer, or Sulphur Burner, the instrument *Fig.* 14. used for the purpose indicated, consists of a wire with a *Fig.* 13. hook at one end, and the other attached to the centre of a long, conical bung (fig. 13). It is convenient to have the upper end pass entirely through the bung, allowing the latter to move up and down on the wire, so that the hook can be raised or lowered, according to the position to be occupied in the cask. This is used by attaching the sulphur match to the hook and lowering it into the cask, after lighting it. The objection to this form of instrument is, that the coal or cinder left on the hook, after burning the

Sulphurer. match, may fall into the cask and give the wine Maumené's an unpleasant flavor. To avoid this, Mr. Maumené Sulphurer.

invented a sulphurer, provided with a deep perforated porcelain cup, into which the match is placed and in which it burns, and which retains the carbonized linen (fig. 14). A piece of wire cloth bent into a cup of a similar form and attached to the lower end of the wire answers the purpose very well.

Sulphur Matches or Bands may be purchased, or they may be easily manufactured. To make them, melt roll brimstone (stick brimstone), or what is better, flowers of sulphur, over a slow fire (sulphur melts at 115° C. or 239° F.); tear linen or cotton cloth into strips an inch and a-half wide and 10 or 12 inches long, and dip them into the melted sulphur, and lay them aside to cool. Then dip again, and repeat the process, dipping and cooling, till the coating of sulphur is of the required thickness, and they should be thickly coated, or it may be necessary to burn too much linen to get sufficient gas. If the sulphur is overheated, the match will be dark-colored.

Sweet scented powders are often added to the sulphur, whose essential oils are disengaged when the sulphur is burned, and the cask is perfumed by their vapors. The substances usually employed are ginger, cinnamon, the flowers of the stock gilly, iris, lavender, thyme, violet, etc., and the matches prepared with the addition of them is generally preferred.

Mr. Maumené says that the smallest amount of this volatile oil gives a perfume to the wine, which is generally advantageous, but Boireau is of opinion, however, that these substances check the combustion of the sulphur, and in a measure neutralize its action, and he prefers the sulphur pure.

To Sulphur a Cask, take a piece of the sulphur match and light it and lower it into the middle of the cask by means of the sulphur burner, and lightly put in the bung of the instrument. By applying the ear to the staves, it can be ascertained if the match is burning. If the air is foul in the cask, and the match will not burn, the noxious gas must be expelled as described under the head of *Casks*. When the fire is extinguished the burner is withdrawn, care being taken, if the hook is used, not to drop any of the carbonized linen into the cask. If that should happen, the cask must be washed again. As the burning sulphur fills the cask with gas, which exerts considerable pressure, care should be taken that the bung is not blown out into the face of the operator.

Sometimes a strip of the sulphured cloth is lighted at one end and lowered into the cask, the other end being secured by putting in the bung. This is objectionable, because it leaves the debris of the match sticking to the bung and the stave, which may give a disagreeable flavor to the wine. As already mentioned under the head of *Casks*, never burn a match in a cask containing alcohol.

To Sulphur Wine, if the cask is only partly full, operate the same as in sulphuring an empty cask, only care must be taken not to lower the match into the wine. Here the sulphur burner with a movable bung comes in play. If the cask is full, the gas may be drawn in by burning a match close to a hole bored in the head of the cask somewhat higher than the faucet, drawing from the latter at the same time. It is evident that while the wine runs from the lower hole, the gas will be drawn in at the vent. Where it is necessary to leave a cask with a vacancy in it for some time, flowers and souring may be prevented by burning in it a piece of sulphur match and bunging it up, and the process should be repeated every two weeks, and besides as often as the bung is removed for any purpose. It is better always to keep the cask full, for in time the sulphurous gas will communicate a disagreeable taste to the wine, which it takes a long time to remove.

Sulphuring should be Avoided in Certain Cases.—Ropy wines should not be sulphured, for the presence of oxygen is necessary in order to help their fermentation; nor should those wines be sulphured which it is desirable to keep in a state of effervescence. Sulphur should be very sparingly used in connection with red wines, as it causes them to lose a portion of their color by rendering insoluble the coloring matter, and precipitating it; and for the same reason it is used for bleaching white wines, and it prevents the latter from turning yellow. Liqueur wines which are slow of fermentation should not be sulphured, for they need all the natural aids to fermentation.

Fermentation is Arrested, sometimes, in the manufacture of white wines, by drawing them off into well sulphured casks, using two or three squares of the match, if the fermentation is not very tumultuous; but if it is very active, it may be treated as mentioned below for musts. And in most cases the proper practice is, where wine needs sulphuring, to draw it off into the sulphured cask, and in this way the oxygen contained in the wine is more thoroughly exposed to the action of the gas.

Unfermented Must.—By sulphuring the must, fermentation is prevented, and thereby is produced what the French call *mute wine;* and it is the must of white grapes as it comes from the press that is more generally subjected to the process. It is first allowed to settle as described in the chapter on white wine, but it must be drawn from the vat as soon as signs of fermentation appear, and bubbles of carbonic acid rise to the surface. And to have the must clear, it must be closely watched, for as soon as fermentation sets in, it becomes turbid. The must should be freed from all fragments of stems, skins, seeds, etc., and should therefore be strained as it runs from the press.

It is Prepared in Two Different Ways.—First, the cask must be scalded, rinsed, and drained in the usual way, and then as much sulphur must be burned in it as can be consumed, or until the match goes out for want of oxygen. Then the cask must be rapidly made half full of the must, and closely bunged. It should then be rolled and thoroughly shaken until the gas has been well absorbed by the juice. The must is then drawn off without allowing it to come in contact with the air (See *Racking*), and into another cask which has been sulphured in the same manner, and is treated as before. While the second cask is being agitated, sulphur is again burned in the one just emptied, until it goes out, and then the must is transferred back in the same manner, and is again shaken. It is subjected to this operation four times, and the cask is finally filled with must treated in the same way, and tightly bunged. The more successful will the operation be, the more the liquid is kept from contact with the air, and therefore this method is preferable to the next. The second method is as follows: burn in an empty cask matches representing a couple of ounces of sulphur; pour in about five gallons of must, bung it up and thoroughly shake; take out the bung and put in another lighted match; if it will not burn for want of oxygen, the air must be renewed by blowing in the cask with a bellows. Then burn the match in the cask, and afterwards pour in five gallons more of must, bung and shake as before. Continue the process till the cask lacks about five gallons of being full. Then five gallons must be sulphured in another cask, and the cask filled up with this and tightly bunged. Of course, the sulphur burner must be shortened as the cask fills up.

Must treated in this manner may be kept for a long time if well clarified, and the cask is well sulphured at each racking, or a portion sulphured when it commences to ferment.

If it is only necessary to keep the must a short time, a portion only, say one-third, need be sulphured. In that case there will be less odor of sulphur, and it will soon pass away.

Clarification and Care of Unfermented Must.—It should be kept in good, strong casks, well hooped and well bunged, in closed cellars of a constant temperature. The casks should be filled every few days with sulphured must; and they should be frequently racked to free them from ferments. They should not be exposed to the air when racking, and should be racked into well sulphured casks. Boireau says that the must may be completely clarified *before sulphuring*, by introducing about one ounce of tannin per 100 gallons of must, and pouring into the casks before completely filling about a quart of water in which has been dissolved about four tablets of gelatine, and which has become cold.

A Sulphur Flavor is sometimes communicated to must treated as above, and is also sometimes acquired by wines which are put into casks which have been sulphured for some time, without first washing them, and also by allowing the debris of the sulphur match to fall into the cask; this flavor is apt to pass away with time it not very pronounced, or in that case may be removed by racking into a clean cask. But if the wine has a very decided sulphur flavor, it must be disinfected by wood charcoal. Several large pieces† of coal well cleaned and well dried are introduced into the cask and soaked in the wine, from which they can be withdrawn by strings attached before putting them in the cask. Forty-eight hours are generally sufficient to remove the flavor; but if necessary, the process may be repeated, by changing the charcoal. In operating on white wines, a large amount of charcoal may be used without inconvenience, but in the case of red wine, there seems to be some danger of depriving it of a portion of its color. Mr. Maumené says, however, that the charcoal is liable to deprive the wine of the carbonic acid dissolved in it, it being an absorbent of that gas, and thereby rendering the wine more subject to the action of oxygen.

Other Substances have been recommended to Prevent Fermentation in a Must, but notwithstanding the disagreeable flavor which is communicated by an excessive use of sulphur, no other agent has been found which is as satisfactory, on the whole.

By Burning Alcohol in the Cask, the oxygen may be removed, but the ferments are not destroyed. Care must be taken to avoid an explosion. Therefore, the spirit must not be poured into the cask and lighted, but must be placed in a small vessel and lowered in through the bung, as in the case of sulphuring.

The Concentrated Aqueous Solution of Sulphurous Acid has been recommended, but Maumené says that not only is its preservation very difficult, but its management is more difficult than the sulphur match, and the chances of its being mixed with dangerous substances are considerable; and therefore no one should think of using it.

The Bisulphite of Lime has been used to prevent fermentation in wine and cider, but it does not always give satisfactory results, and the salt is difficult to keep, and the use for wine, at least, has generally been abandoned. In the experiments of Proust, given

---

† Machard says about 125 grammes to a tonneau, or 4 or 5 ounces to 250 gallons of wine.

by Maumené, the smallest quantity used was 15 grammes to 100 kilogrammes of must, or about one-half ounce to 23 gallons.

Salicylic Acid has been much recommended within the past few years, but like everything else, it affects the flavor, if sufficient is used to prevent fermentation. The quantity necessary depends upon the amount of alcohol, ferments, etc., contained in the wine. Prof. Neubauer, quoted by H. Endemann in *American Chemist*, says that wine which is yet fermenting should not receive any salicylic acid, since too large quantities of the substance are required for effective use, but that it may be used in wine when made to prevent after-fermentation; that it will prevent disease, but will not cure wine when diseased. Though infallible rules as to quantity cannot be given, experiments should be made with from .02 to .06 gramme per litre, or say from 1.165 to 3.5 grains per gallon. A solution of 2 grammes (30.864 grains) of salicylic acid to 100 c.c. (3.38 fluid ounces) of alcohol of 80° is employed; 1 c.c = 0.02 grammes; 3 c.c. =0.06 grammes; 61.44 minims or a little more than one fluidram = 1.165 grains, and 3.7 fluidrams= 3.5 grains. Salicylic acid being but sparingly soluble in water, it is preferable to dissolve in strong alcohol, and these are convenient proportions.

It is said that 100 grammes (3½ Ap. ounces) will stop the fermentation of 1000 litres (about 264 gals.) of must, when nearly completed; 800 grammes are necessary when in active fermentation; and 400 will preserve the wine when made.

But now the intelligence comes that salicylic acid has an injurious effect upon the teeth and bones, it having an affinity for calcareous salts (*Boston Journal of Chemistry*, Vol. XI, 143), and the French Minister of Agriculture and Commerce, on the report of the Committee of Public Hygiene, recommends that the sale of articles of food adulterated with it be prohibited as injurious to the public health. (*Ib*. Vol. XV., 45.)

CHAPTER X.

AGING—EFFECTS OF VARIOUS INFLUENCES.

General Considerations.—Wines, from the time of their first fermentation down to the time of their degeneration and decay, are constantly undergoing change. Until they have acquired a certain age, varying in each case with the quality and nature of the liquid, they do not possess those qualities which make them an agreeable, healthful beverage. The care to be bestowed upon them in their general treatment not only includes what is necessary for their preservation, but also what is necessary to *age* them by developing in them all the good qualities of which they are susceptible, and the means of preventing and remedying their defects and diseases.

A New Wine, when first fermented, is quite different from one even a few months old, in respect to color, flavor, and aroma. But the quality which it may acquire depends upon the proportion of different substances which it contains. Some wines, poor in alcohol and deficient in tannin, will develop their best qualities and begin to degenerate very soon after fermentation. Such should be consumed as soon as their insensible fermentation is completed; it is useless to attempt to age them; while those which are stout, firm and full-bodied must be kept several years to be completely developed.

The Bouquet and Distinctive Flavor of a wine, according to Mr. Boireau, generally, are not perfectly developed until defecation is complete—that is to say, until, after several months' repose under proper conditions, they have ceased to deposit insoluble matters, and no longer mineral and vegetable salts, ferments, and coloring matter are precipitated.

Old Wine, then, differs from a new wine of the same origin by its color, its aroma, and flavor, and the difference is due to several causes.

The Color of old red wine is less dark on account of the precipitation of a part of the coloring matter, which, rendered insoluble by the formation of different combinations, has been carried down with the lees. The red color becomes tawny in time.

The Aroma of old wine is more agreeable, being largely due to ethers which are formed by a combination of the alcohol with the acids, and because the other aromatic principles are no longer masked by the carbonic acid which is disengaged when the wine has been recently fermented.

The Difference in Flavor is due to several causes, such as the loss of a great part of the mineral and vegetable salts, which have become insoluble by combination with the tartaric, acetic, and malic acid, and their consequent precipitation, and also to the deposit of a portion of the coloring matter.

So that when a wine is old, having been well cared for, it contains less coloring matter, vegetable and mineral salts, acids free and combined, tannin, ferments, mucilage, alcohol, etc., than when first fermented.

Influences which Develop, also Destroy.—Pellicot, quoting Béchamp, says that a wine ages and improves under influences analogous to those which spoil it, and he, himself, carries the idea a little farther, and adds, that the influence which produces the amelioration in a wine—which ages it—will, after having brought about the improvement, cause it to deteriorate, unless its action is opportunely suspended.

It must also be understood that certain influences which will greatly improve a strong, alcoholic, or a sweet wine, might in a short time entirely ruin a weaker one, or a dry wine.

Influence of the Air.—When a wine of ordinary strength, a table wine, comes into immediate contact with the air, a portion of its alcohol evaporates, it loses its bouquet and flavor, and if long exposed, a whitish scum is formed on its surface, called *flowers*. These have already been described in the chapter on fermentation as *micoderma vini* and *micoderma aceti*. A disagreeable flavor is communicated to the wine which the French call *goût d' évent*, and the wine is said to be *éventé*, or flat; and it becomes turbid, and loses its transparency. Sometimes when the wine still contains sugar the flowers are not formed, but a second alcoholic fermentation sets in, and it works. If the wine is not immediately freed from contact with the air, it acidifies, becomes pricked, and by degrees turns to vinegar. (See *Acetic Fermentation*.) And if still longer exposed, putrid fermentation sets in.

Sweet wines, whose alcoholic strength exceeds 16 per cent., and which contain a good deal of sugar, are not so liable to be injured by the influence of the air. Not only does their high degree of spirit interfere with acetic and putrid fermentation, but an insensible alcoholic fermentation sometimes takes place, and the supply of alcohol is kept up. But in time, as the sugar disappears, the alcohol becomes enfeebled by evaporation, and then acetic fermentation sets in, as in the weaker wines.

In the sherry countries it is considered necessary that the wine should be exposed to the action of the air, and therefore the casks are not kept full, and flowers are considered a good sign. In a few instances, where the wines are strong enough to bear it, aging may be hastened by some exposure to the air, but great care must be taken that they are not left too long under its influence, or disorganization may ensue. It must, however, be laid down as an almost universal rule, that the casks must be kept full and well bunged. (See *Ulling*.)

Variations of Temperature affect wines like other liquids by contraction and expansion. When a full cask is put in a cold place, the wine contracts and leaves a vacant space; then it must be filled up or the wine drawn into a smaller cask. If the temperature of the wine in a full cask is raised, the liquid expands, and is apt to cause leaks; the sediment is liable to rise and give the wine a flavor of the lees.

Influence of Heat.—Guyot says that the higher the degree of heat to which wines are exposed, the greater their internal activity. Those subjected to 15, 20, 30 degrees, Celsius, (59°, 68°, 86° F.), sooner arrive at maturity, if young, at old age, if ripe, and at decrepitude, if old, than they would at a temperature of 10° C. (50° F.) From which the conclusion is drawn, that wines which have nearly or quite reached their maturity must be protected from heat, or at least from that of an elevated temperature, and that old wines should be kept in as cool a place as possible.

Aging by Heat.—On the other hand, if we wish to hasten the maturity of our wines, we can do so by keeping them in a warm place rather than in a cool cellar. The younger the wines, and the more sugar and alcohol they contain, the more they will gain, and the less risk will they run if subjected to a temperature of from 60° to 86° F. For example, sweet wines which are only ripe at thirty or forty years will mature in fifteen or twenty years, at 68° of heat, and in five or ten years, at 86°; a Bordeaux or a Hermitage wine which at 50° would be made in eight or ten years, would certainly be made in four or five years at from 59° to 68°, and in two or three years at 77° or 86° of heat. He says that a temperature between 40° and 90° C. (104° and 194° F.) will disorganize many kinds of wine, particularly red wines and those which have remained long in the fermenting vat, though it will not have that effect upon all wines.

It is well known that the inhabitants of many southern countries are accustomed to expose their wines to a considerable degree of heat to hasten their maturity, and different methods are employed for the purpose, and it is important to know what kind of wine will be improved and what injured by the practice. On this subject Boireau says, that after many experiments, he can affirm that if the heat exceeds 30° C. (86° F.), it is injurious to the grand *mellow* wines of the Gironde; also to wines of a delicate bouquet whose alcoholic strength does not exceed 12 per cent. Fine wines which possess both an aromatic taste and bouquet, a fruity flavor, and a pronounced mellowness, by heat take on a certain tawny flavor of worn out wine; but they become dry, lose their mellowness, and coolness, and acquire a cooked flavor, which changes their nature and gives them an analogy with the wines of the south of France. This taste covers their natural flavor and renders them common.

He goes on to say that wines subjected to the action of heat in direct contact with the air, lose by evaporation a part of their alcohol; the oxygen deprives them of a part of their color, and if the influence is prolonged, they become weak and greatly deteriorated. Exposed to heat in imperfectly closed vessels, they deposit, and take the tawny flavor (*goût de rancio*) if their alcoholic strength exceeds 16 per cent.; but if feeble in spirit, and they remain long in this condition, the oxygen transforms a part of their alcohol into vinegar. In receptacles kept full and well stopped, they undergo but few constitutional changes, if the heat does not exceed 158° F.; but, nevertheless, a small part of their coloring matter is precipitated, and their taste is sensibly changed. A flavor of cooked wine is found, and a slight odor of the lees, no matter how quick the heating.

Whatever the kind of wine operated upon, care must be taken not to carry the heat too high, for it will decompose and precipitate certain principles in dissolution in the wine, and change its natural flavor. After cooling, voluminous deposits will be found, and the cooking will give the wine a disagreeable flavor and an odor of the residue of a still. The extreme limits of from 113° to 158° F. should not be exceeded, and the greater the heat the shorter should be the exposure to it.

Generally speaking, the wines which gain the most by heating, either by artificial means or by leaving them in casks well bunged, but in ullage, in warm store rooms, are strongly fortified liqueur wines. And in order that they be not injured under those conditions, *they should contain at least* 18 *per cent. of pure alcohol*. And as they will gradually lose a little of their spirit by evaporation, their alcoholic strength should be taken from time to time, and they should be kept up to the indicated degree by fortifying.

Preserving Wine by Heat.—Aside from the question of aging wine by the effect of heat, Pasteur has attempted to show that wines can be kept without change, if the temperature is raised for a short time to 130° or 140° F. This is on the theory that wines become flat, pricked, turned, or rotten, owing to secondary fermentations, and that each change is due to the action of a particular ferment, as stated in the chapter on fermentation; and that this degree of heat destroys the action of these ferments—in fact, kills them. It is owing to the presence of the alcohol, that they are destroyed by this degree of heat, for a must which has been raised to the boiling point still ferments according to the experience of Boireau and of Pellicot. The first named gives the results of his experiments in heating wines according to Pasteur's plan. The wine was in bottles, and the heat was gradually raised to 52° C. (125.6° F.) In comparing the wines treated with unheated wines kept under the same conditions, he found that the wine which had been heated could support contact with the air with less injury than the unheated, but that nevertheless it became flat, covered with flowers, and acidified even in closed vessels which were not completely full; also that fine wines generally are injured by the process. The wines experimented upon had from 10 to 10½ per cent. of alcohol.

It is a costly process to subject wine to a high artificial heat, and owing to the doubt which yet seems to attend the matter, but few are likely to go to the expense.

Influence of Cold.—Most authors have something to say on the subject of congealed wines, and undoubtedly the liquid may be concentrated by freezing a portion of the water, and drawing off the remaining liquid. Those living in cold countries can try the experiment, but it will certainly not be practiced in California.

Mr. Boireau says that the liquid remaining acquires a flavor similar to that possessed by wines which have been heated; that fine wines of a delicate bouquet and flavor acquire a commoner flavor than those in their normal state.

Treatment of Frozen Wines.—It may not be amiss to indicate what treatment a wine should receive in case it has been frozen and has thawed again. It becomes turbid, loses part of its color, and several matters are precipitated, or remain in suspension, and it is liable to ferment when the temperature rises. The last named author says that it should be put in a place of even temperature, and if necessary, it should be fined; in which case it should be fortified with a strong wine of the same nature, or a small amount of brandy.

Influence of Light.—Guyot says that the direct light of the sun causes wine to work, especially red wine, and that it has an injurious effect upon its composition and color; and the coloring matter being decomposed, or modified, acts upon the other elements and makes the wine turn. And hence the wisdom of putting wine in colored bottles. It is only the direct light of the sun, however, that is to be avoided, for a dim light, light reflected or polarized, and moonlight and artificial light are not sufficiently powerful to produce a sensible effect.

Aging by Sunlight.—Exposure to the rays of the sun has been resorted to for the purpose of aging wine, but Boireau says that it is not favorable to all, and is least suited to those whose alcoholic strength does not exceed 15 per cent. He says that the direct rays of the sun falling upon bottled wines will promptly precipitate the coloring matter, and that the effect is greater where the bottles are not completely filled and corked with the needle. If the bottles are wrapped in paper, or if the wine is in casks, the aging is less rapid. He shows by experiment that insolation is advantageous only to wines of more than 15 per cent. of alcohol, to sweet wines, and wines fortified up to 18°, intended to be treated as the wines of Madeira, $i.e.$, baked. But wines of about 10 per cent. of spirit will not endure this method of aging without more or less deterioration by souring.

Effect of the Motion of Voyages.—Wines age more rapidly if kept in motion, and hence, in part, the good effect of a long voyage. Strong, sweet wines, are undoubtedly greatly improved by the motion consequent on transportation, as well as by the heat, but constant agitation will cause weak ones to go rapidly through the periods of their existence, and degenerate.

Wines Suitable for Shipment.—And Dr. Guyot adds that a wine which does not contain 12 per cent. of alcohol and 6 per cent. of sugar, crosses the equator with great difficulty, even in bottles. In wood, it should be young and contain 20 per cent.

of spirit, or sufficient sugar to make up that amount. For a voyage in Europe, or to America direct, he says that the wines of Bordeaux, Burgundy, and of Champagne, of 10 to 12 per cent. of spirit and 2 to 4 per cent. of sugar, behave well if young or in bottles.

Mr. Boireau, however, says that wines proper for exportation, and which will keep in tropical climates, where good cellars and good care are generally wanting, are those which possess naturally or by addition a high alcoholic title, a solid, but bright and handsome color, a clean taste, and perfect limpidity. Sweet, fortified wines best fulfil these conditions. He says that liqueur wines, for shipping to the tropics, should have at least 18 per cent. of pure alcohol; below that they ferment, their saccharine matter is transformed into alcohol, their strength diminishes, and they end by becoming pricked. Dry wines, to be sent to those countries, should have the same strength, unless the casks are kept full. He adds, however, that these remarks only apply to those wines which on their arrival do not receive the usual care, such as filling the casks, clarifying and racking, and are not kept in suitable places; and that a good firm wine of the south of France, which has naturally at least 12 per cent. of alcohol, can be shipped without fortifying.

The motion and the high temperature to which wines are subjected in transportation also cause a loss of color by precipitation, particularly if they lack tannin. Wines which are sufficiently strong in alcohol, but from lack of tannin want firmness and body, are liable to acidify. Therefore, wines too poor in tannin should not be shipped abroad. The greater part of the wines of the Gironde having plenty of tannin, can be safely shipped if fortified to 11 per cent., and the grand wines of less alcohol are safe if shipped in bottles.

In Shipping a New Wine, whose sensible fermentation is finished, the motion often causes a new disengagement of carbonic acid, and sometimes in sufficient force to burst out a head of the cask, unless vented. Of course, such wine should not be shipped, except under conditions which admit of careful supervision. If transported short distances, a small gimlet hole should be kept open near the bung, in which three or four straws may be placed with the heads or spikes on, or a small tin tube with a button at the top may be placed in the hole and bent inside the stave, having sufficient play to allow the gas to escape. Must is shipped in the same way.

Other Motion, such as Jarring and Trembling, produced by loud noises and by passing teams and by factories, act injuriously upon wines, causing them to behave badly and to deteriorate. Guyot also says what may be by some deemed fanciful, that musical sounds hasten the development of wine; and that most old wines will turn in a cellar transformed into a music hall.

Fining is also resorted to for the purpose of aging wine, producing results somewhat similar to the effects of time. But it should be performed with the care and subject to the conditions mentioned in the proper place. (See *Fining*.)

Aging Generally.—Before subjecting a wine to any of the processes for artificial aging, care should be taken, says Mr. Boireau, to precipitate the matters held in suspension, and to render it perfectly limpid.

Grand wines, however, should never be subjected to the treatment, for if a premature development of bouquet is obtained, it is at the expense of that precious quality, mellowness. For to-day, *gourmets* and consumers of refined taste do not select wines which have a bouquet, if they are also dry and harsh to the palate; such wines are only too plenty. They esteem above all those wines which in aging have kept their fruity flavor, their velvety smoothness, that unctuosity which can only be preserved in keeping them in a place having a regular temperature (aveaging 60°), in well closed receptacles, by bringing about the defecation of their lees and the deposit of their ferments by opportune rackings without contact with the air, and by fining them as little as possible.

If, for want of care or suitable places, the wines work, enter into fermentation, their mellowness diminishes, and when neglected they become dry.

The Wines which Gain the Most by the Aging Processes mentioned, are: 1st, Wines excessively rough and overcharged with color; 2d, fortified wines, whose minimum degree of alcohol is 18 per cent.; 3d, sweet wines fortified to 18 or 20 per cent.

Those which remain too harsh should be fined with a strong dose of gelatine; continued agitation after this will make them smoother.

Fortified wines, dry or sweet, age very quickly, if subjected to agitation and afterwards to insolation, if followed by a complete clarification; but it is important to fortify them anew, for the alcohol evaporates, and below 15 per cent. they would sour instead of acquiring bouquet. It is also sometimes necessary to add sugar to sweet wines so treated.

CHAPTER XI.

GENERAL TREATMENT—CELLARS.

Unfortified, or Table Wines.—After what has been said in the last chapter of the different effects produced by the various influences to which wine may be subjected, it remains to point out the proper care and treatment to be bestowed upon unfortified table wines, whose alcoholic strength does not exceed 15 per cent. The three essential conditions indicated by Mr. Boireau are:

1. They should be protected from the contact of the air.
2. They should be kept in a uniform temperature.
3. They should be freed from their lees, ferments, and deposits; they must become perfectly clear, and their degeneration be prevented.

It is very important to taste them, and keep close watch over them by frequent visiting, in order to prevent secondary fermentations and their consequent injurious results, particularly in the case of mellow wines, which thereby transform into alcohol the mucilages and pectines which they contain, and lose their fruity flavor. (See *Red Wine, White Wine, etc.*)

Deposits, Lees, etc.—It is important that they should be freed from ferments and deposits, for muddy, troubled wines are predisposed to secondary fermentations, alcoholic or acetic; they readily contract the bad taste of the lees, bitterness, etc. In all wines, the work of clearing is constantly going on; different matters, among others, coloring matter, several mineral and vegetable salts, etc., which were dissolved in the wine, become insoluble, and these with a portion of the tannin are precipitated to the bottom of the vessel or remain in suspension. It is these matters with the ferments which constitute the lees. Wines deposit more or less, according to their nature and the care bestowed in their making. The most voluminous deposits take place during the first year, and they diminish in volume and consistency at each racking, if properly cared for. When they have become well settled and bright, and have achieved their complete development, the deposit is almost nothing. But it increases anew when the wine declines and begins to degenerate.

To Prevent this Degeneration, and to keep fully developed wines, they must be put into bottles. (See *Wine in Bottles*.)

CELLARS.

What has been said in the preceding chapter naturally leads us to the subject of the proper place for storing wine after it has completed its active fermentation. Cellars proper are constructed entirely under ground, and should have vaulted roofs of masonry. If the cellar is under a building, the arch can safely come within two or three feet of the level of the ground, but if no building is over it to protect it from the heat of the sun, it should be four or five feet under ground. Many storehouses for wine are constructed partly above and partly below ground, and others again, entirely above. Undoubtedly those below ground are the best adapted for keeping wines which have arrived at maturity, and for those of little alcoholic strength, but when it is desired to rapidly develop and age an immature wine, it can be sooner accomplished in a place of a higher temperature, and there also can a strong wine be safely kept.

Temperature.—Whatever the degree of temperature, all agree that it should be as nearly uniform as possible; and to insure this, the cellar should face the north or east when practicable. The outer door should not open directly into the cellar or storehouse, but it is better to have the entrance through an outbuilding, or at least with an outer and an inner door, at a considerable distance. If the wine-house is above ground, its walls should be of sufficient thickness and of suitable material to prevent changes of temperature, and it should have a loft or room above, so that the wine may be protected from the effects of the rays of the sun falling upon the roof; and it may also be shaded by trees. Some of the older writers say that the proper temperature for a cellar is 50° or 52° F., but so low a degree can only be obtained in a well constructed cellar wholly under ground, and deep, and is not likely to be obtained in this State. Boireau, however, says that in the Gironde the average temperature of the cellars is from 15° to 17° C., or 59° to 62½° F., and if a person can maintain the temperature of his cellar or storehouse in this State uniformly at 60° he will do well.

Dampness.—Formerly, when wooden hoops for casks were used, it was necessary to guard against dampness, for they soon rotted, and required to be frequently renewed; but now with the use of iron in place of wood, less care is necessary in that respect. It is best, however, that they should be sufficiently dry that mould will not form on the cask, for a bad taste may thereby be communicated to the wine. Therefore, cellars should not be constructed in very damp places, should have the soil of the floor well compacted, should be well drained, and well cemented, and if necessary, the floor may be covered with a bed a foot deep composed of a mixture of lime, sand, and gravel, or cinders, or the like, well beaten down, and the whole covered with dry sand. Nothing should be left in the cellar which naturally gathers moisture. All mould should be frequently removed, and the sand removed and replaced with dry sand when necessary. Sawdust should not be used on the floor. In San Francisco, the best cellars have a good asphaltum floor, and I know of nothing better after the odor has passed away.

Ventilation is necessary at times to prevent too much dampness, and also to change the air which may become foul. Underground cellars can be ventilated by means of a large tube, such as is used on shipboard, provided with a broad opening at the top which can be turned in the direction of the wind, conducting the air into the cellar. Storehouses may have small, movable windows. In order to keep down the temperature, the proper time to ventilate is during the coolest part of the night in the warmer parts of this State.

Evaporation of the Wine, however, must be guarded against, which may vary from 3 to 10 per cent. per annum, according to whether the place of storage is open or closed. In France the government makes an allowance in favor of the wholesale merchant of 8 per cent., for loss. And Boireau says that in dry storehouses where the air is continually renewed by ventilation, the loss equals the allowed per cent., and even exceeds it, particularly if the casks are weak and poor, hooped in wood, and if the hoops are not driven when they become dry. The loss may then reach 10 per cent., without extraordinary leakage. By guarding against too free access of air and heat, not only will a very considerable loss by evaporation be avoided, but also other defects which may seriously affect the wine, such as acidity, bitterness, too great dryness, etc. And moreover, in poor cellars the wines require much more attention, such as ulling, racking, and frequent tasting, to protect them from secondary fermentations.

Other Precautions.—From what has been said concerning the influence of light, motion, etc., it results that wine cellars should not be too light, nor be situated under wagon roads where vehicles frequently pass, nor near blacksmiths' shops, or other noisy industries, such as boiler making, etc. The vicinity of sinks, cesspools, sewers, and the sources of noisome odors generally, should be avoided; and cellars should not be used for storing milk, cheese, vinegar, or any matter liable to ferment, such as fruit, vegetables, etc.; nor should new wines be stored there until their active fermentation has ceased, for these things may either communicate a bad odor and taste to the wine, or set up in it secondary fermentations.

The Casks and Tuns should be supported by strong timbers or masonry, and should be sufficiently elevated, so that the wine may be easily drawn off, and should be securely blocked. Fig. 15 represents a cask supported by timbers resting on brick work. Where the casks are arranged in piles, those in the lower tier should have four blocks

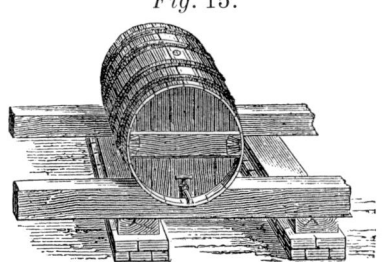

Fig. 15.

Cask and Support.

or chocks each, for if they are blocked only on one side, they are liable to be disturbed, and the outer ones should also have a large block under the bulge. Of course, the outer blocks should be so adjusted that they cannot be knocked out in passing by, and in rolling barrels, etc. The casks of the upper tiers are rolled up on skids, or inclined planes, and are then rolled along over scantlings, laid on the tier below; and hoisting tackle is often of use in this connection. When, however, the cellar is furnished with sufficient large tuns, the piling of casks may be dispensed with.

CHAPTER XII.

RACKING.

The Racking of Wines, or drawing off, is performed for the purpose of freeing them from the lees. Some of the older writers recommend that wine should be allowed to remain on the lees till February or March, but the better practice is to draw it off as soon as it has cleared. If it is allowed to remain long upon the lees, variations of temperature and secondary fermentations, storms, etc., are apt to cause it to become troubled and muddy, and acquire a flavor of the lees. Boireau says that he has constantly observed that wines in general, and especially those which have been fined, if racked as soon as well cleared, say from two weeks to a month after fining, according to the kind of finings used, place of storage, nature of the wine, etc., are generally more limpid, have a cleaner taste, and are much less liable to work than if left on the finings for six months, from one racking to another. Wines not fined, which have become clear naturally by repose, exhibit the same results; those which are racked as soon as bright, are, in every respect, of a quality superior to those which have been left upon their lees from one equinox to another.

The Conditions Indispensable to Good Racking are stated by Mr. Machard as follows:

1. To perform the operation when the weather is dry and clear, and if possible during a north wind, for it is only during such weather that the precipitation of the lees can be really complete.

2. To avoid the operation during damp and rainy weather, and while violent winds are blowing from the south.

3. Not to proceed during a storm, because then the lighter parts of the lees rise and produce fermentive movements which are always to be guarded against.

4. Never to draw off a troubled or muddy wine, for then it must be racked again; and in that condition the deposits are always mixed with the wine.

5. Moreover, never rack at the following periods of the vegetation of the vine: when the buds begin to swell, at the time of flowering, and especially at the time when the fruit commences to change color, in ripening.

6. Never to proceed during the heat of the day, or a south wind, but always in the cool of the morning and during a north wind.

7. To always make use of the sulphur match.

8. Never to leave the wine long exposed to the air.

9. Not to allow the wine to fall too far, so as not to deprive it of its carbonic acid, which exerts a conservative effect, and thus also to avoid too great agitation, which may be prejudicial.

10. Finally, to use the greatest care to free it from the least traces of sediment.

I have repeated nearly the language of the author quoted, at the expense of some repetition, because the rules are laid down by him more minutely than by the other authors who agree with him in general terms.

It is agreed that the most critical periods for wine on the lees are the different periods of the vegetation above mentioned, which vary somewhat in different climates, and they should therefore be racked before these epochs arrive.

New Red Wines, says Mr. Boireau, which have been properly made, which are clear, which do not work, and which are kept in closed cellars, should be drawn off four times during the first year; the first racking is performed as soon as the insensible fermentation has ceased, and the wine has become clear, *i.e.*, during the first cold weather of December; the second in March, before the sprouting of the vine, or at the vernal equinox; the third before the flowering of the vine, in June; and the fourth at the autumnal equinox, in September. Machard considers that no racking is so important as that of March, and he insists upon it that it should never be omitted, and that it should be well done, for if the lees are all removed then, it may even go safely till the next vintage, and the June or July racking be omitted, except in warm climates; and then, as before observed, it should be done in the cool of the day. Instead of waiting till September, the operation is often performed in August, when the grape begins to turn. Of course, the periods change somewhat in different climates, as already observed, so that the cellar-man must familiarize himself with the conduct of the wine in his locality, and govern himself accordingly, racking before the period arrives when the wine usually works.

Old Red Wines are racked only twice a year, in the spring and fall, before the equinoxes, except in case of their becoming turbid by secondary fermentations, when they must be racked, whatever the time of year, except also in case of certain diseases. If, however, the wine has not been well made or properly cared for, it may show signs of fermentation and alteration, and need racking at periods different from those above mentioned. If the wine does not clear of itself by the time it should be drawn off, it may be necessary to clarify it by fining (which see). But if well made and properly cared for, it will ordinarily clear itself.

New White Wines are racked as soon as they become clear, and no precise epoch can be fixed for the operation, because the duration of the fermentation depends essentially upon the density of the must and the temperature. In any case, it is much more prolonged than that of red wines. It often happens that it continues till the month of February, when the must is very rich in sugar, especially if the weather is cold late in the fall; while wines made of grapes from the same vineyard, made in the same way, but less rich in the saccharine principle, may terminate their fermentation in December.

The racking should always be performed before the weather becomes warm, for the elevation of the temperature will set the wine working, and the lees will become mixed with it. Ordinarily the most favorable time is the month of February.

Subsequent Rackings.—White wine, new or old, requires to be racked three times a year, as stated in the chapter on White

Wine; *first*, in March, at the time of the sprouting of the vine, before the equinox; *secondly*, at the flowering of the vine, in June, before the summer solstice; and *thirdly*, in September, at the ripening of the grape, before the autumnal equinox. (See *White Wine, Racking*.)

Care to be Observed.—Contact with the air should be carefully avoided during the operation. The same care should be observed as in racking red wine, and the operation is performed in the same manner, always keeping in view that what may be essential to keep a mellow wine in condition, may to a certain extent be neglected where dryness is desired.

A sulphur match ought always to be burned in the cask before wine, either red or white, is racked into it, for thus the germs of fermentation which may be in the cask will be rendered inactive by the sulphurous acid formed, and which will also absorb with avidity the oxygen, and thereby in two ways tend to prevent fermentation. The cask, however, should not be sulphured till well drained, or the water remaining will be impregnated with the gas, which is liable to give a disagreeable sulphur taste to the wine which will not disappear for some time. (See *Sulphuring*.) A cask which has been put away sulphured must for the same reason be washed before using; and in fact no cask should be used without washing.

Other Precautions.—Great care must be taken in all cases not to disturb the sediment by moving the cask, by pounding on the stave to loosen the bung, or by driving in the faucet. The latter ought to be opened before inserting it, so as to allow the air contained in it to escape, and not to force itself into the cask and trouble the wine, which it is liable to do by contraction and expansion, forcing in the faucet. It should be closed as soon as the wine begins to run. It is hardly necessary to say that an empty bucket should be kept under, when putting in the faucet, to catch the wine that may escape. Care must also be taken that the cask to be filled, and all the utensils used in and about the racking, are scrupulously clean, and buckets, hose, funnels, siphons, etc., must be washed carefully every day, for if allowed to stand with wine in them, they will become sour. Siphons and short tubes can be scoured by means of a brush, such as is used for cleaning bottles and lamp chimneys, by attaching it to a long, stiff wire.

Different Methods of Racking.—The commonest way is to draw the wine through a faucet into a bucket, and pour it into the empty cask by means of a funnel. The faucet is placed in a hole bored in the end of the cask, an inch or more above the lower stave. After the faucet has been placed in position, vent the cask of wine, but not before. When the wine no longer runs, the cask should be slightly tipped forward, but by a very easy and gradual movement, so as not to disturb the lees. This may be done by a man carefully lifting the rear end. A kind of hoisting-jack (fig. 16) is used for this purpose. The lower end rests on the ground, near the rear end of the cask, and the upper end of the movable rod is placed under the upper chime. On turning the crank the cask is tipped gently forward, and a ratchet catches the pinion and prevents the return. If there is not sufficient space between the wall and the cask to operate in the manner stated, one end of the jack is placed against the wall above the cask, and the power is applied to the upper forward part of the cask by placing the other end behind a forward hoop.

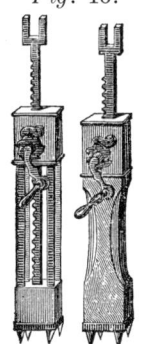

The fork (fig. 17) is used in the same way, being lengthened by means of the screw. Fig. 18 represents another contrivance for the same purpose.

If only one man is employed, a lever supported above the cask by two legs straddling it, and forming the fulcrum, the rear end provided with a

96   RACKING.

hook which hooks under the chime, and the other end extending forward beyond the front, may be used (fig. 19). The workman, by bearing down on the lever, or by pulling the strap at the end, tips the cask forward. When the wine has nearly all run out, it should frequently be examined by holding a small quantity to the light in a small, thin glass, and as soon as the slightest appearance of lees presents itself, the operation should cease, and none of the muddy wine should be poured into the other cask. This method has its advantages, in that the first appearance of cloudiness can be detected, for the liquid is always under the eye of the operator, but it has the disadvantage of greatly exposing the wine to the air.

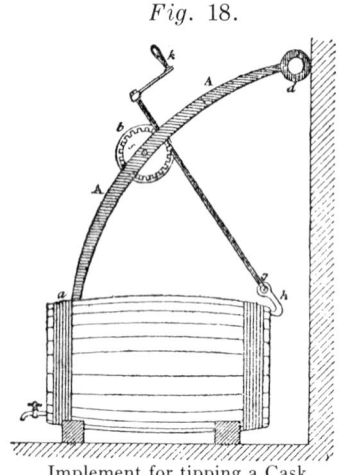

Fig. 18.

Implement for tipping a Cask.

Fig. 19.

Implement for tipping a Cask.

Another method which avoids the last objection, is to securely connect the faucet of the cask of wine with the faucet of the empty one, to open them both, and let the wine run from one to the other. If they are both on the same, or nearly the same level, a portion only will be transferred, and then the rest may be forced over by connecting the tube of a hand-bellows tightly with the bung-hole of the cask of wine, and blowing into it. This is easily done by attaching the bellows by means of a hose to a long, hollow, conical bung. (See fig. 20.) As soon as the air is heard in the tube, close the faucet, and before removing it, bung the cask

RACKING. 97

tight. The remaining wine is removed as in the first method.

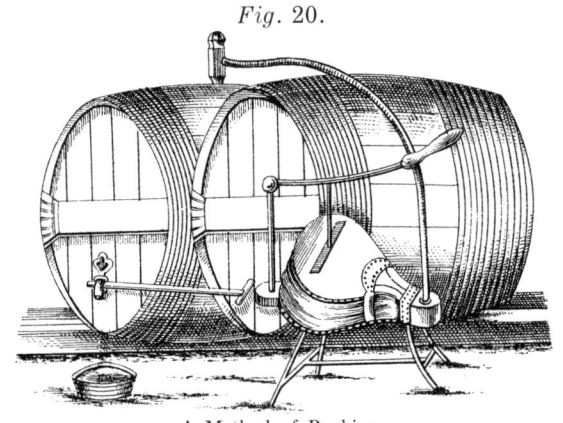

Fig. 20.

A Method of Racking.

Pumps and Siphons are very useful where wine is to be merely transferred from one cask to another, but they are not

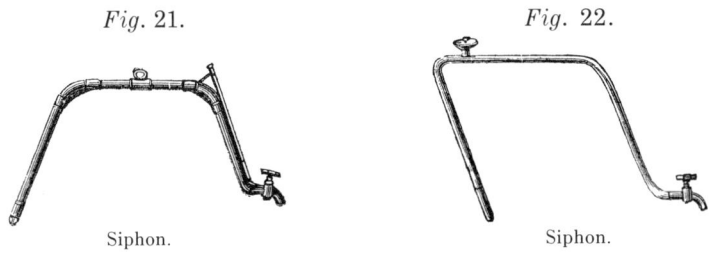

Fig. 21.   Fig. 22.

Siphon.   Siphon.

well suited for racking it from the lees, for it is difficult to make use of them without disturbing the sediment, and thereby troubling the liquid.

Figs. 21 and 22 represent two forms of siphons. They may also consist simply of a bent tube.

Fig. 21 shows an exhausting tube attached, by which the air is sucked out with the mouth.

Fig. 23 shows a rotary force pump for transferring wine from
Fig. 23.

Rotary Force Pump.

one cask to another. Lever force pumps are also used for the same purpose.

CHAPTER XIII.

CLARIFICATION — FINING.

When Necessary.—Wines do not always acquire the desirable state of brightness and limpidity by repose and racking, and it becomes necessary to clarify them. They may become cloudy through secondary fermentations, which cause the lees once deposited to rise and become again mixed with the liquid, or through changes of temperature, by transportation, by careless racking, etc., and by mixing different kinds together; or they may fail to clear naturally, because not possessed of sufficient tannin or albumen to precipitate the different matters held in suspension. Weak wines of poor years may contain ferments in excess of their sugar, which may be removed by clarification, and so fermentation be checked or retarded. Wines, however, which are well made and properly cared for, ought to become bright without recourse to clarification, and such will be found preferable to, and will possess more fruitness, unctuosity, and color, than those which have been clarified by several finings. And for these reasons—although it may be necessary to fine such wines as do not naturally clear themselves—care must be observed not to carry the process too far, and deprive them of the tannin necessary to their preservation, as well as of too much of their color, fruity flavor, and mellowness.

The Different Substances Employed for Clarifying act either chemically and mechanically, or simply mechanically. Among the latter are blotting paper, either in sheets or in pulp, fine sand, and powdered stone, which are placed in the cask, and which in falling, carry down with them the matters which are held in suspension. Wine is sometimes clarified by filtering it through woolen bags. Those substances which act both chemically and mechanically are albumen and gelatine, and similar substances.

Of Gelatinous Substances, two kinds are used, gelatine, so-called, and isinglass, or fish glue, and they act in two ways.

They are not entirely dissolved in water; thin, transparent pellicles remain in suspension, which form a sort of network in the wine, and in settling they carry with them other insoluble matters. Thus, their action is mechanical. The portion which is fully dissolved is pure gelatine, and acts chemically. It combines with the tannin of the wine and forms an insoluble substance, tannate of gelatine, which is readily precipitated.

Gelatine, so-called, is prepared from the bones, skin, and tendons of animals, and is sold in tablets or sheets, and is sometimes chipped or broken into small fragments. It is one of the most powerful of finings, and causes a loss by precipitation of a considerable portion of the tannin and of the coloring matter of the wine. It should not, therefore, be used in clarifying red wines, except when it is desirable to deprive them of a portion of their roughness caused by an excess of tannin, or of a portion of their color; and it should always be employed with caution. It produces more sediment than the two substances next named, and leaves a bad taste in the wine, unless perfectly fresh matters have been used in its preparation. For the latter reason, wine clarified with it should be racked from the finings as soon as cleared. It may be profitably used to clarify common white wines; and if they are difficult to clarify, tannin should be added as described below.

Preparation.—Take about two tablets, or one ounce, for one hundred gallons, or double the quantity, if the greatest possible effect is desired. Dissolve it in a dish over the fire with a little water, constantly stirring, and do not allow the water to boil. If previously soaked a few hours in water, it will dissolve all the more easily. Use as directed below.

Isinglass, Fish Glue, or Ichthyocol (*Ichthyocolla* of the pharmacists), is prepared from the swimming bladder of the sturgeon, and usually comes from Russia. It acts in the same way as gelatine, mechanically, and also by combining with the tannin. This is preëminently the fining for white wine. One ounce or more may be used for 100 gallons. It should be broken up by pounding it with a hammer on a block of wood, and should be chopped into small fragments, so that it may be easily dissolved. Put it in a vessel of crockery, and pour over it of the wine to be clarified sufficient to cover it. Add another glass or two of the wine in a few hours, when the first has been absorbed. After about twenty-four hours it forms a jelly. This should be thinned by adding more wine or warm water, and it should be thoroughly worked with the hand until completely dissolved, and then be strained through a piece of linen, using sufficient pressure to squeeze out the mucilage. It should be thoroughly whipped or beaten, and more wine is added if too thick. After being prepared, it may be kept for some time in bottles, by adding a little brandy. In clarifying sweet white wines, it is recommended that an ounce or two of cream of tartar be added, which must first be dissolved in warm water.

Albuminous Substances.—Among these are mentioned the *blood of animals*, dried or fresh, and it is a powerful clarifier. About two quarts to 100 gallons are used, beaten up with an equal quantity of wine. It is liable to deprive the wine of a portion of its color, and sometimes conveys a disagreeable flavor, particularly unless used when quite fresh. It should not be used to clarify old or fine wines, but may be employed for new and common ones. It is of use in clarifying white wines which have turned yellow, for it effectually removes this color. It should be used sparingly, if at all, for red wines, and the wine should be drawn from the finings as promptly as possible.

Milk is also used in the same way and in the same quantity as blood. It is liable to sour, and a small quantity is apt to remain in the wine. By its use sugar of milk is introduced, which is liable to undergo lactic and butyric fermentations, and the flavor of sour milk and rancid butter may be communicated to the wine. This may also be used to decolor white wine which has become yellow.

The White of Eggs is the best of the albuminous substances used for clarifying. It is coagulated by the alcohol and tannin, and forms a precipitate heavier than the liquid, and as it falls, carries with it the matters remaining in suspension. If the eggs are fresh, as they always must be, there is no danger of communicating any foreign flavor to the wine by their use; but it is not advisable to use the yolks, for they injure the wine by decoloring it, and the sulphur contained in them may communicate the odor of sulphuretted hydrogen. This is preëminently the fining for red wine. It is also used for the clarification of white wine, but Machard says that it is subject to be condensed in the form of splinters (*esquilles*), which obscure rather than clarify the liquid. The whites of ten or a dozen eggs are used for 100 gallons. They are beaten up in a small quantity of wine or water before using.

Clarifying Powders.—In addition to the subtances mentioned, there are special preparations in the form of powders, sold for the purpose, which are highly recommended by some authors. They are supposed to consist mainly of dried blood; directions for using are given on the package.

Gum Arabic, about 10 ounces to 100 gallons, is also used, but it is not readily precipitated, and is apt to remain in dissolution in the wine.

Salt is often added to the different finings, by first dissolving a small handful in water. It renders them heavier, and as it is insoluble in alcohol, it becomes precipitated, and thus acts in two ways. Many authors recommend its use, but Boireau says it should only be employed in clarifying common or very turbid wines.

Alcohol is added with great advantage if the wines are so weak in spirit that the finings do not act.

Tannin, however, more frequently requires to be added, for upon it and the alcohol depends the action of the substances employed. If the wine is not lacking in alcohol, and the finings do not act, sufficient tannin must be added to produce the desired effect. If the ordinary tannic acid of commerce is employed, one-half to one ounce for 100 gallons may be used. Dissolve ½ lb. in a quart of the strongest alcohol, 95°, by thoroughly shaking in a bottle of double the size. After standing twenty-four hours it is filtered, and one gill of the solution contains one ounce

CLARIFICATION.   103

of tannic acid. This preparation of tannin, which is prepared from nutgalls, is used for tannifying sparkling wines, because it does not adhere to the inside of the bottle. It is preferable, however, in general to employ the tannin derived from the vine itself. For this purpose a strong decoction is made by steeping grape seeds, which have not undergone fermentation, in water. They should be coarsely broken, or bruised, and boiled for several hours. By adding from one-fourth to one-fifth of its volume of strong alcohol of 85 per cent., it can be kept for future use. The liquor may be filtered before adding the alcohol. Instead of the seeds, sometimes a handful of stems are steeped, and the liquid is used. Tannified wine may be prepared by soaking 50 or 60 lbs. of the bruised seeds in 100 gallons of white wine, for one or two months. It is cared for as white wine. If only one cask is to be treated, say 100 gallons, one-half pound of grape seed may be reduced to powder and put in.

It is difficult to lay down a definite rule as to the amount of either preparation to use, for the reason that the amount of tannin contained in the wine itself varies. Three or four gallons of the tannified wine are recommended for 100 gallons, and a much smaller quantity of the first mentioned decoction would be equivalent in its effects, on account of its additional strength. If, however, it is found that sufficient has not been used, the wine must be clarified anew, and tannin added again. By experimenting on a small quantity of the wine, the proper quantity may be ascertained.

Fig. 24.
Fig. 25.   *Fig.* 26.

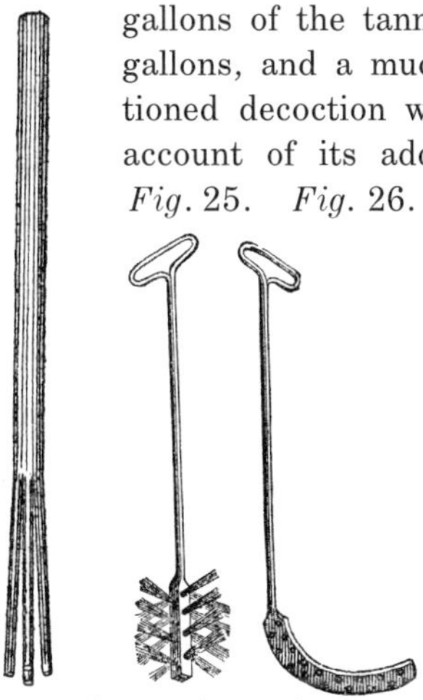

Implements for stirring.

Method of Operation. — After preparing the finings as described under the head of each of the substances already mentioned, two or three gallons of wine are drawn from the bung by the aid of a siphon, pump, or other suitable implement, the finings are poured in, and the wine is stirred until thoroughly mixed with them. This may be done with a stick split at the end into three or four prongs (fig. 24), or by a sort of brush consisting of several small bundles of bristles inserted in a stick and at right angles to each other (fig. 25), or with a sort of bent paddle, pierced with holes, called a whip (fig. 26). The wine drawn out should then be replaced in the cask, which should be completely filled, and left to rest till the wine is bright. In filling a cask which has recently been agitated, or into which finings have been put, a good deal of froth is frequently found which will run out at the bung before the cask is full, and will prevent the operator from filling it. A few smart blows on the bung stave with a bung starter will break the bubbles and remove the foam. The time required to clarify a cask of wine depends somewhat upon the quality of the wine itself, and also upon the kind of finings used. The usual time is from two weeks to a month. In no case, however, should it be allowed to remain on the finings after it has cleared and has ceased to deposit, for the sediment may work up again and cloud the wine, and if left too long in contact with the deposit, the wine may acquire a disagreeable flavor.

If, after leaving the wine a suitable time, it still remains turbid and continues to deposit, it should be racked into a clean cask and fined again, adding tannin, if necessary.

CHAPTER XIV.

SWEET WINES—FORTIFIED WINES.

Generally.—The French give the name *vins de liqueur*, liqueur wines, to sweet wines, and it is also sometimes applied to fortified dry wines. Sweet wines are those which, after terminating their active fermentation, still retain a quantity of sugar. In order to produce natural sweet wines, it is necessary that the must should contain a large amount of sugar; Boireau says, from 16° to 25° Baumé, or about 29 to 46 per cent. It would seem that the latter figure is too high for a *natural* sweet *wine*, for it probably would not ferment at all, and to make *a wine* from a must containing over 35 per cent. of sugar, the alcohol must be added. (See *Musts*.) He goes on to say that these wines will contain from 15 to 16 per cent. of natural alcohol, without addition; the sugar which they contain makes them heavier than water.

To Increase Sugar.—In order to augment the amount of sugar, the grapes are left on the vine till they become excessively ripe; in some places the stem of the bunch is twisted on the vine to interrupt the rising of the sap; the must is also sometimes concentrated by boiling; sometimes the grapes are picked and exposed to the sun on screens or straw mats, until they become shriveled, and sometimes they are dried in ovens.

Without Fermentation.—Sometimes sweet wines are made without allowing the must to ferment at all, by adding alcohol till it contains 18 or 20 per cent. of spirit; thus all the sugar is preserved. Again, they are made by mixing with dry wines grape syrup or concentrated must, and fortifying.

Care Required.—It has already been stated in the chapter on keeping wine that these wines require less care than weaker ones. But Mr. Boireau says that wines, whether sweet or dry, whose strength does not exceed 16 per cent., require the same care as ordinary wines.

106 SWEET WINES.

In order that sweet and fortified wines may be kept in storehouses subject to great changes of temperature, in bottles upright, or in casks in ullage—in other words, under the conditions in which brandy can be kept, they must contain 18 or 20 per cent. of alcohol. They age sooner in casks than in bottles. (See *Aging*.)

Clarification of these wines is effected by fining or by filtering. The best finings for the purpose are those containing albumen, such as the whites of eggs, though fresh blood may be used, but only for the commoner wines. If they are very pasty, tannin should be added, and then they should be clarified with a strong dose of gelatine.

Small quantities of wine may be filtered through paper or flannel, in closed filters.

These wines should always be allowed to rest for a while, and then be racked before shipping, for it is rare that they do not make a deposit. (See *Fining*.)

Boiling Must.—Pellicot says that the common practice in making sweet wines, is to reduce the volume of the must by one-third, or even one-half, by boiling. They clear sooner, and retain less of the cooked flavor if only a part is boiled, that is, if, after boiling, one-fourth to one-third of the volume is added of must from the sweetest varieties of grapes. In this way the wines are more agreeable, and sooner matured. When the boiled must is taken from the cauldron, it must be briskly stirred with a bunch of twigs, or the like, till it ceases to smoke, in order to remove a disagreeable flavor which wines so made may contract. He gives it as his opinion that the greater part of the sweet wines, even of southern countries, are made by boiling the whole or a portion of the must, in spite of allegations to the contrary; and he considers it an innocent and legitimate operation, the only objection being the cooked flavor, which disappears with age. He excepts, however, wine made from very sweet varieties, which are ripened artificially. He also recommends that when kept in a large cask, the lees should not be removed, as they contain a good deal of sugar. As a certain quantity is drawn off, it may be filled each year with new wine of the same quality.

Sweet Muscat.—In making sweet Muscat, fermentation should be checked by the addition of alcohol, for if allowed to continue too long, the Muscat flavor will disappear. And this is usually necessary, as before stated, to keep the wines sweet.

Pressing.—Where the grapes are quite ripe, and somewhat dry, it may be difficult to extract the juice without a very powerful press; under such circumstances Machard recommends that, after crushing, the grapes be put into a vat for twenty-four or forty-eight hours, according to the temperature, and until fermentation commences, which fluidifies the must and makes it run more freely from the press.

The Marc of Sweet Wines is useful to mix with poor white wines to give them more sugar and more strength.

The amount of Alcohol to be added varies from two to five per cent., or more, depending upon the amount developed by fermentation, and the degree of sweetness desired. If the must is not allowed to ferment at all, it must be fortified up to 18 or 20 per cent.; if, however, it is so sweet that it will not ferment, it may be kept without the addition of alcohol, but it will be syrup, and not wine.

Density.—Dubief says that sweet wines should mark a density of from 4° to 5° Baumé, and the best of them even 7°.

Furmint Wine.—The following is the method given by Pellicot as practiced by him in making wine from the Furmint grape. He gathers the grapes when they are very ripe, and the small berries are half dried, and then exposes them to the rays of the sun for six or eight days, upon screens. When ready to crush, he takes the screens to the crusher. The dryest berries are then removed by shaking the frame, or with the hand, and put by themselves; and the remainder are crushed in the usual manner. Then the dry ones are crushed as well as possible, and the two kinds are mixed together and fermented. Owing to the syrupy nature of the must, it ferments for a long time, and without much effervescence. When it acquires a suitable flavor, it is drawn off, and is then racked several times till clear.

Where the grapes are trodden, it is probably necessary to separate the dry grapes from the rest, and crush them by themselves, in order that they may be well crushed; but if a good crusher is used, it would seem entirely unnecessary.

Straw Wines, according to Machard, are made as follows: The ripest bunches are chosen, and preferably from old vines. They are gathered when the weather is warm and dry. They are spread upon straw, or hung up in the upper room of a house. They are visited from time to time, and the rotten berries removed. They are thus left till February or March, the time when straw wine is usually made. Some, however, press in December, but the wine has not the quality of that made later.* When sufficiently dried the grapes are stemmed, and the remaining rotten berries are removed. They are then crushed and pressed. The pressings are all mixed together. To arrive at perfection, such a wine, he says, must be kept ten, twelve, or more years; that it need not be racked, nor the casks made full, and that it requires no fining.

PORT WINE.

The Musts of the port wine grapes grown in the Upper Douro, Portugal, show from 24 to 29 per cent. of sugar, according to the variety. There are others cultivated in the district which contain less sugar. The sweetest of all is the Bastardo. The fermentation takes place under cover, in what is called a *lagar*, which is a large stone vat, about three feet deep. According to Dr. Bleasdale, it is necessary to gather the grapes as soon as they are completely ripe; that the *lagar* or fermenting vat should be filled as promptly as possible; that the mass should be thoroughly stirred; that the fermentation should be tumultuous and uninterrupted, and that the wine should be drawn off when it has developed a vinous smell and flavor, and astringency and roughness

---

*It must be remembered that he is writing for the cold climate of the Jura, where the grapes do not naturally acquire that degree of maturity necessary for sweet wines.

to the taste, though all the sugar has not been fermented. The defective grapes are picked out, and only good ones put into the vat. As soon as the fermenting vat is filled, a sufficient number of men enter into it to complete the treading. Three men to each 120 gallons of must are employed, who with bare feet tread and dance upon the grapes. If fermentation is slow in starting, more men are put in to impart warmth, or a quantity of warm must is added. The first treading lasts, in the instance given by Dr. Bleasdale, six hours during the first night, and is continued next day with two men, where three were employed the first night. Men enter again during the active fermentation and tread to keep down the pomace, and to extract as much coloring matter as possible. Then the treaders leave the *lagar*, but the fermentation is closely watched.

The following graphic description, which differs in no essential respect from that of Dr. Bleasdale, is from Vizitelli:

"When the mid-day meal is over, the grapes having been already spread perfectly level in the lagar, a band of sixty men is told off to tread them. The *casa dos lagares** is a long building with a low pointed roof, lighted with square openings along one side, and contains four lagares, in the largest of which sufficient grapes can be trodden at one time to produce thirty pipes of wine.† As is universally the case in the Upper Douro, these lagares are of stone, and about three feet in depth. In front of each, and on a lower level, is a small stone reservoir, called a dorno, into which the expressed juice flows after the treading of the grapes is concluded, and which communicates by pipes with the huge tonels‖ in the adega below, although not beneath the lagares, being in fact in the face of the reservoirs, but on a level some twelve feet lower, with a long, wooden staircase leading to it. In front of the lagares runs a narrow stone ledge, to which ascent is gained by a few steps, and here while the treading is going on the overseers post themselves, long staves in hand, in

---
*Fermenting house.
†A pipe is 138 wine gallons, or 115 Imperial.
‖ Tuns.

order to see that every one performs his share of labor. The treaders, with their white breeches well tucked up, mount into the lagar, where they form three separate rows of ten men each on either side of the huge, overhanging beam, and placing their arms on each other's shoulders, commence work by raising and lowering their feet alternately, calling out as they do so, '*Direita, esquerda!*' (Right, left!) varying this after a time with songs and shoutings in order to keep the weaker and lazier ones up to the work, which is quite as irksome and monotonous as either treadmill or prison crank, which tender-hearted philanthropists regard with so much horror. But the lagariros have something more than singing or shouting to encourage them. Taking part with them in the treading is a little band of musicians, with drum, fife, fiddle, and guitar, who strike up a lively tune, while their comrades chime in, some by whistling, others with castanets. Occasionally, too, nips of brandy are served out, and the overseers present cigarettes all round, whereupon the treaders vary their monotonous movements with a brisker measure. This first treading, the 'sovar o vinho,' or beating the wine, as it is called, lasts, with occasional respites and relays of fresh men, for eighteen hours. A long interval now ensues, and then the treading or beating is resumed. By this time the grapes are pretty well crushed, and walking over the pips and stalks strewn at the bottom of the lagar, becomes something like the pilgrimages of old, when the devout trudged wearily along with hard peas packed between the soles of their feet and the soles of their shoes. The lagariros, with their garments more or less bespattered with grape-juice, move slowly about in their mauve-colored mucilaginous bath in a listless kind of way, now smoking cigarettes, now with their arms folded, or thrown behind their backs, or with their hands tucked in their waistcoat pockets, or raised up to their chins, while they support the elbow of the one arm with the hand of the other. The fiddle strikes up anew, the drum sounds, the fife squeaks, the guitar tinkles, and the overseers drowsily upraid. But all to no purpose. Music has lost its inspiration, and authority its terrors, and the men, dead beat, raise one purple leg languidly after the other. In the still night time, with a few lanterns dimly lighting up the gloomy casa dos lagares, such a scene as I have here attempted to sketch has something almost weird about it. By the time the treading is completed, the violent fermentation of the must has commenced, and is left to follow its course.* Accordingly, as the grapes are moderately or overripe, and the atmospheric temperature is high or low, and it is intended that the wine shall be sweet or dry, this fermentation will be allowed to continue for a shorter or a longer period, varying from fifteen hours to several days, during which time the husks and stalks of the grapes, rising to the surface, form a thick incrustation. To ascertain the proper moment for drawing off the wine into tonels, recourse is usually had to the saccharometer, when, if this marks four or five degrees, the farmer knows that the wine will be sweet; if a smaller number of degrees are indicated, the wine will be moderately sweet, while zero signifies that the wine will be dry. Some farmers judge the state of the fermentation by the appearance of the wine on the conventional white porcelain saucer, and the vinous smell and flavor which it then exhibits. When it is ascertained that the wine is sufficiently fermented, it is at once run off into the large tonels, holding their 10 to 30 pipes each, the mosto extracted from the husks of the grapes by the application of the huge beam press being mixed with the expressed juice resulting from the treading. It is now that brandy—not poisonous Berlin potato spirit, but distilled from the juice of the grape—is added at the rate of 5½ to 11 gallons per pipe,† if it is desired that the wine should retain its sweetness. Should, however, the wine be already dry, the chances are that it will receive no spirit at all. The bungs are left out of the tonels till November, when they are tightly replaced, and the wine remains undisturbed until the cold weather sets in, usually during the month of December. By this time the wine has cleared and become of a dark purple hue. It is now drawn off its lees, and returned again to the tonel, when it receives about 5 gallons of brandy per pipe.§ In

---

* It will be noticed that Dr. Bleasdale says that the treading is repeated during active fermentation. Probably different practices prevail in different localities.
† About 4¾ to 9½ per cent—say 5 to 10.
§ 4.35 per cent.

the following March it will be racked into pipes preparatory to being sent down the Douro to the wine shippers' lodges at Villa Nova de Gaia," a suburb of Oporto.

These Lodges or Storehouses are large, one-story buildings above ground, dimly lighted through small windows, for Mr. Vizitelli informs us that it is considered that ports mature less perfectly when subject to the influence of the light. But like other fortified wines, exposure to the air is considered beneficial to them; and in racking, they are drawn off into a wooden pitcher holding about five gallons, and poured into the cask to be filled, coming freely in contact with the air.

All Wines of Similar Character are Blended together at the lodge, by mixing in largs vats, sometimes stirred with a large fan operated by machinery. The blending is also performed in casks, by pouring into each one successively a certain number of gallons of each kind of wine, so that the contents of all the casks will be uniform. A small quantity of spirit is usually added at the time of cutting. After blending the wine is racked every three months, until in a condition for shipment, which may be in from fifteen to twenty-four months, according to quality.

Port loses its Color rapidly in Wood, and much of its fullness, and wines five years old cease to be regarded as shipping wines, and are then kept in store and used to give age and character to younger wines. It is then a valuable, old, mellow, and tawny wine, which the merchants of Oporto themselves drink.

Port Wine Contains from 18 to 23 per cent. of absolute Alcohol after fortifying, the amount of spirit added depending upon how much is developed by fermentation, and the amount of sugar in the grapes. It is customary to add a small amount whenever it is racked, and before shipping. The object of these frequent additions is to keep up the necessary strength, for a certain amount of alcohol is constantly evaporating while the wine is in casks, and it may fall below the required strength if these additions are not made.

Mr. Vizitelli has fallen into the error of stating that in dry climates wine becomes stronger by the evaporation of its *watery parts;* but this is impossible, for alcohol is more volatile than water, and whenever there is evaporation in a wine, it becomes weaker from the loss of alcohol; and whenever a wine gains strength by keeping, it is because the sugar contained in it has been transformed into alcohol, etc., by fermentation, as stated in other parts of this work.

MADEIRA.

Making.—In the island of Madeira it is the practice, according to Mr. Vizitelli, to tread the grapes thoroughly in a large, square wooden trough, or lagar, in which they are also pressed, as in sherry making. A great part of the juice is extracted by treading, being strained through a basket as it runs off into casks. After the grapes have been thoroughly trodden, the pomace is gathered together and piled in the centre of the lagar, and pressed and patted with the hands to extract the must, and this is repeated three times, and finally the pomace is again raised in a mound, wound with a rope, and pressed by means of a heavy beam suspended over the lagar. This primitive method, however, can have but little interest for the wine maker, as the essential practice in making Madeira, or rather in the aging of it, is the application of heat.

Casks, Treatment.—The must is fermented, the wine racked and heated, in casks holding 130 gallons. After heating, it is stored in casks holding about 400 gallons. It is fermented in these smaller casks with the bung open, simply covered by a leaf, till the month of November. Either before or after the fermentation, a small quantity of brandy is added, varying in quantity according to the quality of the must, but seldom exceeding three per cent. When the wine has well cleared, it is racked and lotted, according to quality, and forwarded to the heating house, or estufa.

Heating House, Heating.—One of these at Funchal, described by Vizitelli, consists of a block of buildings of two stories, divided into four compartments. "In the first of these, common wines are subjected to a temperature of 140° F., derived from flues heated with anthracite coal, for the space of three months. In the next compartment wines of an intermediate quality are heated up to 130° for a period of four and a-half months, while the third is set apart for superior wines, heated variously from 110° to 120° for the term of six months. The fourth compartment, known as the 'calor,' possesses no flues, but derives its heat, varying from 90° to 100°, exclusively from the compartments adjacent; and here only high-classed wines are placed." They receive a further addition of spirit, after leaving the estufa, varying in quantity from one to three gallons per cask, presumably to supply what has evaporated during the heating. Wines are also heated by exposing them to the rays of the sun in glass houses. In the day time a temperature of 120° to 130° is secured, which becomes considerably less during the night, which change is by many considered detrimental. Some again, put the casks out of doors in the full sunshine. In the estufas mentioned, the pipes are placed on end in stacks of four, with smaller casks on the top, a gangway being left between the different stacks. The casks are vented with a small hole during the process. Leaking is common during the exposure to so great a heat, and it is necessary to inspect the casks once during every day and once during the night.

Each compartment is provided with double doors, and after it is filled with wine, the inner door is plastered so as to stop all the cracks. In entering the estufa, only the outer door is opened, entrance through the inner one being made through a small door for the purpose. The man who examines the casks, coming out after a stay of an hour, drinks a tumblerful of wine, and cools off in a tight room provided for the purpose. From 10 to 15 per cent. of the wine is lost by evaporation while it remains in the heating house.

General Treatment—Alcoholic Strength.—The solera system is somewhat in vogue in Madeira, as in the sherry country. The practice also of leaving the casks in ullage prevails—a vacant space of ten or a dozen gallons is left. On the south side of the island 5 per cent. is the largest amount of alcohol added, and on

SWEET WINES.

the north side a little more, which is added at different times. Most Madeira is dry, or nearly so, and contains about 18 per cent. of alcohol on the average.

SHERRY.

Climate.—According to General Keyes, the climate of the sherry districts of Spain is a trifle warmer in winter and about the same in summer as that of Napa Valley. But the seasons are not so distinctly wet and dry as in California, and the grapes are sometimes rained on while growing, and are frequently wet while ripening. Neverthless, the south of Spain is a dry country.

The Vintage begins in the early part of September, at which time the grapes are ripe, but by no means overripe, but sweet and luscious. The grapes are picked in the early part of the day, and spread upon mats in the sun, where they remain till the evening of the same day, when they are crushed. General Keyes says that they are invariably crushed in the evening of the same day, but Mr. Vizitelli states that they remain on the straw mats from one to three days. As both write from observation, it would seem that the practice varies, the time of the exposure to the sun probably depending upon the degree of maturity when picked. The defective berries are carefully removed. The cool of the night for crushing is preferred to the heat of the day, and to avoid the precipitation of fermentation.

Crushing.—Mr. Vizitelli's description is as follows: "The pressing commenced between seven and eight o'clock, and was accomplished in a detached building under a low tiled roof, but entirely open in front. Passing through the gateway, and stumbling in the dim light afforded by an occasional lamp fixed against the wall, over a rudely paved court-yard, we found ourselves beside a row of large, stout wooden troughs, some ten feet square and a couple of feet deep, raised about three feet from the ground, and known in the vernacular of the vineyards as lagares. The bottoms of these receptacles were already strewn with grapes, lightly sprinkled over with yeso (gypsum), which if spread over the whole of the bunches, would not have been greatly in excess of the amount of dust ordinarily gathered by a similar quantity of grapes conveyed in open baskets on the backs of mules from the vineyards to the pressing places in the towns. At Torre Breva, the sixty or more arrobas of grapes (1500 lbs.) required to make each butt of wine, were having from two to four pounds of yeso sprinkled over them, or about half the quantity which would be used in a moist season. I was assured that at last year's vintage here not a single ounce of yeso was employed in the manufacture of upwards of 700 butts of wine. * * * Rising perpendicularly in the centre of each of the four lagares to a height of about seven feet, is a tolerably powerful screw, which is only brought into requisition after the grapes have been thoroughly trodden. A couple of swarthy, bare-legged pisadores leap into each lagar, and commence spreading out the bunches with wooden shovels; and soon the whole eight of them, in their short drawers, blue-striped shirts, little caps, red sashes, and hob-nailed shoes, are dancing a more or less lively measure, ankle-deep in newly-crushed grapes. They dance in couples, one on each side of the screw, performing certain rapid, pendulum-like movements which are supposed to have the virtue of expressing the juice more satisfactorily from the fruit than can be accomplished by mere mechanical means. Their saltatory evolutions ended, the trodden grapes are heaped up on one side and well patted about with the shovel, like so much newly mixed mortar. This causes the expressed juice to flow out in a dingy, brown, turgid stream through the spout fixed in front of the lagar, into a metal strainer, and thence into the vat placed beneath to receive it. Fresh grapes are now spread over the bottom of the lagar, and, after being duly danced upon, are shoveled on one side; and this kind of thing goes on until sufficient trodden murk has been accumulated to make what is called a pile."

Pressing.—His description goes on to show that the treaders give place to the pressers, who, with wooden shovels, build up a mound of marc under the screw, conical in form, some five feet high, which is neatly dressed and trimmed, and then wound around with a straw rope or band, about four inches wide, from base to summit. A circular piece of wood is placed on the top, and the pressure is applied by means of the screw, the must passing through the intersterstices of the straw band.

Treading and pressing goes on nightly for fourteen hours, with occasional intervals for refreshment.

The wine from the press is invariably fermented separately from that of the first run during the treading.

All agree that the grapes are crushed without stemming, but it seems that the practice of pressing with the stems on is not uniform. General Keyes says that he made careful inquiry on this subject, and was informed that only a few of the larger stems were removed, while Mr. Vizitelli states that the sherry wine maker is so much afraid of tannin and roughness in the wine, that the stems are all removed before the pomace is pressed. This is not important, however, as the press wine is inferior, and is usually distilled.

It is almost a universal custom to sprinkle each pressing of grapes with two or three handfuls of gypsum, or from two to six pounds to a butt of wine of 130 gallons, and in wet seasons, even more. Gen. Keyes gives an instance of one wine maker who made several casks of sherry one year without the use of gypsum, and he found no material difference in the product, but he still follows the custom of the country. (See *Plastering*.)

Fermenting.—The must is run into casks of about 150 gallons capacity, which are filled only to within ten or fifteen gallons of their full capacity, and is left to ferment in a cool shed, or in a place separate from the storehouse or bodega; new wine is not fermented in the same room with the old.

As soon as the wine falls bright, which it does at any time from January to April, it is racked and placed in the bodega, with still a vacant space in the cask, and brandy is added equal to one or two per cent. to the stronger wines, and three or four per cent. to the commoner ones.

If the wine is deficient in sugar, it may clear by January, but if rich, it may not become bright till April. During the active fermentation, the bungs, of course, are left open, and in the bodega they are left loose, or laid over the hole.

Sometimes the wine is left undisturbed in the bodega until required for shipment, when it is racked, clarified, and again fortified. It is considered best, however, to rack it once a year. The wine is now well fermented, and dry, or nearly so, and the sugar that may be found in it after shipment, has been put in by adding a small quantity of sweet wine.

The Bodegas, or Storehouses, in which these wines are stored, are entirely above ground, have very thick walls and double doors, the roof is covered with tiles, and the floor may consist only of a mixture of sand and loam, which, when moistened, is not muddy, and when dry, is not very dusty. They are kept well ventilated, even at the expense of a good deal of loss by evaporation, and are comparatively cool, the rays of the sun being excluded by shutters. As only old or seasoned casks are used for shipment, the new ones are used for fermenting the must, and so they are seasoned.

Changes in the Wine.—The young wine in the bodega now, during the first two years, undergoes extraordinary changes. That made from the same vineyard and of the same varieties of grapes, crushed at the same time, placed in casks side by side, receiving apparently identical treatment, developes totally different characters in different butts, and is classed according to these several characters, as Fino, Oloroso, and Basto.

The best is *fino*, of a delicate, soft, mellow flavor, and pale in color, and only from ten to twenty per cent. take this form. The *fino*, at times, develops into a still finer quality, producing what is known as *amontillado*, the most valued of all.

Oloroso is a nutty flavored development rather deeper in color, and of a stouter character; when old, it is of great body, and perfectly dry.

The coarse, inferior kind is called *basto*.

There are still other casks which by bad behavior, poor fermentation, or weakness, are only fit for the still.

Flowers.—Sherry produces the phenomenon known as flowers of wine (*micoderma vini*), of which a writer under the assumed name of Pedro Verdad, whom I have frequent occasion to quote, says: "At every period, about the flowering of the vine, and at about vintage time, the wine begins to 'breed;' that is, throw up a *flor* (flower), which remains for some time on the surface, and then falls in sediment to the bottom, when the wine once more becomes bright. This phenomenon is looked for with great anxiety in the bodegas, for if it does not occur, the wine may be assuming some other and less valued character. Strange as it may appear," he says, "I have seen the actual *flor* rise in a bottle in England, just as in the butt in Spain."

Vino Dulce, or Sweet Wine, is made from the sweeter kinds of grapes, especially the Pedro Jimenes. The grapes are exposed to the sun, sometimes for a fortnight, and till they almost become raisins, and they then go through the ordinary modes of crushing and fermentation. To each butt of this wine about six or seven gallons of spirit are added, while the must of other grapes have as much as twenty gallons mixed with each cask of must to check the fermentation, and keep the wine sweet. One-third of the spirit is poured in as soon as a small portion of the must has been put into the cask, a third when the cask is half full, and a third when nearly three-quarters full. The reason is obvious, as the spirit is lighter than the must, and would otherwise remain on the top. Soleras of *vino dulce* are of a sweet, luscious flavor, and of an oily and slightly glutinous consistency. The finer kinds resemble a liqueur, and are of great value.

Vizitelli says that sweet wine is used to give softness and roundness to old and pungent wines, as well as to the cruder, youthful growths, and it is remarkable how very small a quantity suffices perceptibly to modify these opposite characteristics. As little as one per cent. of dulce will impart a softness to the drier wines, which otherwise they only acquire after being several years in bottle.

Color Wine (Vino de Color) is composed of a mixture of white wine and *arrope*. The latter is a must of white grapes boiled down over a slow fire till it is reduced to one-fifth or one-sixth of its orginal quantity, great care being taken to skim it while boiling. This is a dark-colored, almost black fluid, of a bitterish taste. It is mixed with from three to five times its volume of white wine, and the "color" is formed.* It is chiefly used for giving color to young and undeveloped wines. With great age, the solera of this wine is very valuable, being of a deep brown color, and a perfect essence.

Mature Wines.—When the wines have assumed their distinctive characters—and this requires from three to five, or even more, years—they are used to replenish the soleras. In the shippers' bodega are kept many soleras, each containing a given number of butts. A solera, whether classed as *fino*, *oloroso*, or otherwise, has its distinctive quality required in the preparation of a wine for shipment. It has been reared and nursed for years with careful attention; each butt has been tasted from time to time, and any cask in which a material deterioration has been detected is rejected from the solera, and probably fortified with spirits, or distilled.

THE SOLERA SYSTEM.

The distinctive feature in the production of sherry is the *solera*, which signifies foundation, and means old wine kept in casks, which are never moved as long as the solera exists, and on the foundation of which younger wines are reared.

The casks are arranged in groups, piled in tiers, and the groups into scales. The distinctive feature of the system is a series, commencing with a very old wine, followed by a younger one, and so on down the scale to the youngest, so that when wine for blending and shipment is drawn from the group of casks constituting the oldest solera, they are replenished from the group of casks of the next younger solera, and these again from those of the next younger, and so on through the scale, thus keeping up the characters of the soleras.

Establishing a Solera.—The following from the address of

---

* Vizitelli says the arrope is mixed with nine parts of must, and fermented to make the color, but the other authors say "white wine," instead of "must."

Mr. Pohndorff before the Viticultural Convention held at San Francisco in September, 1882, gives a good idea of how to establish a solera:

Select the finest wines of a year's vintage, put them away by themselves, and carefully care for them and nurse them by racking, etc., during the year. The next year, separate the finest wines from the vintage, always leaving ullage in the casks of three to five gallons, according to size, and the bungs loose, simply laid over the hole. Go on in this way for five years. Now a fifth of this five-year-old wine may be drawn off for, and used to establish another solera, and the casks refilled from the four-year-old wine, which, of course, must be as nearly as possible of the same nature. With the younger wines, you may do the same, except those of one and two years old, which are not yet soleras, but young wines. You have then a solera of this five-year-old wine, which is one-fifth four-year-old wine, and this may be called the mother solera. At the end of ten years more, you can say that you have a solera fifteen years of age; though during the period, you have drawn off periodically a small portion of it and replaced it with the next younger, always providing that the younger wine is similar, for this quality is of much greater importance than the difference of a year or two in age, for wine a year or two younger or older, if of the same kind, will not injure the solera, but its character may be destroyed by mixing with it wine of a different nature.

A solera, then, really consists of a mixture of wines of different years. The head of each cask is inscribed with the distinguishing mark of its solera, and the number of butts of which it is composed.

"The Standard Soleras," says Gen. Keyes, "are those from which the wine is drawn for shipment, and their contents have rested in, and permeated through, a series of groups called feeders"—a solera sometimes dating back a century, it is said. "At every stage the wine is graded, so that the best young wine passes ultimately into the oldest and highest priced solera. When there is only a small number of feeders, say two or three, in the group next behind the standard solera, the wine ought not be drawn out for shipment oftener than twice a year; but when there are many, say twelve, the wine for shipment may be drawn out every two months. To make myself understood in this complicated process, I must explain the principle upon which it is founded. When wine is needed for shipment, a portion is drawn out by siphons from the standard soleras. The amount which may be drawn out with safety, and the kind of younger wines which are to replace it in the old solera, requires great skill and experience, and, I may say, a natural aptness for the business. The end in view is to draw off from a standard solera such a number of gallons, that, being replaced by an equal number of gallons of the younger wines, the standard of the solera may remain intact. If too much is drawn out, or if it is replaced from the wrong feeders, the standard may be injured, or even destroyed. But if the proper number of gallons are drawn out and replaced by the right sorts from the other casks, the old solera soon transmutes the younger wines to its standard, the bodega retains its reputatation, and the owner grows rich." He quotes Mr. Davis, of Jerez, as follows: "The age of the first step of a solera scale depends entirely upon the character and price of the oldest grade of that particular solera. For instance, the first group of wine in a scale of six, ending in a medium priced sherry, might be two years old; whereas, the first group of wine to permeate through a scale of, say four, ending in a wine of great age or value, would, perhaps, require to be fifteen or twenty years old. In proportion to the number of the scale behind the final solera, so is the frequency with which the wine can be drawn determined. In a scale of twelve, the final solera might be drawn, perhaps, every two months. In a scale of three feeders, perhaps twice a year."

Blending for Shipment.—In the cellar a book is kept in which is recorded the blend of each shipment made, the history of the shipment, and all the facts necessary to its identification, and a sample bottle of every shipment is also preserved. When an order is received for a quantity of wine of the same kind as a former shipment, reference is made to the blend book, and recourse is had to the sample bottle, due allowance being made for the bottle flavor acquired by the sample, and the blend is prepared accordingly, the necessary quantity being taken from each solera, of which there are many in a shipping bodega, and allowance is also made for the change that may have occurred in the solera by replenishing. It is needless to add that only experience and natural aptitude fit a man for this delicate operation.

If the order is by a sample whose blend is not known, the sample is brought into the tasting office, and the blend glass brought into requisition. It is a graduated glass tube, with forty markings, corresponding to the number of *jarras*, or jars, which a butt contains, all shipments being by the butt. The shipping butt contains 130 gallons, and the cask for storing is about 20 gallons larger.

The cellar-man dips out and puts into the graduated glass amounts corresponding to the number of jars to be taken from each solera, sweet wine being added for sweetness, and color wine for color. As the sugar added in the sweet wine would excite fermentation, sufficient *aguardiente*, spirit, must be added to bring its alcoholic strength up to at least 18 per cent.

The right blend having been ascertained, it is left for a while, and tasted once or twice to make sure that it is correct. If it does not match the sample, a little of this and that solera is added till it exactly corresponds. The blend is then entered in the blend book, which gives the number of butts required, and the amount to be taken from each solera. The book is then handed in to the bodega for the execution of the blend. Supposing it to be a ten-butt shipment, ten butts are brought into the cellar, having been most carefully examined and rinsed out with spirit. If ten jars are required from a solera of fifty butts, two jars would be drawn from each of the fifty butts of the solera, and put into the ten butts, and so on from each solera; whatever the number of butts in a solera, an equal quantity of wine is drawn from each cask.

The following samples of blends are given by Verdad:

ORDINARY PALE SHERRY.

Pale soleras,	20 jarras
Fino soleras,	16 "
Vino dulce,	3 "
Aguardiente,	1 "
	40 jarras

ORDINARY GOLDEN SHERRY.

Pale soleras,	22 jarras
Oloroso soleras,	8½ "
Vino de color,	2 "
Vino dulce,	6 "
Aguardiente,	1½ "
	40 jarras

ORDINARY BROWN SHERRY.

Pale soleras,	23 jarras
Oloroso,	4 "
Vino de color,	5 "
Vino dulce,	6 "
Aguardiente,	2 "
	40 jarras

Fining.—After the blend is complete, the wine is fined with the whites of eggs and fuller's earth, a kind of earth found at Lebrija, near Jerez, and called *Tierra de Lebrija*. For a butt of wine, a handful of this earth is made into a paste with the whites of ten eggs. The paste is thrown into the cask, and the wine is stirred in the usual manner. (See *Fining*.)

CHAPTER XV.

DEFECTS AND DISEASES.

These are Divided by Boireau into *two classes:* 1. Those defects due to the nature of the soil, to fertilizers employed, to bad processes in wine making, and to the abundance of common, poor varieties of grapes. It is evident that defects of this class may exist in the wines from the moment when they leave the fermenting vat, or the press, and they are as follows: earthy flavor, greenness, roughness, bitterness, flavor of the stems, acidity, want of alcohol, lack of color, dull, bluish, leaden color, flavor of the lees, and tendency to putrid decomposition. 2. Those vices which wines acquire after fermentation, and of which the greater part are due to want of care, or uncleanness of the casks, and they are: flatness, flowers, acidity (pricked wine), cask flavor, mouldiness, bad flavors communicated by the accidental introduction of foreign soluble matters, ropiness, bitterness, acrity, flavor of fermentation, degeneracy, and putrid fermentation.

General Considerations.—Before entering on the subject of the correction and cure of defects and diseases, it is proper to say, that whatever be the nature of the malady or defect, especially if the bad taste is very pronounced, wine once hurt, however completely cured of the disease, will never be worth as much as a wine of the same nature which has always had the correct flavor.

It is, therefore, wiser and more prudent, says our author, to seek to prevent the maladies of wines, than to wait for them to become diseased in order to cure them.

Of course, the wine maker should use every endeavor to remedy the natural defects of his wines. And as for the wine merchant and the consumer, they should reject all vitiated wines, unless they can be used immediately, for they lose quality instead of gaining by keeping.

Moreover, when a wine has a very pronounced defect, it can rarely be used alone, either because deficient in spirit or in color, or because the vice cannot be entirely destroyed.

It would also be a mistake to suppose that the flavor of a diseased wine would be rendered inappreciable by mixing and distributing it throughout a large number of casks of sound wine; oftener the latter would be more or less injured by the operation. The defect of such a wine should first be removed by treating it by itself, and then it should be mixed only with the commonest wine in the cellar.

Each defect and disease will be treated under its proper name, the cause indicated, with the means to be employed to prevent, diminish, or to remove it.

The doses in all cases, unless otherwise indicated, are according to Mr. Boireau, who gives what is required to treat 225 litres, but we have increased the dose to what is necessary for 100 gallons of wine in each case.

Any one can first try the experiment on a gallon or less by taking a proportional amount of the substances indicated, leaving the sample corked, in a cool place, for at least two days in ordinary cases, or for eight days in case the wine is fined.

NATURAL DEFECTS.

Earthy Flavor—Its Causes.—It is a natural defect in the wine, and consists of a bad taste by which the pulp and the skins of the grapes are affected before fermentation. It occurs in wine made from grapes grown on low, wet, swampy land, and on land too heavily manured, or fertilized with substances which communicate a bad flavor. He says that this must not be confounded with the natural flavor and bouquet of the wine. Contrary to the opinion of those œnologues who attribute this defective flavor to the presence of essential oils, he believes that there is a sensible difference between the natural flavor (*séve*) and the earthy flavor. In fact, the flavor and bouquet of wines made from grapes of the same variety, but grown in different vineyards, present considerable differences, which are due to the different natures of the soils, to the different processes in wine making, to climate, exposure, age of the wine, etc. On the other hand, the taste and odor produced by the natural flavor and bouquet are not entirely developed till the wine is old, and the clearing is complete ; while the bad taste transmitted from the soil through the sap, instead of increasing with age, diminishes, and often finally disappears. The reason is that this taste being communicated principally by the coloring matters of the skins, diminishes with the deposit of these matters, according as the wine becomes clear. It follows that certain wines may have a good flavor, and even acquire a bouquet in aging, which while young had a disagreeable earthy flavor.

He instances the wines of several crops, treated by him, having a fine color, mellowness, and 10 per cent. of alcohol, which in their early years had an earthy flavor so pronounced that it might almost have been taken for a mouldy taste. This taste diminished gradually, with proper care, and finally disappeared toward the third year; the natural flavor then developed itself, and the wines acquired an agreeable bouquet in bottles.

Grapes from young vines planted in moist land, have an earthy flavor more pronounced than those from older vines, grown in the same situations, and this flavor is generally more developed in the heavy-yielding common varieties than in the fine kinds.

How Prevented.—This flavor may be sometimes diminished or destroyed by draining the soil of the vineyard, aerating the vines when too crowded, and by avoiding the planting of trees in the vineyard. If it comes from too much manure, less should be used, and less wood left on the vines.

Great care should be taken to draw such wines from the fermenting vat, as soon as the active fermentation is finished, for a long sojourn in the tank with the stems and skins aggravates the defect.

The Treatment of wines so affected differs according to their origin, their nature, and their promise of the future; but the condition necessary in all cases is to promptly obtain their defecation or clarification, and never to allow them to remain on the lees. They should therefore be drawn off as soon as clear, and frequently racked to prevent the formation of voluminous deposits.

Red wines, which in spite of this defect, have a future, and may acquire quality with age, should be racked at the beginning of winter, again in the beginning of March, and after the second racking should be fined with the whites of 12 eggs to 100 gallons of wine; they are then racked again two weeks after fining.

Common red wines, without a future, dull and poor in color, and weak in spirit, are treated in the same manner, but before fining, a little more than a quart of alcohol of 60 to 90 per cent. is added to facilitate the coagulation of the albumen.

In treating wines which are firm, full-bodied, and charged with color, after the two rackings, an excellent result is obtained by an energetic fining with about three ounces of gelatine.

Earthy white wines should be racked after completing their fermentation, and after the addition of about an ounce of tannin dissolved in alcohol, or the equivalent of tannified white wine. After racking, they should be fined with about three ounces of gelatine.

These rackings and finings precipitate the insoluble matters, and part of the coloring matter, which is strongly impregnated with the earthy taste, and the result is a sensible diminution of the flavor. When not very pronounced, it is removed little by little at each racking. But if it is very marked, the wine after the first racking should have a little less than a quart of olive oil thoroughly stirred into it. After a thorough agitation, the oil should be removed by filling the cask. The oil removes with it a portion of those matters in the wine which cause the bad flavor. The wine is afterwards fined as above.

Some writers recommend that wine having an earthy flavor should be mixed with wine of a better taste, as the best method of correcting the defect; but from what has been said in the preceding part of this chapter, it would seem to be an unsafe practice.

The Wild Taste and Grassy Flavor are due to the same causes, and are removed in the same way.

Greenness—Its Causes.—This is due to the presence of tartaric acid, which it contains in excess. It gives a sour, austere taste to the wine, which also contains malic acid, but in a less quantity. When tasted, it produces the disagreeable sensation of unripe fruit to the palate, sets the teeth on edge, and contracts the nervous expansions of the mouth.

Greenness, as the term imports, is caused by want of maturity of the grapes. We all know that acids abound in unripe fruit, and it is only at the time of maturity, and under the influence of the heat of the sun, that they disappear and are changed into glucose or grape sugar.

A green wine, then, is an imperfect wine, which, besides this defect, generally lacks alcohol, body, mellowness, firmness, bouquet, and color, because the incompletely matured grapes contain much tartaric and malic acid, and but little grape sugar and other mucilaginous matter, and because the matters destined to give color to the skins, as well as the aromatic principles, are not completely elaborated.

The only way to Prevent this Defect is to resort to means necessary to increase the maturity of the grape, or to add sugar to the must, neither of which will scarcely ever be found necessary in California, where the defect is not likely to exist, if the grapes are not picked too green.

Treatment.—Where the sourness is not insupportable, the wine may be ameliorated by adding a quart or two of old brandy for each 100 gallons.

The wine as it comes from the vat contains much more free tartaric acid than it contains after the insensible fermentation in the cask, because it combines with the tartrate of potash in the wine and forms the bitartrate of potash, or cream of tartar, which is deposited with the lees, or attaches itself to the sides of the cask. It follows that the wine will be less green after insensible fermentation, at the first racking, than when it was new; but if the greenness is excessive after the insensible fermentation, the wine still contains much free acid. The excess of acid may be neutralized in wines which are very green by adding the proper amount of tartrate of potash, which combines with a part of the tartaric acid to form the bitartrate, which after a few days falls

130 DEFECTS AND DISEASES.

to the bottom, or adheres to the cask. The dose varies from 10 to 24 ounces per 100 gallons of wine. Five or six gallons of wine are drawn out of the cask, and the tartrate of potash is thrown in by the handful, stirring the while as in the case of fining. This treatment does not always succeed; hence, the necessity of preventing the defect when possible.

When the greenness is not very marked, the wine may also be mixed with an older wine, which contains but little acid and plenty of spirit.

Lime and other alkaline substances will surely neutralize the acid, but they injure the wine and render it unhealthy, and should never be used.

Machard lays great stress upon the addition of brandy to such wines, because, he says, the alcohol will precipitate the excess of acids, and will also combine with them to form ethers which give a delicate, balsamic odor to the wine, which is most agreeable. (See *Ethers, Bouquet.*)

Roughness is due to the astringency given to the wine by the tannin when in excess. Tannin is useful for the preservation and the clarification of wines, and those which contain much, with an equal amount of alcohol, keep much longer than those which contain less, and undergo transportation better, and are considered more healthful.

Roughness is Not a Fault, it is rather an excess of good quality, if the rough wines have no after-taste of the stems, bitterness, earthy flavor, acrity, and possess a high degree of spirit, a fruity flavor, and a good color. Such wines are precious for fortifying, and to assist in aging those which are too feeble to keep a long time without degenerating. When kept without cutting, they last a long time, and end well. But they are long in developing.

The Roughness Disappears in Time, because the tannin is transformed into gallic acid, and besides is precipitated by other principles contained in the wine, and by finings.

An Excess of Tannin is Avoided in strong, dark-colored, full-bodied wines by removing all the stems, and by early drawing

DEFECTS AND DISEASES.

from the tank. If the wines are inclined to be soft, weak, and with but little spirit, no attempt should be made to avoid roughness.

When wines are put into new casks, their roughness is increased by the tannin derived from the oak wood of which they are made; but during insensible fermentation a good deal of the tannin is thrown down with the vegetable albumen contained in the new wine.

How Removed.—If the wines are of good body and color, the roughness may be removed by fining them with a strong dose of gelatine, two or three ounces to 100 gallons. As this removes a portion of the color, it should only be resorted to in the case of rough and dark-colored wines, to hasten their maturity.

Bitterness and Taste of the Stems—Causes.—Bitterness is a disagreeable taste which, *in new wines* attacked by it, comes from the dissolution of a bitter principle contained in the stems, a principle entirely different from tannin. Sometimes it is communicated by the skins of certain varieties of grapes.

This is Prevented by allowing the grapes to reach complete maturity, and above all by stemming them all, and by not leaving the wine too long in the fermenting vat.

The Treatment is the same as for the earthy flavor, and also afterwards pouring in a quart or more of old brandy.

The bitterness here mentioned is only that met with in new wines, and its cause is entirely different from that found in old wines, which is described further on.

The Taste of the Stems, which often accompanies bitterness, is due to a prolonged immersion of the stems in the wine. It is supposed that this defect, which gives the wine a wild and common flavor, comes from an aromatic principle contained in the stems. It is prevented by stemming, and like natural bitterness, diminishes with time. The treatment is the same.

An unreasonably long vatting is one of the principal causes of bitterness and stem flavor.

Sourness—Its Causes.—Sourness, or heated flavor, as it is also called, is due to the presence of acetic acid in the wine. All wines, even the mellowest, the best made, and the best cared for, contain some acetic acid, but in so small a quantity as to be inappreciable to the taste. Acetic acid is produced in wines during their fermentation in open tanks, and is due to the contact of the air with the crust of the pomace. This crust or cap, formed of skins and stems, brought to the surface by bubbles of carbonic acid rising from the liquid, is exposed directly to the air, and the alcoholic fermentation of the liquid part is soon completed, and under the influence of the air and ferments, the alcohol is transformed into acetic acid. This transformation is so rapid that when the vatting is too prolonged, and the temperature is high, the exterior crust rapidly passes from acetic to putrid fermentation.

As long as the tumultuous fermentation continues, the crust is kept up above the surface by the bubbles of rising gas, but when it ceases, the cap falls, and settles down into the liquid, and the wine becomes impregnated with the acetic acid. The wine also, by simple contact with the crust, acquires a vinegar smell and taste.

Wines which become pricked by contact with the air after fermentation are treated further on under the head of *Pricked Wines*.

How Prevented.—The formation of acetic acid during fermentation is prevented by fermenting the wines in closed or partly closed vats, by avoiding contact of the air, by keeping the pomace submerged, and by confining the carbonic acid in the vat. If open vats are used, they should be only three-fourths full, so that a layer of gas may rest upon the pomace and protect it from the atmosphere; or the cap may be covered with a bed of straw as soon as formed. Care should be taken to draw off as soon as fermentation is complete.

Treatment.—Wines affected in this manner cannot be expected to acquire good qualities with age. They may be rendered potable, but their future is destroyed. Therefore, every precaution

DEFECTS AND DISEASES. 133

should be taken to guard against the defect. They should be separated from their first lees as soon as possible; consequently, they should be drawn off as soon as the gas ceases to rise. If they are still turbid, they should be clarified by an energetic fining, and they should be racked from the finings the very moment they are clear. They should be afterwards racked to further free them from ferments. If the wines are only *heated*, the odor of acetic acid will be sensibly diminished by the above operation; but if they are decidedly pricked, the means to neutralize their acid when drawn from the vat, as indicated for *Pricked Wines*, should be resorted to.

Alcoholic Weakness is due to a want of sufficient spirit, caused by an excess of water of vegetation, and the consequent lack of sugar in the grapes. In France this defect is generally found in wines coming from young vines planted in very fertile soils, or from the common varieties, pruned with long canes, and producing a great quantity of large, watery grapes. When wines weak in alcohol contain but little tannin and color, they rapidly degenerate, often commencing their decline during their first year, and before their clarification is completed.

How Avoided.—This defect can be corrected by planting the proper varieties of vines, and by avoiding rich soils; but in the climate of California there is but little danger of the wines being too weak, unless the grapes are late varieties, and grown in very unfavorable situations.

The Treatment of weak wines is to rid them of their ferments as soon as possible, in order to avoid acid and putrid degeneration, to which they are quite subject. This result is obtained by drawing them off as soon as the lees are deposited. If they remain turbid after the second racking, they should be gently fined with the whites of nine or ten eggs to 100 gallons. The coagulation of the albumen will be facilitated by adding one or more quarts of strong alcohol to the wine before fining, and by adding to the eggs a handful of common salt dissolved in a little water. But as these wines, by themselves, are short lived, it is necessary, in order to prolong their existence, to mix them with firm wines, strong in body and rich in color. By adding alcohol, they are still left dry and without fruity flavor, while if mixed with a wine of a flavor as nearly like their own as possible, and having a fruity flavor, and being firm and full-bodied, but not fortified, they will acquire mellowness as well as strength.

Want of Color—Causes.—As coloring matter is not found in the skins of grapes till they are ripe, green wines produced in years when the grapes do not ripen well, lack color.

The amount of color may be diminished if by excess of maturity the skins of the grapes decay.

The method of fermentation also influences more or less the richness of the color. Those wines, in the fermentation of which the pomace is kept constantly immersed in the liquid, dissolve out more coloring matter than those fermented in open vats in which the crust is raised above the surface of the must.

Some kinds of grapes naturally develop more color than others.

How Guarded Against.—It is therefore obvious, that the lack of color may be guarded against by gathering the grapes when they are just ripe, planting the proper varieties, and keeping the pomace submerged during fermentation, stirring it up, if necessary.

The Treatment should be such as to avoid as much as possible the precipitation of the coloring matter. They should, therefore, be fined as little as possible, and gelatine should be carefully avoided. If they must be fined, use the whites of eggs and in the quantity mentioned for weak wines—10 to 100 gallons.

Of course, their color may be increased by mixing them with darker colored wines, but in order not to affect their natural flavor, they should be mixed only with wines of the same nature and of the same growth.

It is not to be supposed that any one will resort to artificial coloring of any kind.

Dull, Bluish, Lead-colored Wine, and Flavor of the Lees— Causes.—Certain wines remain turbid, and preserve a dull, leaden-color, even after insensible fermentation. This state may be due to several causes. Oftentimes young wines remain turbid because, for want of racking at proper times, and for want of storing in proper places, secondary fermentation has set in, which has stirred up the lees which had been deposited at the bottom of the cask. This also takes place when new wines are moved before racking.

Treatment.—In these cases, put them into a cellar of a constant temperature, leave them quiet for a couple of weeks, and see if they settle naturally. If not, clarify them by using the finings appropriate to their nature.

If they are turbid on account of an unseasonable fermentation, the first thing to do is to stop the working by racking, sulphuring, etc. When, in spite of all the cares that have been bestowed upon them, they still remain dull and difficult to clarify, while undergoing no fermentation, the cause must be sought in the want of tannin or alcohol.

If the difficulty is due simply to lack of spirit, the treatment consists in adding two or three quarts of strong alcohol to each 100 gallons, mixing with the wine a fifth or a tenth of a good-bodied wine of like natural flavor, and then by fining it with eggs as mentioned for weak wines.

If the dull wine has sufficient alcohol, as shown by a pronounced color, add about an ounce of tannin dissolved in alcohol, or the equivalent of tannified wine, and fine it with one to two ounces of gelatine.

Bluish or violet color, accompanied by a flavor of the lees, often occurs in wines of southern countries, and is due to an abundance of coloring matter and a lack of tartaric acid. When the violet-colored wine has a good deal of color, and more than nine per cent. of alcohol, the color may be changed to red by mixing with it from one-sixth to one-fourth of green wine, which contains an excess of tartaric acid, the natural blue color of the grape being changed to red by the action of the acid; then about an ounce of tannin, or the equivalent of tannified wine, should be added, that the color may become fixed, and that clarification may subsequently take place in a proper manner. In default of green wine, crystalized tartaric acid may be used, which is very soluble in wine. A small amount should be first experimented with, in order to learn just how much to use to change the blue of the wine to red, for we must not forget that this acid gives greenness to the wine and thereby renders it less healthful.

If the wines are so weak in alcohol that they have but little color, and that is blue and dull, they have a tendency to putridity. In this case, the blue color is in fact only a commencement of decomposition. It is due to an internal reaction which transforms a part of the tartrate of potash into carbonate of potash. Such wines have a slightly alkaline flavor, and left to themselves in contact with the air, they become rapidly corrupt, without completely acidifying. These wines are of the poorest quality. This disease, which is very rare, may be prevented by using the proper methods of vinification, and by rendering them firmer and full-bodied by the choice of good varieties of vines. In the treatment of such wines, some propose the use of tartaric acid to restore them. This will turn the blue color to red, but will not prevent the threatened decomposition. Mr. Boireau prefers the use of about one-sixth of green wine, which contains an abundance of the acid, and the subsequent mixing with a strong, full-bodied wine.

Putrid Decomposition—Causes.—Wines are decomposed and become putrid, on account of little spirituous strength and lack of tannin. The weakness in alcohol is due to want of sufficient sugar in the grapes—to the excess of water of vegetation. We see, then, that wine is predisposed to putridity when it is wanting in these two conservative principles, alcohol and tannin. Such wine quickly loses its color; it never becomes brilliant and limpid; it remains turbid, and never clears completely, but continues to deposit. The tendency to decomposition is announced by a change of color, which becomes tawny and dull, which gives it, though young, an appearance of worn-out, turbid, old wine. Its red color is in great part deposited, and it retains only the yellow. If the defect is not promptly remedied by fortifying, it acquires a nauseous, putrid flavor of stagnant water; and it continues turbid, and is decomposed, without going squarely into acetous fermentation.

How Avoided.—To avoid this tendency, which is rare, means should be employed to increase the natural sugar in the must, and by planting proper varieties of grapes, which will produce good, firm wines, and by choosing proper situations for the vineyard, and employing the best methods of vinification.

Treatment.—Decomposition may be retarded in several ways: First, by fortifying the wines, by adding tannin to them, and by adding a sufficient quantity of rough, firm, alcoholic wine; second, in default of a strong, full-bodied wine, brandy may be added, or better, the tannin prepared with alcohol, so as to give them a strength of at least ten per cent.; third, fining should be avoided as much as possible, especially the use of finings which precipitate the coloring matter, such as gelatine; albumen should be used in preference, as for weak wines; fourth, the movements of long journeys, and drawing off by the use of pumps, should be avoided, for they are apt to increase the deposition of the coloring matter.

The treatment mentioned will retard the decomposition, but will not arrest it, and such wines can never endure a long voyage unless heavily brandied.

Several Different Natural Vices and Defects may attack the same wine, when it should be treated for that which is most prominent.

ACQUIRED DEFECTS AND DISEASES.

Flat Wine—Flowers—Causes.—Flowers of wine are nothing but a kind of mould, in the form of a whitish scum or film, composed of microscopic fungi, the *mycoderma vini* and *mycoderma aceti*, already mentioned under the head of *Fermentation*, and which develop on the surface of wine left in contact with the air. This mould, or *mother*, communicates to the wine a disagreeable odor and flavor, and also a slight acidity, which the

French call *évent* odor, or flavor *éventé*, and which may be called *flatness*. The development of these organisms is due principally to the direct exposure of the wine to the air, which favors their growth by the evaporation of a portion of the alcohol which exists at the surface of the liquid which is exposed, and a commencement of oxidation of that which remains. The result is that the surface of the wine becomes very weak in alcohol, and having lost its conservative principle, it moulds. This mould consists, as before remarked, of a vast number of small fungi. They have a bad flavor, and are impregnated with an acidity which comes from the action of the oxygen of the air upon the alcohol, converting it into acetic acid.

This disease develops more or less rapidly, according to the alcoholic strength of the wine and the temperature of the place where it is kept. Those common, weak wines, which have only from 7 to 8½ per cent. of alcohol, are the first attacked; on them flowers are developed in three or four days. Stronger wines, which contain from 10 to 11 per cent. of spirit, resist twice as long as the weaker ones. Fine wines of an equal strength resist better than the common kinds; and wines which contain more than 15 per cent. are not affected. During summer they are much sooner affected.

Machard is of the opinion that this flavor is due to the commencement of disorganization of the ferments remaining in the wine, which, as they begin to putrify, give off ammoniacal emanations. Maumené says that it is due to the loss of carbonic acid.

To Prevent Flatness, all agree that wines should be protected from the air; for this purpose they should be kept in casks constantly full, or in well corked bottles lying in a horizontal position. When it is necessary to leave ullage in the cask, a sulphur match must be burned, and the cask tightly bunged. (See *General Treatment, Wine in Bottles, Sulphuring,* etc.)

In frequently drawing from the cask, the deterioration is retarded by taking care to admit the least possible amount of air, just enough to let the wine run, but the evil cannot be entirely prevented in this way; and by frequent sulphuring the wine will acquire a disagreeable sulphur flavor; therefore, ullage should never be left when it is possible to avoid it.

Treatment.—When the wines show flowers, but have not yet become flat, as in the case of new wines which have been neglected, and have not been filled up for a week or more, and are only affected at the surface, by filling up, the flowers may be caused to flow out at the bung. The cask must then be well bunged. It must afterwards be kept well filled, for besides the flat flavor that the flowers may give the wine, they will render it turbid on account of the acid ferments introduced, and cause it to become pricked in the end.

Wine badly flowered, and which has acquired a decided flavor of flatness, without being actually sour, should be filled up, and the flowers should be allowed to pass out of the bung; it should then be racked into a well sulphured cask, which must be completely filled. The flowers must not be allowed to become mixed with the wine. After racking, two or three quarts of old brandy to each 100 gallons should be added, or a few gallons of firm, full-bodied wine, as near as possible of the same natural flavor. It should then be well fined, using in preference the whites of eggs (one dozen for 100 gallons, and a handful of salt dissolved in a little water), and then it must be racked again as soon as clear.

The object of this treatment is to extract from the wine by racking the mould which causes the bad taste; to replace by fortifying, the alcohol lost by evaporation; and finally, by fining, to remove in the lees the acid ferments, which have developed in the form of flowers.

Yet those wines which have become badly affected through negligence are never completely restored, and if they are fine, delicate wines, they lose a large part of their value. Therefore, great care should be taken to prevent this disease, which in the end produces acidity, for, often, neglected wines are at the same time *flat* and *pricked*.

Some authors recommend that such a wine should be again

mixed with a good, sound, fresh pomace, which has not been long in the vat, and allowed to ferment a second time; this is called *passing it over the marc*. Of course, this can only be done in the wine making season, and cannot be resorted to by those who do not make wine themselves, or who are at a distance from a wine maker.

When all else fails, they recommend that several large pieces of dry, fresh charcoal be suspended in the wine, attached to cords to draw them out by, Maigne says, for forty-eight hours, and Machard says, one or two weeks, renewing the charcoal from time to time till the taste is removed.

If the wine has already become acid, charcoal will not remove the flavor.

Sourness, Acidity, Pricked Wine—Causes.—Acidity is a sour taste caused by the alcohol of the wine being in part changed to acetic acid by the oxygen of the air. It is due to long contact with the air, and it is the oxygen which produces the change, as described under the head of *Acetic Fermentation*, and it is the more rapid, according as the temperature is more elevated, and the wine contains more ferments.

What Wines Liable to.—All wines whose fermentation is completed, and which have been fermented under ordinary circumstances—that is, those which have received no addition of alcohol, and no longer contain saccharine matter, are subject to this affection when left exposed to the air.

When they have been fortified up to 18 per cent. of alcohol, whether sweet or not, they do not sour until the alcohol has been enfeebled by evaporation.

If they contain sugar, although not fortified, a new fermentation takes place, and they do not acidify until the greater part of the sugar has been transformed into alcohol. Machard, however, says that wines which contain a good deal of sugar do often acidify, and in the experience of others, there is a continuous fermentation, which renders them very liable to become pricked.

As the acetic acid is formed at the expense of the alcohol, the more the wine contains of the former the less will it have of the latter.

Acidity is Prevented by giving wines proper care and attention, and by keeping them in suitable places, and by using the precautions indicated for *flat* or *flowered wines*, *i.e.*, by avoiding long contact with the air. Flowers are the forerunners of acidity; yet they do not always appear before the wine is pricked, especially if the temperature is elevated, and the alcoholic strength considerable. In general, wines become pricked without producing flowers when they are exposed to the air at a temperature of 77° to 100° F.; acidity is produced under these conditions in a very rapid manner; and this is why extra precautions should be taken during hot weather. It should also be remembered that this vice comes *either from the negligence of the cellar-man to guard the wines from contact with the air, or from the bad state of the casks, and storing in unsuitable places*.

Treatment.—Acetic acid in wine may be in great part neutralized by several alkaline substances; but, if used, there remain in solution in the wine certain salts (acetates and tartrates) formed by the combination of the acetic and tartaric acid with the alkaline bases introduced. These alkaline substances not only neutralize the acetic acid, but also the vegetable acids contained in the wine. These neutral salts are not perfectly wholesome, being generally laxative in their nature. Moreover, the acetic acid cannot be completely neutralized by the employment of caustic alkalies (potash, soda, quicklime), and these bases decompose the wine and cause the dissolution and precipitation of the coloring matter, and render it unfit to drink by reason of the bitterness which they communicate. It is necessary, therefore, to choose for the treatment of pricked wines, those alkaline matters which are the most likely to neutralize the excess of acetic acid without altering the constitution of the wine, without precipitating their color, and which produce by combination the least soluble and least unwholesome salts.

Those which should be employed in preference to others are, carbonate of magnesium, tartrate of potassium, and lime water.

The following substances should only be employed when it is impossible to obtain those last mentioned, for the reason that the salts remaining in solution in the wine may cause loss of color, and even decomposition, if used in large doses, *i. e.*, wood ashes (ashes from vine cuttings being preferred as containing much of the salts of potash); powdered chalk and marble (composed of the subcarbonates of lime, marble dust being the purer); solutions of the sub-carbonates of potash, and of the subcarbonate of soda, and plaster.

In Using the Substances, it is always best to experiment with a small quantity of wine, being careful to employ a dose proportioned to the extent of the degree of acidity. Thus, to a quart of wine add 15 or 20 grains of carbonate of magnesia (1 or 2 grammes per litre), little by little, shaking the bottle the while; again, but only when the wine is badly pricked, slack a suitable quantity of quicklime in water, and let it settle till the surface water becomes clear. Then add to the wine which has already received the carbonate of magnesia, 5 or 6 fluidrams of the lime water (2 centilitres), and shake the mixture; then pour in 2 or 3 fluidrams of alcohol (1 centilitre), and finally clarify it with albumen, using fresh milk in preference, from 1½ to 3 fluidrams to a quart (½ to 1 centilitre to a litre); cork the bottle, shake it well, and let it rest for three or four days, when by comparing the sample treated with the pricked wine, the effect will be seen.

This treatment varies according to the nature of the wine. If it is green and pricked, add 15 grains (1 gramme per litre) of tartrate of potassium to the magnesia; and if the wine has a dull color, after having added the milk, put in about 3 grains (22 centigrammes) of gelatine dissolved in about a fluidram (½ centilitre) of water; if the wine is turbid and hard to clarify, add a little more than a grain (8 centigrammes) of tannin in powder, before putting in the milk and gelatine.

Of course, the same proportion should be used in operating upon a larger quantity of wine.

If carbonate of magnesium, which is preferable to all others, cannot be obtained, the dose of lime water may be doubled, and in default of lime, powdered chalk, or marble and vine ash may be used, but with great prudence, and in smaller proportions, or solutions of the sub-carbonates of potash and soda. Great care should be exercised as to the quantity of the latter used, and they should not be employed in treating wine slightly attacked.

Mr. Boireau prefers the carbonate of magnesium to any other alkaline substance, because it affects the color less, and does not give bitterness to the pricked wines, nor render them unwholesome, as do the salts formed by alkalies with a potash, lime, or soda base. In medicine, carbonate of magnesium is used to correct sourness of the stomach (so also, we might add, is carbonate of sodium). For the same reason, decanted lime water is preferred to the sub-carbonate of lime, employed in the form of marble dust and powdered chalk; nevertheless, lime water in large doses makes a wine weak and bitter.

Brandy is added to these wines in order to replace the alcohol lost in the production of acetic acid. The preference given to milk for fining is founded upon the fact that it is alkaline, and therefore assists in removing the acid flavor of the wine while clarifying it. It is alkaline, however, only when it is fresh; skim-milk a day old is acid, and should not be used. Finally, the tartrate and carbonate of potassium employed to treat green and pricked wines, are used to neutralize the tartaric acid, and gelatine and tannin to facilitate the clarification and the precipitation of acid ferments.

Wines whose acid has been neutralized should be clarified, and then racked as soon as perfectly clear, according to the methods pointed out.

The acetic acid being formed at the expense of alcohol, the more acid the less alcohol, and hence the necessity of adding spirit, or, if the acidity is not too pronounced, of mixing with a full-bodied but ordinary wine; but those wines should not be kept, as they always retain acid principles, become dry, and turn again at the least contact with the air. If they are very bad, and their alcoholic strength much enfeebled, they had better be made into vinegar.

Machard's Treatment.—Machard says that the most successful treatment for sour wine employed by him, is that founded upon the affinity of vegetable substances for acids, and that he has succeeded beyond his hopes in completely removing the acid from a wine which was so sour that it could not be drank without seriously disagreeing with the person drinking it. This is his method of proceeding.

He formed a long chaplet, six feet or so in length, by cutting carrots into short, thin pieces, and stringing them on a cord. This he suspended in the wine through the bung for six weeks, and at the end of the time he did not find the least trace of acetic acid, thereby accomplishing what he had for a long time in vain attempted. He says that this is the only treatment that succeeded with him, and he confidently recommends it to others. But he advises that the carrots be left in the wine at least a month and a-half, protecting the wine from the air. And he says that there is no danger of injuring the wine by long contact with the carrots, or by using a large quantity of them.

Other Methods.—Maigne says that if the wine is only affected at the surface from leaving ullage in the cask, the bad air should be expelled by using a hand-bellows; when a piece of sulphur match will burn in the cask, the air has been purified. Then take a loaf of bread, warm as it comes from the oven, and place it upon the bung in such a way as to close it. When the loaf has become cold, remove it, rack the wine into a well sulphured cask, being careful to provide the faucet with a strainer of crape or similar fabric, so as to keep the flowers from becoming mixed with the wine. It will be observed that the bread absorbs a good deal of the acid, and the operation should be repeated as often as necessary.

Another plan is to take the meats of 60 walnuts for 100 gallons of wine, break each into four pieces, and roast them as you would coffee; throw them, still hot, into the cask, after having drawn out a few quarts of wine. Fine the wine, and rack when clear, and if the acidity is very bad, repeat the operation.

A half pound of roasted wheat will produce the same effect.

He also gives the following method for using marble dust. Take of

White marble,	12 lbs.
Sugar,	18 lbs.
Animal charcoal, washed with boiling water,	6 ozs.

Take of this from 3 to 6 lbs. to 100 gallons of wine, according to the degree of acidity; dissolve it in two or three gallons of the wine and pour into the cask. Shake it well, and continue the agitation from time to time, for twenty-four or thirty-six hours, till the wine has lost its acidity, taking care to leave the bung open to allow the escape of the carbonic acid which is generated. At the end of the time, add of cream of tartar one-half as much as the dose employed; shake again, from time to time, and at the end of five or six hours, draw the wine off and fine it. If, at the end of the first twenty-four hours, the wine is still acid, add a little more of the powder before putting in the cream of tartar.

In answer to the objections that the charcoal removes the color and bouquet of the wine, and that the acetate of potassium formed injures the wine, he says that the charcoal would not hurt a white wine, and would have but little effect upon a red wine; and as to the bouquet, that wines which have become sour have none, and that the acetate of potassium has no perceptible effect upon the health.

Instead of the preceding powder, the following may be employed:

White marble, in fine powder,	12 lbs.
Animal charcoal { for ordinary wine,	4 ozs.
{ for fine wine,	2 ozs.
Sugar,	1 lb.

From 5 to 7 lbs. of this are used for 100 gallons of wine, and one-half the quantity of cream of tartar in fine powder is then added, in the manner above mentioned.

Cask Flavor, or Barrel Flavor—Causes.—This, says Mr. Boireau, should not be confounded with the *wood flavor* derived from oak wood, and which wines habitually contract when stored in new casks, and which comes from aromatic principles contained in the oak. This barrel flavor is a bad taste, which appears to come from an essence of a disagreeable taste and smell, and which is the result of a special decay of the wood of the cask. This vice is rare. It is impossible for the cooper to prevent it, for he cannot recognize the staves so affected, so as to reject them. For those pieces of wood which have a disagreeable smell when worked, or show reddish veins, blotched with white, often produce casks which give no bad taste to the wine, while other staves selected with the utmost care, sometimes produce that effect, and even in the latter case it is impossible to point out the staves which cause the trouble. When such a cask is found, the only way is to draw off the wine, and not use the cask a second time.

The Treatment for wines which have contracted a bad taste of the cask, is to rack them into a sweet cask, previously sulphured, to remove them from contact with the wood which has caused the trouble. The bad taste may be lessened by mixing in the wine a quart or two of sweet oil, and thoroughly stirring it for five minutes, first removing a few quarts of wine from the cask to permit of the agitation. The oil is removed from the surface by means of a taster, or pipette, as the cask is filled up. The wine should then be thoroughly fined, either with whites of eggs or gelatine, according to its nature, and racked at the end of one or two weeks.

The reason for the treatment is that the fixed oil takes up the volatile essential oil, which apparently produces the bad flavor. The olive oil used contracts a decided flavor of the cask.

This treatment diminishes the cask flavor, but rarely entirely removes it.

Maigne says that to succeed well by this process, the oil should be frequently mixed with the wine, by stirring it often for two or three minutes at a time, during a period of eight days. It is also necessary that the oil be fresh, inodorous, and of good quality, and of the last crop.

The same author gives another process, that of mixing with the wine sufficient sugar or must to set up active fermentation. After the fermentation has ceased, fine and rack.

This author also mentions other methods of treatment, but as olive oil is the remedy more generally used, it is not worth while to give them at length; suffice it to say, that the substances recommended are, a roasted carrot suspended in the wine for a week; a couple of pounds of roasted wheat suspended in the wine for six or eight hours in a small sack; the use of roasted walnuts, as mentioned for sourness; and two or three ounces of bruised peach pits, soaked two weeks in the wine.

Mouldy Flavor—Bad Taste Produced by Foreign Matters.—Wine contracts a musty or mouldy flavor by its sojourn in casks which have become mouldy inside, on account of negligence and want of proper care, as by leaving them empty without sulphuring and bunging. (See *Casks*.) The mould in empty casks is whitish, and consists of microscopic fungi, which are developed under the influence of humidity and darkness. The bad flavor appears to be due to the presence of an essential oil of a disagreeable taste and smell.

Prevention and Treatment.—It is prevented by carefully examining the casks before filling them, and by avoiding the use of those which have a mouldy smell. Wines affected by this flavor require the same treatment as those affected with cask flavor.

Maigne says that this taste may also be corrected by applying a loaf of warm bread to the open bung, or by suspending in the wine a half-baked loaf of milk bread. The operation should be repeated in three or four days.

Foreign Flavors.—Wines which have contracted foreign flavors, either by being kept in casks which have been used for liquors of decided flavors and odors, such as anisette, absinthe, rum, etc., or from contact with substances having good or bad odors, owe their taste to the dissolution in them of a part of the essential oil which those substances contain, and should be treated in the same manner. The chief thing is to remove the cause, by changing the cask, for if the foreign taste and smell become very marked, they cannot be completely destroyed; they can only be rendered tolerable by mixing them with sound wines.

Ropiness is the name applied to a viscous fermentation which takes place in wine, making it slimy in appearance. It is met with more particularly in white wines, which contain albuminous matters in suspension, and but little tannin. It is not a very serious difficulty, for it can be easily corrected. It is only necessary to tannify the wine by adding 12 or 15 quarts of tannified wine, well stirred in with a whip as in fining, or an ounce or two of tannin dissolved in alcohol for each 100 gallons. The tannin combines with the viscous matter and precipitates it, so that in removing the ropiness the wine is fined at the same time. It should be racked from the finings after about two weeks' repose.

And we may add that grapes which produce wines predisposed to ropiness ought not to be stemmed, or the must should be fermented with at least a portion of the stems.

Mr. Machard says that this disease is also due sometimes to lack of tartaric acid, and that it may be cured by supplying this substance, and setting up fermentation again. For 100 gallons of wine, about a pound of tartaric acid should be dissolved in hot water, to which the same quantity of sugar is added, and when dissolved, the whole is poured warm into the cask containing the ropy wine. Then replace the bung, and give the cask a thorough rolling for six or eight minutes. A small hole is previously bored near the bung and closed with a spigot, which is removed after rolling the cask, to allow the gas to escape. After resting two or three days, the wine, which we suppose to be a white wine, should be fined with isinglass.

Ropy Wines in Bottles generally cure themselves, but they must not be disturbed until the deposit changes color and takes a brownish tinge. Then is the time to decant them for drinking.

Ropiness may also be Cured by passing the wine over the marc again. But only good, fresh pomace should be used, which is but a few days old. This is done by mixing the wine with the marc of three times the quantity of wine, and stirring from time to time till fermentation is established. After the fermentation, the press wine may be mixed with the rest.

The author does not state whether this is to be done in the case of white wine or red wine, or both, but it is apparent that it would be subjecting a white wine to a very unusual operation. Fresh lees may also be mixed with the wine instead of the marc. Sometimes it is only necessary to let the wine fall into one vessel from another at a little height, several times, or to give it a thorough agitation by stirring it, or by driving it about for a few hours in a vehicle over a rough road.

Alum has been sometimes recommended, but it is now condemned as unwholesome.

Other means have been suggested, but these will suffice; and it is agreed by all that tannin is the sovereign remedy.

It is best to avoid the use of sulphur in treating ropy wines, for fermentation is to be encouraged rather than checked.

Acrity.—An acrid taste, with which certain wines are affected as they grow old, is a sign of degeneration. Mr. Boireau says that he has reason to believe that this disease is due to the presence of acetic acid, coupled with the precipitation of the mucilages which give the mellow flavor to wine. It is more often observed in old, dry wine, improperly cared for, and consequently deprived of its fruity flavor.

The Proper Treatment is to remove the acetic acid by using a gramme or two per litre (60 to 120 grains to a gallon) of carbonate of magnesium. (See *Sourness, Pricked Wines*.) If the acrity is not too great, wines may be fortified, or mixed with a strong, young, clean-tasting wine of the same nature, after which they should be fined.

Bitterness, which is often a natural defect (which has already been considered), becomes an accidental defect when developed in old wines which were previously sound. It is almost always a commencement of degeneration. This bitter taste comes principally from those combinations which are formed by the dissolution of the coloring matter, and by the precipitation of the mucilaginous substances, the pectines, which give the wine unctuosity and its fruity flavor.

Treatment.—The way to diminish this bitterness is to fortify and regenerate the bitter wine which has entered on its decline, by mixing it with wine of the same nature, but young, stout, and full-bodied, and which have not yet reached maturity. The mixture should be fined with albumen, and racked after resting a fortnight. The wine may be improved in this way, but the bitterness will reappear in a few months. It should, thererore, be used as soon as possible.

Machard recommends the following: Fine the wine with eggs, and let it rest till clear. Burn in a clean cask a quarter or a half of a sulphur match (for 60 gallons), and pour in the bitter wine at once with the smoke in the cask, after having added to each litre of the wine about one gramme of tartaric acid (say 60 grains to the gallon), dissolved in warm water. It must then be mixed with from a fourth to a half of old wine, firm and well preserved. He says that a new wine to mix with it is not suitable, not having sufficient affinity for the old.

Where there is such a difference of opinion as there is between these two authors, one recommending the mixture of new wine, and the other forbidding it, every one had better experiment for himself with a small quantity, and after the cut wines have become thoroughly amalgamated, a choice can be made.

And yet, Mr. Machard says that if the bitterness is not very great, it is better to give them no other treatment than simply mixing them with younger ones, but which have a tendency to become sour, or are already slightly pricked.

Mr. Maumene Distinguishes Two Kinds of Bitterness:
1. The nitrogenous matters, under certain circumstances not well understood, appear to be changed into a bitter product, and entirely spoil the best wine. This effect depends especially upon the elevation of the temperature and the old age of the wine. He says that he knows of but one way to remove this bitterness, and

that is to add a small quantity of lime. For example, 25 to 50 centigrammes per litre (say 15 to 30 grains per gallon). The lime should be perfectly new and fresh. It is slacked in a little water or wine, and poured into the cask; after stirring well, it is left to rest for two or three days, and then racked and fined. Probably the lime combines with the nitrogenous matters, gives an insoluble compound, which separates from the wine, and restores to it its former flavor. The wine ought to remain acid after this treatment. He says that it has succeeded with him a great number of times. 2. Another cause of bitterness appears to him to be the formation of the *brown resin* of ammoniacal aldehyde, under the influence of oxygen. The ferment which adheres to the inside of the cask gives a little ammonia by decomposition.

We see how the wine, under the influence of the air, produces a little aldehyde, the ammoniacal aldehyde, and finally the very bitter brown resin, whose formation was made known by Liebig. It is under these circumstances that sulphuring may be employed as a remedy. The sulphurous acid destroys the resinous matter in taking its oxygen to become sulphuric. There is then made sulphate of ammonia and pure aldehyde. These two substances by no means communicate to the wine the disagreeable flavor of the brown resin from which they are derived.

Another origin of bitterness is given, that of the oxidation of the coloring matter, but there is no positive proof of this any more than there is of the two causes mentioned by him. Unfortunately, the whole matter is hypothetical.

Fermentation and Taste of the Lees—Yeasty Flavor.—By the term *fermentation* in this connection we mean the malady which is known in different parts of France by various names, such as *la pousse, vins montés, tournés, tarés, à l'échaud*. It generally attacks those wines which are grown in low places, which come from poor varieties of grapes, or are produced in bad seasons, are weak, full of ferments, and thereby liable to work.

Mr. Boireau gives it the name of *goût de travail*, working taste, or fermentation flavor. He says that the taste is due to the presence of carbonic acid, disengaged during secondary alcoholic fermentation, by reason of saccharine matter contained in the wine, or of mucilaginous matters which give them their mellowness. The principal cause of fermentation is the presence of these matters joined with ferments, and takes place in an elevated temperature.

The *yeasty flavor* comes from the mixture in the wine of the lees and deposits already precipitated, and which are again brought into suspension by the movement of fermentation.

How Prevented.—Fermentation and the consequent taste of the lees are prevented by making and fermenting the wines under proper conditions, keeping them in an even temperature, and by separating them from their lees by well-timed rackings, as detailed in the chapters on *General Treatment, Racking, etc*.

Treatment.—The working is stopped by racking the wines into sulphured casks, and placing them in cellars of a cool and even temperature. (See *Sulphuring, etc.*) If they have become turbid, they must be fined, and they must be left on the finings only as long as is strictly necessary for their clarification.

Machard recommends that about a quart of alcohol for 100 gallons of wine, or its equivalent of old brandy, be introduced into the sulphured cask before drawing the wine into it, and that it be fined in all cases.

Degeneration—Putrid Fermentation.—We are warned of degeneration in wines a long time in advance, in divers manners: by the loss of their fruity flavor, by bitterness, acrity, etc.; but the true symptoms in old wine are, the more abundant precipitation of their blue coloring matter, a heavy and tawny aspect, with a slightly putrid flavor. The principal causes are the same as those mentioned in speaking of the putrid decomposition in new wines, that is, feebleness in alcohol, and lack of tannin.

We know that by the time the tannin is transformed into gallic acid, the alcohol is diminished by slow evaporation, and it follows that wines which are too old have lost a part of those principles which give them their keeping qualities, alcohol and tannin.

The Duration of Different Wines is exceedingly unequal,

DEFECTS AND DISEASES. 153

and, like animate beings, they display marked differences in constitution. There are very feeble wines, as we have already seen, which are in the way of degeneration the first year, while others, firm and full-bodied, gain in quality for four, six, ten, and more years. As soon as it is seen that a wine, by its taste and appearance, has commenced to degenerate, it is important to arrest the degeneration at once.

Treatment.—Degeneration may be retarded by adding tannin, but it is preferable, in most cases, to mix the wine with younger wines of the same nature, firm, full-bodied, which are improving, and consequently possess an excess of those qualities which are wanting in the degenerating wine. (See *Wine in Bottles.*)

CHAPTER XVI.

WINE IN BOTTLES.

When Ready for Bottling.—Wines should not be bottled till their insensible fermentation is entirely completed, have become entirely freed from deposits, excess of color, salts, and ferments, and have become perfectly bright. If they are bottled before these conditions are fulfilled, deposits are made in the bottles, the wines may contract bitterness and a taste of the lees, and if fermentation is violent, the bottles may burst. When they are bottled too young they are sure to deposit, and then they must be decanted.

The Length of Time that They Require to Remain in Wood before being ready for bottling, depends upon the strength and quality of the wines, and the conditions under which they are kept.

Weak wines, feeble in color and spirit, mature rapidly, while firm, full-bodied wines, rich in color and alcohol, require a longer time to become sufficiently ripe to admit of bottling.

The older writers say that wines should not be put into glass until they have become fully ripe, and have become tawny (if red), and have developed a bouquet. But Boireau says that this is not the proper practice. He says that wine is fit for bottling when freed from its sediment, and when there is hardly any deposit formed in the cask at the semi-annual racking—when its color is bright, and it has lost its roughness or harshness, which it possesses while young, and at the same time preserves its mellowness. If left in the cask till a bouquet is developed, wines will often be found to be in a decline by the time they are bottled, and will not keep as long as those bottled previous to the development of their bouquet, and while they still possess their fruity flavor. But greater precautions must be taken to insure their limpidity, or they will be liable to deposit heavily in the bottle. And Machard, who indicates aroma and color as signs of proper maturity, though laying more stress upon the taste, says that it is always better to be a little too soon than to wait till the wine passes the point.

Some wines are fit for the bottle at one year old, others require to be kept from two to six years, and some even ten years, or longer, in wood. White wine, generally speaking, matures earlier than red.

How Prepared for Bottling.—Although a wine may appear perfectly limpid to the eye, yet, when bottled, it may make a considerable deposit, and therefore, the only safety is to carefully rack and fine it to get rid of the insoluble matters in suspension. If it is not clear after one fining, it must be drawn off and the process repeated. When fined and cleared, it is better to rack again into a cask slightly sulphured, and allow it to rest for three or four weeks before drawing into the bottles; for if drawn from a cask still containing the finings, the sediment is liable to be stirred up by the movement of the liquid. If this is not done, the faucet should be fixed in place at the time of fining and before the wine has settled, and at the same time the cask should be slightly inclined forward and blocked in that position, and other precautions must be taken not to disturb the cask after the wine has cleared. If the wine is too feeble to allow of fining without injury, and one is sure of its perfect limpidity, the fining had better be dispensed with. Very young wines may be bottled after subjecting them to repeated finings, but it will deprive them of some of their good qualities. (See *Fining*.) It often happens that a well-covered, or dark-colored wine will deposit considerable color in the bottle after one fining; such wine should be twice fined, and twice racked before fining, say, once in December or January, and again in March.

The Most Favorable Time for Bottling is during cool, dry weather, but in cellars of uniform temperature, it may be done at any time. It is better, if possible, to avoid warm or stormy weather, and those critical periods in the growth of the vine referred to in the chapter on Racking. Of course, the wine should not be bottled if it shows signs of fermentation.

WINE IN BOTTLES.

Bottles should always be carefully washed and drained before using. They are best washed by the use of a machine made for the purpose, which scrubs them inside—and sometimes, also, outside—with a brush (fig. 27). If only a small number of bottles are to be cleaned, it may be done by using the chain made for the purpose, or by putting in coarse sand or gravel and water, and thoroughly shaking them. Shot must not be used, for a portion of the lead will be dissolved by the water, and if any remains in the bottle it will be acted upon by the wine, and lead poisoning may result. In many cases it will be necessary only to rinse them out with clean water. Whether new or second-hand, they must be scrupulously clean before using. After the bottles are rinsed, they should be allowed to drain by leaving them inverted for an hour or two in a dry place; if they are left in a damp cellar, they are liable to contract a musty flavor within. They may be drained by placing the necks downward through holes bored in a plank, by inverting them in boxes or baskets, or by placing them upon pegs or nails driven into a post, and inclining upwards sufficiently to leave the opening of the bottle down, when the neck is slipped over the peg or nail. Figs. 28 and 29 show devices for the purpose. The bottles are sometimes rinsed out with wine, or if intended to contain very poor, weak wine, with a little brandy. This is done by pouring the liquor from one bottle to another.

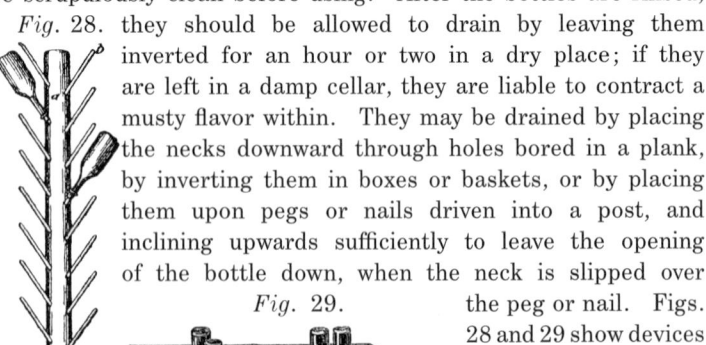

Fig. 27. Bottle Washer.

Fig. 28.

Fig. 29. Bottle Drainers.

WINE IN BOTTLES. 157

It is best to use bottles uniform in size for each lot of wine, and certainly to reject those which are cracked, have large blisters, and those which are very thin. These latter, however, may be employed, if but little pressure is used in corking, but they should be placed by themselves, or on the top of the pile. No one would make use of such bottles except to store wine for his own consumption.

Clear and transparent bottles are used for white wine, and those of colored glass for red. Hock, however, is often put in brownish bottles, conical in shape. White wines which are perfectly limpid show to advantage in clear bottles, but red wines, if stored in such, are liable to lose their color by the action of light.

It is important that the glass of which wine bottles are made should not contain too much soda, potash, or lime, or they may combine with the acids, and injure the wine. By the use of crude soda, alkaline sulphites may be formed in the glass, and communicate an odor of sulphuretted hydrogen to the wine.

Filling the Bottles.—If the faucet has not previously been placed in the cask, it must now be done with great care, so as not to disturb any lees that may have remained at the last racking. The faucet should be put into the cask *open*, as for racking, and with very light blows of the hammer. A shallow dish or bucket is placed under the faucet in which the bottle stands. An ordinary brass faucet may be used, or the bottles may be filled much more rapidly by drawing the wine from the cask into a reservoir provided with as many faucets or tubes as bottles which it is desired to fill at the same time (fig. 30). The cask must be vented either by making a gimlet hole or two near the bung, or the bung

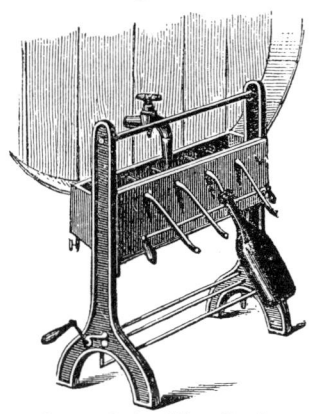

Fig. 30.

Reservoir for filling Bottles.

must be removed. The latter, however, must not be done by blows with the bung-starter, but by using the bung-screw (fig. 31), or the lees will be stirred up. The bottle should not be placed upright so that the wine will fall directly to the bottom, but should be slightly inclined so as to permit the wine to trickle down the inside, or a foam will be formed, and it will be difficult to fill the bottle. The workman having his empty bottles within reach, allows a little of the first wine to run into the dish, or into a bottle, which is put aside, as there may be some impurities in the faucet. The workman is seated in front of the cask, and the empty bottles are placed one at a time under the faucet as described. As soon as one bottle is filled, it is removed and another put in its place, without closing the faucet, and without loss of wine. The sediment would be disturbed by the shocks caused by opening and shutting the faucet.

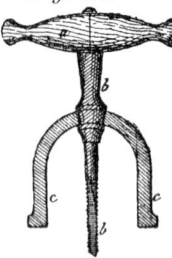

Fig. 31.
Bung Screw.

If the needle is used in corking the bottles, they should be filled within a little more than an inch of the top, and if corked in the ordinary manner, only to within about two inches of the opening, leaving an inch of vacancy below the cork; always, however, depending somewhat upon the length of the corks used. This is continued, placing the full bottles in a convenient place, until the wine ceases to run at the faucet. The cask must then be slightly inclined forward, as described in the case of racking. At this stage, great care must be taken not to trouble the wine; and if a few bottles at the end contain that which is not clear, they should be put aside, to be decanted after settling. In drawing from the upper tiers of casks in piles, the basin must be elevated sufficiently to bring the bottle placed in it up to the faucet, or the latter may be connected with it by a hose.

Corks.—Only good corks should be used. They are supple and uniform in texture. Poor corks are sold in the market, in which is found a good deal of the dark, hard portion of the bark, which are not only liable to break the bottles by the great amount of pressure required to insert them, but also to discolor the wine, affect its flavor, and to permit it to leak out. Straight corks are used now-a-days, somewhat larger than the neck of the bottle, and are forced in by means of

Corking Machines.—These machines are of different forms and make, but are provided with a hollow cone through which the cork is forced by a piston, compressing it so that it easily goes into the neck of the bottle. Some work with a lever, and some with a crank. In the small hand-machine, the piston is

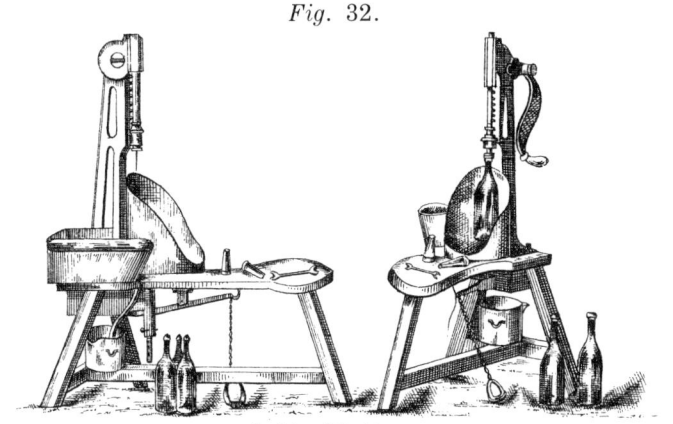

Fig. 32.

Corking Machines.

pushed by the hand. The bottles may be made full enough so that the wine will touch the bottom of the cork, leaving no vacant space, if the *needle* is used in corking. This is a small, tapering, half-round, steel instrument, one-tenth of an inch in diameter, with a groove along the flat side. By placing this in the neck with the groove next the glass, the cork may be forced down to the wine, the air and surplus wine escaping by the groove. After the cork is driven home, the needle is removed. A piece of wire, provided with a handle, will answer the purpose. The handle of the needle (either a ring, or like that of a gimblet), is attached by a hinge, and turns down out of the way of the tube and piston of the machine. Some bottling machines have a needle attachment. Bottles corked by the use of this instrument do not con-

160   *WINE IN BOTTLES.*

tain a vacant space, and the wine keeps better, not being exposed to the action of the air, which would otherwise remain in the neck of the bottle, and not being shaken in transportation.

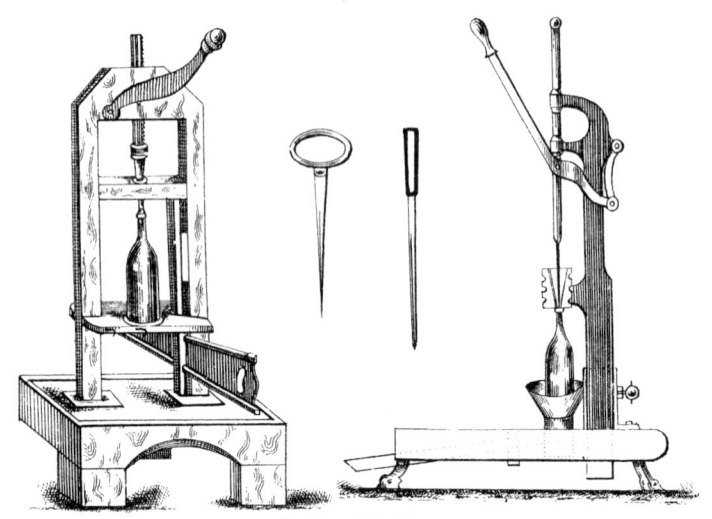

Fig. 33.

Corking Machines.

Figures 32 and 33 show corking machines with and without needles. In fig. 33 two needles are also shown.

If the old-fashioned conical corks are used, they may be driven home with a small mallet, or wooden paddle, but the cylindrical corks are preferable, if the wine is to be kept long.

Preparation of the Corks.—In order to render them more supple, they are soaked for several hours in water. What is far better, however, is to steam them for two or three hours, or soak them in hot water. They should be allowed to drain, and then be dipped in wine like that to be bottled. Some dip them in alcohol to render them more slippery, and some again, put a drop or two of sweet oil on the surface of the water in which they are wet.

The Corks may be Driven down Flush with the opening of the bottle, or they may be left projecting a quarter of an inch, and if much larger than the neck of the bottle, a shoulder will be formed, as in the case of sparkling wines. The object of leaving the corks projecting a third of their length in bottling sparkling wines is, that they may be forced out with an explosion; and the shoulder completely closes the bottle, being wired down.

Sealing the Corks.—If the bottles are stored in a damp place where the corks are liable to rot, and also if they are to be kept more than two years, it is well to cover the ends of the corks with wax. This also prevents attacks by insects.

The Sealing Wax used should be sufficiently adhesive, but not too hard and brittle. Various receipts are given for its preparation, and the following is given by Boireau: Melt common pitch or turpentine over a slow fire, taking care not to allow it to boil over. When it is well melted, remove whatever impurities it contains, add a little tallow—a little less than an ounce of tallow to a pound of pitch. Its natural color is reddish, and is used without addition of coloring matter. Rosin may be substituted for the pitch. Instead of making this preparation, the fruit wax of commerce may be used. About the same quantity of tallow, however, should be added, if sealing wax is used, or otherwise it will be too brittle. The tallow may be replaced by beeswax with advantage.

An excellent bottle wax is said to be made by melting together two pounds rosin, one pound Burgundy pitch, one-fourth pound yellow wax, and one-eighth pound red wax. The wax may be replaced by three ounces of tallow. If too much tallow is added the cement will be too soft.

The Cement is Applied Hot.—It must be melted, and the bottle reversed and dipped into it, so that the wax will cover the end of the cork and a small part of the neck of the bottle, say down to the ring. It is entirely unnecessary to cover more of the neck of the bottle.

Coloring Matter may be added to these different cements, and any desired color produced. A little more than half an ounce of

162   *WINE IN BOTTLES.*

the following named substances is stirred in to one pound of the melted wax.

A brilliant red is produced by vermilion, a duller red by red ochre, black with animal black, yellow with orpiment, dark yellow with yellow ochre, and blue with Prussian blue. Green is made by mixing equal parts of blue and yellow, and other shades may be made by mixing the different colors to suit the taste.

Capsules are now much used instead of wax. In preparing the bottled wine for shipment, where the corks have previously been waxed for storing in the cellar, capsules are also used. In this case, the wax is removed before the capsule is put on by means of a pair of pincers with roughened jaws (fig. 34). These capsules in different colors are sold by dealers in corks.

Fig. 34.

Pincers for Removing Wax.

They are Put on by slipping one over the neck of the bottle as far as it will go, and then pressing it down closely all round. For this purpose, one turn is made around the end of the capsule with a stout cord fastened at one end, and the bottle is pushed forward with one hand, while the loose end of the string is pulled tight with the other, thus sliding the loop over the capsule and the neck of the bottle, and pressing it firmly in place. Instead of holding the cord with one hand, it may be attached to a pedal worked by the foot. A machine (fig. 35) is made with two posts or standards, one solid, to which one end of the cord, A, is attached, and the other playing on a hinge, to which the other end is fastened, and pulled tight by a pedal, B.

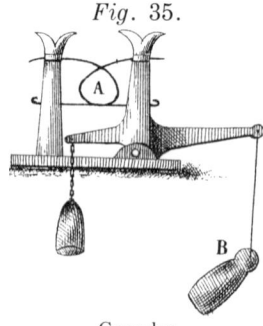

Fig. 35.

Capsuler.

Piling of Bottles.—Bottles may be stacked on the floor of the cellar in piles consisting of a single or a double range. The bed should be made level by arranging the soil, or by laying down strips of wood, and leveling them. The bottles should be laid horizontal. If the neck is down, the deposit will be on and near the cork, and will trouble the wine as it runs from the bottle. If the bottom is lower than the neck, the cork will not be kept wet, and the wine is liable to be injured by the air, as the cork is not perfectly air tight. The bottles should be supported at two points, the neck and the bottom; the belly of the bottle needs no support. If two tiers of bottles are put in a pile, the bottoms are on the outside, with the necks at the middle of the pile. Laths are used to support the bottles, about three-eighths of an inch thick, and one inch or more wide. The lower row of one tier is made by laying down at the outside of the pile two laths to support the bottom end of the bottle, and one thick strip or sufficient laths are laid down to support the neck, inside the ring, and keep the bottle level. The next tier may be commenced by laying one or two laths on the necks of the bottles of the first one to support the necks of those of the other, the necks of the bottles of one tier lapping over those of the bottles of the other; the bottoms of those of this tier must be sufficiently elevated by laths to keep the bottles level. The next row of bottles is supported by laths laid on those below, one or two near the outer end of the lower ones, and a larger number on their necks. In this case the necks all point in, the bottoms being together (fig. 36). The bottles of each row should be sufficiently separated to allow those of the next row above to be supported by the laths without touching each other, and should be blocked after adjusting the distances. The piles may be made from three to six feet high, and must be supported at the ends, either by the cellar walls or posts.

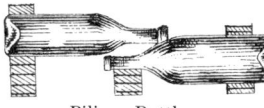

Fig. 36.

Piling Bottles.

Each tier may be made entirely independent of the other, by supporting the necks of the bottles of the next upper row on laths laid near the bottoms of those of the first row, one row having the necks pointing out, and the next one having them pointing the other way. In this case the bottles in a row may be separated an inch or more from each other, and blocked with bits of cork.

Racks and Bins for Bottles.—Instead of piling the bottles, they may be arranged in bins constructed for the purpose. The simplest is a frame of wood or iron of the desired length and height, and deep enough to accommodate one or two tiers of bottles. The lower bars on which the first row of bottles rests, should be so arranged as to support them in a level position, as already described for piling. If only one tier is to be made, only two bars at the bottom are necessary, but if double ranges are to be made, the frame must be deeper, and have a middle bar to support the necks of the bottles, the bottoms all being outside. The bottles are piled in these frames in the manner already described.

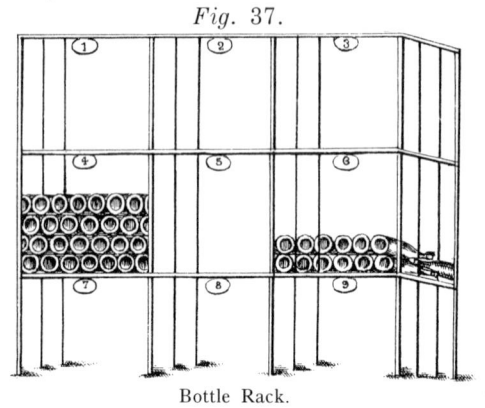

Fig. 37.

Bottle Rack.

Fig. 38.

Bottle Rack.

Instead of piling them in simple frames with the use of laths, racks are made with bars to support each row of bottles by itself, and so that any one bottle can be taken out without disturbing the rest. If the supports are of wood, they may be cut, or if of iron, bent in a form to fit each bottle, that is, in small half-circles in which the bottles rest, with smaller ones for the necks, or they may be straight. These bins may be made portable, and of any size to suit. (Figs. 37 and 38.)

Burrow's Patent Slider Bin, made in England, has a separate compartment for each bottle.

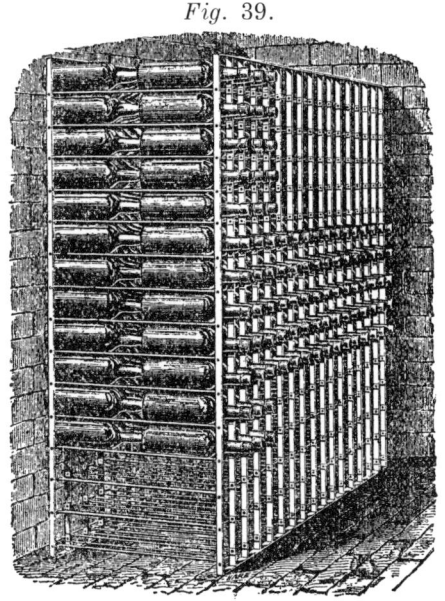

Fig. 39.

Burrow's Slider Bin.

Treatment of Wine in Bottles.—Sometimes it will be found that wine ferments in the bottle, becomes turbid, and makes a voluminous deposit, or may contract various maladies, such as bitterness, harshness, ropiness, or may become putrid. These effects result principally from bottling the wine too young, before insensible fermentation and the natural clearing has been completed, or they may be caused by changes of temperature, or too great age.

Fermentation in the Bottles is due to the same causes as fermentation in casks—changes of temperature, contact of the air, etc. It may be avoided by bottling at the proper time, carefully protecting the wine from the air by corking the bottles hermetically by the use of the needle, and keeping them in a cellar of even temperature. Boireau says that sweet and mellow wines are liable to ferment in bottles, especially if exposed to a high temperature, unless their alcoholic strength exceeds 15 per cent. Still wines which ferment in the bottle generally must be emptied into casks, and there treated as indicated in the chapter on *Diseases*. Temporary relief may be given by putting the bottles in a cooler place, and uncorking them for an hour or two to allow the gas to escape.

Deposits and Turbidity.—Wine, after being some time in glass, forms more or less deposit, according to its age, quality, and degree of limpidity at the time of bottling. The deposits consist almost entirely of coloring matter, and vegetable and mineral salts; sometimes they adhere to the sides of the bottle, and in some cases they render the wine turbid, and again they present the appearance of gravel when the wine contains much tartar.

In wines bottled too young, or which are made by mixing those of different natures, quite a voluminous deposit may be formed after they have remained a few years in glass. But good, natural wines, of good growth, well cared for, and bottled under proper conditions, scarcely commence to deposit at the end of one or two years. The deposit, however, will be increased, if the bottles are frequently disturbed, are transported long distances, undergo changes of temperature, or are kept so long that they begin to degenerate. If there is much deposit, it is apt to give the wine a *bitter* or *acrid* flavor, or a *taste of the lees*. Therefore, if the wines are of high quality, they should be decanted.

Mr. Boireau proceeds to say that if the deposit is small, and we are dealing with grand wines in bottles, which have contracted no bad taste, it is better not to decant them, for the operation is liable to cause a loss of a portion of the bouquet, especially if not done with proper precautions.

These directions only apply to those bottled wines which have deposited sediment, but which are nevertheless clear, and bright, and of a lively color. Those, however, which become and remain turbid, must be fined, and for this purpose they must be put into casks. If wines containing sediment are brought to the table without decanting, they are kept in nearly the same position as they occupied in the cellar, by using small baskets contrived for the purpose. (See *Decantation*.)

Bitterness and Acrity, when not caused by deposits, are due to loss of the fruitiness and mellowness of the wine, which then has commenced to decline. The only remedy in case of fine wines which have preserved their bouquet, is to mix them with younger wines, mellow and perfectly bright. This should be done by decanting without contact with the air; but if they are seriously affected, they must be put into casks and the operation there performed; then they should be well fined before re-bottling.

Ropiness in bottled wines, which is due to lack of tannin, generally occurs in white wines which have been bottled before perfectly clear, and while they contained considerable nitrogenous and albuminous matters in suspension. The treatment is indicated elsewhere.

In most cases, if the wines are worn out, it will be necessary to put them into casks, and mix them with younger ones of the same quality.

Degeneration and Putridity.—Wine may be kept and improved in bottles, if properly treated, as long as its constituent principles remain soluble and in combination; but with the lapse of time, varying with different kinds, it begins to lose quality. This degeneration, says the author last quoted, announces itself a long time in advance, in the grand wines, by a loss of their unctuosity, of their fruity flavor, and by a bitter and sometimes acrid taste; and if they are kept for several years more, the fragrance of the bouquet is lost, and they contract a *rancio* or tawny flavor, which masks their natural flavor; they rapidly lose color, and form a deposit much more considerable than in the earlier years of their sojourn in bottles; and finally, when their degeneracy is advanced, they give off a slightly putrid odor.

As soon as high priced wines have attained their entire development in bottles, in order to prevent their decline, they should be carefully decanted into bottles with ground glass stoppers, previously rinsed with wine of the same kind.

Loss of color, joined with an abundant deposit, which is a sure sign of degeneration in the wines of the Gironde, do not mean the same in all other kinds. For instance, the red wines of Spain (and we may add, Portugal), and the sweet wines of Rousillon, which have a very dark color when young, almost entirely lose it after three or four years in bottle; they become tawny, without degenerating; but, quite to the contrary, their quality is improved.

It is observed, however, that in wines of these latter classes, whose alcoholic strength exceeds 15 per cent., the deposit is not so great, compared with the amount of coloring matter precipitated, as in wines of the first mentioned growth, and that the coloring matter adheres to the sides of the bottle, instead of falling to the bottom. Some of our California wines deposit a good deal of color in the bottle, even when fined. Probably a double fining would be advantageous in many cases.

As alcohol and tannin are the preservative principles of wines, those last longest which are best provided with them.

The cause of the degeneration of wine is the decomposition of its constituent parts, which thereby become insoluble, and are precipitated. The loss of tannin, which in time is transformed into gallic acid, takes from feeble wines their best conservator, and causes precipitation of the coloring matter. And it is observed in practice that wines which contain a great quantity of tannin last longer than those of the same alcoholic strength having less tannin.

Decantation consists in drawing a wine from the bottle containing it, so as to leave the sediment behind. It should be done without exposing the wine to the air.

WINE IN BOTTLES. 169

The bottles should be brought from the cellar without changing their position, for if the deposit is disturbed, and the wine becomes cloudy, the bottles must rest till it has settled again. For this purpose they are laid in a basket, or other suitable receptacle,

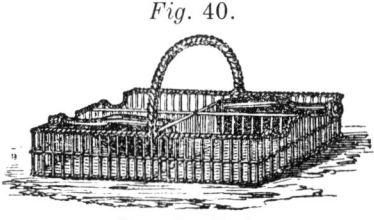

Fig. 41.

Fig. 40.

Decanting Basket.   Corkscrews.

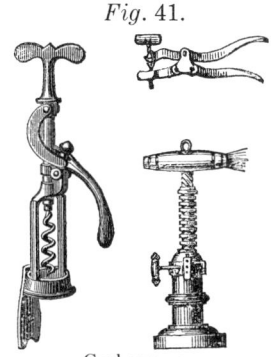

where they are inclined just enough so that the wine will not run out when the cork is removed (fig. 40). The cork must be drawn without disturbing the sediment, by using a corkscrew, which by means of a screw or lever, gradually removes it, and without a shock (fig. 41). The wine is slowly run into another clean bottle previously rinsed with the same kind of wine. If the wine is in its decline, rinse the bottles with old brandy.

The Operation may be Performed by carefully pouring the wine into the empty bottle through a small funnel, which is provided with a strainer. By means of a light placed below the bottle, the sediment can be watched, and as soon as it is about to run out with the wine, the operation must cease. The new bottle must be filled up with the same kind of wine and immediately corked. In decanting in this manner, the bubbling of the air passing into the bottle as the wine runs out, is very apt to disturb the lees. This may be prevented by using a small tube, slightly curved, which connects the air outside with the vacant space in the bottle. In order to prevent access of the air, however,

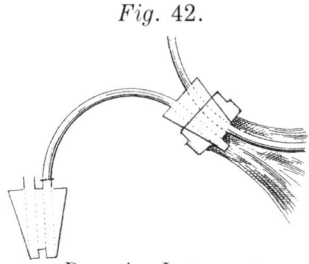

Fig. 42.

Decanting Instrument.

an instrument is used consisting of two conical corks, connected by a small rubber tube. Each cork is pierced with two holes; the one placed in the bottle to be emptied, besides the hole which receives the rubber hose through which the wine runs, is provided with one through which a bent tube is placed to admit the air; the hose passes through the other cork and conducts the wine into the other bottle, and this cork has another hole for the escape of the air (fig. 42).

CHAPTER XVII.

CUTTING OR MIXING WINES.

Most French Wines Mixed.—Maigne, speaking of the wines of France, says, that of one hundred wines in the market, perhaps there are not ten which are not produced by mixing several different kinds. Without doubt, he says, we should as much as possible preserve the products of the vine as they are given to us; but there are a multitude of cases where it is absolutely impossible to render them drinkable without mixing, or as wine men say, without *cutting* them with other wines.

When Necessary — Effect of.—In good years, almost all wines can be drank in their natural condition, but when the grapes have not become sufficiently ripe, the wines, even of good growths, lack quality, or preserve for a long time a roughness more or less marked, and always disagreeable. It is then necessary to mix them, especially if common wines, with better ones, to make them tolerable. It is not always necessary, however, that the season should be bad, in order that cutting should be proper. Wines naturally have, for a certain time, an earthy flavor and greenness which are unpleasant, which disappear by mixing. This is why ordinary wines of a moderate price, which have been mixed, are preferred by a great number of consumers to others which are higher in price but left in a state of nature. For example, a new, very dark-colored wine of good growth is not an agreeable drink; but if an old white wine of an inferior growth, but of good taste and constitution be added, it will be drank with pleasure.

Mixing the wine produces results similar to those caused by mixing the fruit, and it may be done by the wine maker as well as by the merchant. As they come from the vat, wines manifest the qualities and defects communicated by the vintage, and which are varied by a multitude of circumstances, such as the nature of the soil, varieties of grapes, temperature of the season, and the like.

CUTTING OR MIXING WINES.

Wines endowed with qualities which fit them to be kept in their natural condition, of course, are not mixed. But those which, on the other hand (and they are in the majority), have too much or too little color, are weak, flat, coarse, green, pasty, rough, lacking in bouquet, too strong, or too light, cannot be put on the market till they have been cut with other wines capable of giving them the qualities which they lack, and of remedying their defects. It will be understood that the mixture of a weak wine with a stronger one, of one lacking color with one which has too much, a light wine with a generous one, of a hard wine with a flat one, etc., a wine will be produced superior in quality to any one of those used.

For these reasons, in a viticultural district, when a producer cannot sell his wine of a bad year, he mixes it with that of the following year, if the latter is of a better quality; if he cannot mix it all, he may use it for ullage. In the same way, if he has new white wines which become discolored and turn yellow, he mingles them with very dark red wines, which then become more agreeable to drink.

It is said that the tithe wines used to be of superior quality. In certain communes of France, the inhabitants contributed to the priest's cask a certain amount of their new wine, and this wine which represented a mixture of all the wines of the commune, had the reputation of being superior to any one of the others.

And the following case, quoted by Maigne, is given for what it is worth. A cask lay in a cellar into which they were accustomed to throw the leavings of all kinds of wine, such as from broken bottles, drippings, etc. It was intended to use the liquid upon diseased trees, but it was for some time forgotten. When found and brought out, the cellar-man tasted the singular mixture out of curiosity. It was found to be a delicious liquor, which gave delight at dessert; and it was with true grief that they saw its end approach!

In order to perform the operation successfully, an experienced man is required, who will be guided by his educated taste; and therefore, precise rules cannot be laid down, but there are certain general principles which it may be useful to state.

Wines of the same General Nature and Flavor should be used, and two of such wines may nevertheless be deficient in some particular respects, so that by mixing, the defects of the two will be corrected. Such wines are mixed, because they are said to *marry* better, and produce a more homogeneous liquid than those of different natures.

Fine Wines.—All agree that fine wines which have a bouquet and a future are best left in their natural condition, for their distinctive character will be destroyed by mixing with wines of a different nature and quality. Boireau says that experience proves that if such wines are mixed while young, even with old wine of good quality, they will never acquire that degree of fineness which they would have obtained if left by themselves; that they sooner loose their fruity flavor, and are more liable to make a deposit in the bottles.

There are cases, however, when cutting becomes necessary, as when the wine from being kept too long in casks, has commenced to decline, has lost its fruity flavor, has become acrid and dry; when made in a bad, cold season; and when they are too poor, green, or too feeble to keep well.

When wines are too old and worn out, they should be fortified with young wines of the same kind, produced, if possible, from the same vineyard, one or two, or at most, three years old, and possessing great mellowness. The amount of new wine to be used will depend upon the degree of degeneracy and the length of time they are to be kept. (See *Degeneration*.)

Poor, weak wines, whose keeping qualities are doubted, should be mixed with young wine of a good year, firm and full-bodied, possessing as nearly as possible the same natural flavor.

The foregoing is intended to apply to feeble, delicate wines which have a flavor and bouquet, but *which are not too green*. Wines which have a future should not be sacrificed by using them to fortify others which are both *feeble and green*, for the excess of tartaric acid contained in the latter will totally destroy the mellowness of those used to fortify them. To mix with such wines, clean-tasting wines of the south should be used.

If the wines are too green, a portion of the acid may be neutralized, as described under the head of *Greenness*.

Ordinary Wines should be treated in such a way as to give them as much as possible the qualities sought in fine wines, and they should be cut with suitable wines of the same age to give them bouquet, flavor, and mellowness, or at least to remove their excessive dryness—a very difficult thing to do. It may be accomplished, in part, by mixing them with wines of the same growth, but whose bouquet and flavor are very expansive, and by adding neutral, mellow wines.

Sufficient Time Must be Given to the mixture to allow the different wines employed to become intimately combined, or their different flavors may be detected, which will not be the case when thoroughly amalgamated.

When Large Quantities of wine are used, the mixture is more nearly perfect than if mingled, cask by cask; and by operating upon the whole amount at one time in a large vat, a perfect uniformity will be insured.

An Entirely New Wine should not be mixed with an old one, as there is not sufficient affinity between them.

In an old wine, says Machard, all the constituents are in a state of complete quiet; they are well combined (melted) and homogeneous. If there is mixed with it a wine whose principles are equally well combined, no ulterior action will result. But if new principles are introduced, elements of a different nature, the equilibrium will be disturbed, there will infallibly result a reciprocal action and disorganization.

Very Green Wines should not be mixed with those containing much sugar for similar reasons, for the mixture is liable to be thrown into a state of violent fermentation, which it will be difficult to arrest. The reason given is that the green wine contains a good deal of ferment; but if both the wines are produced in the south, where the ferment contained in the dry wine is not abundant, the mixture may safely be made. So that, after all, we get back to the principle, that wines of widely different natures and origins should not be mixed, but keeping this in in mind, a sweetish and a dry wine may be used to correct each other.

White Wines may sometimes be mixed with advantage with red ones, as before mentioned, but the former should not be employed too liberally.

Diseased Wines must not be mixed with sound ones, except in the few cases mentioned under *Defects and Diseases*. It is especially dangerous to cut a soured or pricked wine with a sound one, for the whole mass is liable to be lost.

Mixing Grapes.—It is doubtless always better, when practicable, to correct defects by mixing the grapes and fermenting the different kinds together, for then a more homogeneous wine will be formed; and, therefore, the intelligent grape grower will find out the defects of his wine, and remedy them by planting a sufficient quantity of other varieties for the purpose.

Precautions.—Care, however, must always be taken not to spoil a good wine by cutting it with a very common one, nor by mixing poor varieties with grapes of fine kinds.

Cheap wines, however, for immediate consumption, may admit a certain proportion of poor, common wine, into their composition, without inconvenience. In that case, the ferments of the common sorts will not have time to act and produce serious results.

If, however, they are to be kept for some time, or bottled, the effect will be bad, for the ferments always abundant in wines from the commoner varieties, are liable to become decomposed, and cause a disagreeable, nauseating flavor.

Whenever there is a doubt in the mind of the cellar-man as to whether certain wines should be mixed, it is always best to make a small sample first, clarify it, and leave it for a sufficient length of time, and judge of the result, before operating upon a large quantity.

CHAPTER XVIII.

WINE LEES, MARC, AND PIQUETTE.

The Residue of Wine Making, pomace and lees, are often placed immediately in the still, and their alcohol distilled off directly, but the result is better if the wine is first extracted, and distilled without putting the residue into the boiler, for it is liable to burn and give a disagreeable burnt flavor to the brandy.

I am indebted to Mr. Boireau, so often quoted, for what follows:

WINE LEES.

The Lees should not be neglected, because, for want of proper care, the wine which is extracted from them will contract a very disagreeable taste, which is due to its too long sojourn on the deposit, and which would be prevented by drawing it off in time.

Therefore, in order that the wine extracted from them should not lose all its value, the lees should receive particular attention, and be stored in places free from variations of temperature.

The Quantity of Wine Contained in the Lees varies from 30 to 90 per cent. From those of fined wines an average of 70 per cent. may be extracted without pressing.

The Dry Parts of the Sediment contain a great quantity of insoluble matters, tartar, or argol, several other vegetable and mineral salts, divers compounds, ferments, mucilaginous matters, and the residue of animal and vegetable matters (albumen and gelatine), which have been employed in fining.

An Analysis of Dry Lees by Mr. Braconnot, a distinguished chemist, establishes the presence of the following substances: bitartrate of potash (cream of tartar), tartrate of lime, tartrate of magnesia, nitrogenous animal matter, fatty substances, coloring matter, gum, and tannin.

The Composition of Dry Lees varies with the age, nature, and quality of the wine which produces them; but in all, the bitartrate of potash or cream of tartar predominates. The lees of mellow wines contain mucilages, and we find in the lees deposited by sweet wines great quantities of saccharine matter which may be utilized. The different uses to which dried lees may be put will be mentioned further on.

Treatment of the Lees.—Lees will settle by repose, but the wine which comes from them, if left long upon the heavy lees, contracts a disagreeable flavor, owing to its contact with the insoluble matters forming the sediment, and with the ferments found in the lees with the residue of the substances used in fining. The surface wine is often in a state of fermentation, and remains turbid, contracting at the same time a disagreeable bitterness, unless soon withdrawn from the influence of the ferments.

By proper care and attention, not only can all the liquid be extracted from the lees, but the wine so extracted will have no bad flavor, no vice, in a word, will partake of the same qualities as the wine from which the heavy lees were deposited. The casks into which they are to be put should be washed in the same manner as those destined to contain limpid wine, and double the quantity of a sulphur match employed in the case of racking new red wines, should be burned in each. As fast as the casks are emptied in drawing off, the lees are turned into a pail, and immediately poured into the cask intended for them. In emptying them into the pail, care should be taken not to introduce dirt, mould, etc., and if there is debris around the bung-hole, it should be swept away before removing the bung. As soon as the cask is full of lees, it should be stored, bung up, in a proper place, as mentioned, and should then be ulled and bunged, and the date of storing may be marked on it, with the kind and age of the wine from which it came.

When the casks are not completely filled the same day, and it is necessary to leave them with ullage, they should be bunged tight, after having again burned a square of a match in each, and the sulphuring should be renewed as often as the lees are added, if left so for several days, in order to avoid access of air, and to prevent the action of ferments. In a word, casks containing lees, without being full, should always be well bunged and sulphured, and guarded from variations of temperature.

The casks, when stored, should be regularly ulled once a week with limpid wine, and re-bunged, and after two weeks' repose, the first drawing off takes place, and should be renewed once or twice every month. All the clear wine will be drawn off at each racking, by following the precautions indicated further on. By drawing off thus frequently, fermentation, to which such wine is subject, will be avoided, even in summer. Thus, also, will be avoided the disagreeable taste of the lees, of acrity and bitterness, which wine contracts when left long on the deposit, and moreover, much more clear wine will be withdrawn. Lees from diseased wine should not be mixed with the rest, but should be put aside and treated according to the malady by which the wine was affected.

Extraction of Wine from the Lees.—Lees preserved under the conditions indicated naturally free themselves from a great part of the foreign substances which they contain, by rest, for they are insoluble, and specifically heavier than wine, and settle of their own accord. The wine should not be fined till drawn from the heavy lees.

The racking off of the clear wine may be performed in two ways, either by the use of a glass siphon or of a faucet. For the first rackings the glass siphon is most appropriate, and by its use the boring of holes high up in the end of the cask is avoided. It is introduced about eight inches into the full cask, a proper vessel to catch the wine is placed under the end, with another vessel close at hand, and the wine is started by the breath; but the siphon must be held with the hand, or otherwise sustained so that it will not go too deep into the cask. By holding a candle below, it can be seen if the wine is any way clear; and as long as it runs sufficiently limpid, the siphon is lowered into the cask, little by little, till the level of the turbid wine is nearly reached. When one bucket is filled, the other is slipped under the stream without stopping it. Two men are usually required, one to attend the siphon, and the other to empty the buckets. As soon as the wine runs muddy, it is stopped. If the cask of lees is sufficiently elevated, the stem of the siphon may run into a funnel placed in the empty cask.

When the casks have all been drawn from, the remaining heavy lees are filled into those containing the greater quantity, so as to transfer the least quantity. Before filling, however, the casks should have a double square of sulphur match burned in each, to prevent subsequent fermentations.

The use of the faucet is preferred, when the lees are thick, and the casks which contain them are near the ground, and are only used for storing lees. In the latter case, the injury to the cask by boring holes in the head at several heights, is of little consequence. A greater quantity of wine may be drawn off by the use of the faucet than with the glass siphon, but it is generally less clear than if carefully done with the latter; and one man can do the work.

First, it is necessary to ascertain how far down the clear wine reaches, by means of gimlet holes, and the faucet hole should then be bored just above the level of the heavy lees. If the faucet has been placed too low, the sediment which runs through it at first may be put aside.

After the drawing of the clear wine has been repeated several times, and the thick lees united as above mentioned, the casks should not be filled until heavily sulphured, and they must not be disturbed, for the least agitation may stir up the sediment already formed, and cause bad flavor in the wine, and even produce putrid fermentation, especially in those from fined wines which contain large quantities of animal matter introduced in the finings. Casks emptied of heavy lees should be washed with a chain, to remove the sediment clinging to the inside, which must not be allowed to dry on.

Fining Wines Extracted from the Lees.—These wines often are not sufficiently clear; and they are generally more difficult to clarify completely by the usual methods than the wines which produced the lees.

It is noticeable that these wines have less color and less alcohol than other wines produced in the ordinary way.

The difficulty in obtaining their complete clarification arises from the great quantity of insoluble matter which they still hold in suspension, and their relative feebleness in alcohol and tannin.

The want of color is due to the mechanical action of the insoluble matters which the lees contain; these matters in precipitating carry down a part of the coloring matter remaining in solution in the liquid. It follows that the older the lees, and the oftener the wine has been drawn from them, the feebler the color.

Red Wines extracted from the lees, to be completely clarified, should be fined with a heavy dose of albumen (the whites of 16 or 18 eggs to 100 gallons), previously well beaten up in a pint of water in which half an ounce of sea salt has been dissolved to give it density. If the alcoholic strength is below nine per cent. they should be fortified by the addition of two or three quarts of brandy or alcohol to each 100 gallons. Red wines from this source should not be fined with gelatine, or it will diminish the color too much.

White Wines of this kind may be fined with albumen also, if strong in alcohol; but otherwise, they should be fined with a heavy dose of gelatine, three tablets. But before fining they must be tannified by adding 4 or 5 gallons of tannified wine, or an ounce of tannin for each 100 gallons.

Wines from lees should remain on the finings only long enough to precipitate the matters used, about ten days; after which they must be carefully racked, and cared for like other wines.

Pressing the Thick Sediment.—After the lees have undergone three or four semi-monthly rackings, the rest of the wine which they contain may be extracted by pressure, and this amounts on the average to fifty per cent. More wine might be extracted by further racking, but by allowing the wine to remain longer in contact with the finings and other sediment, it will contract the disagreeable flavors already alluded to, which may be avoided by pressing the lees after the first three or four rackings; and an excellent result is obtained by using a filter press after the first racking, and the wine obtained will have no bad taste.

The pressing is performed in small sacks about eighteen inches long. They should be made of cotton cloth, as those made from hemp, even after being used several times, give a disagreeable flavor to the wines passed through them.

It is not necessary to provide more than sacks enough for one cask of lees. The cloth of which they are made should be fine, and of close and regular texture.

To make a cheap press, one head of a cask is removed, and the pieces of this head are fastened together by nailing on two cross pieces to keep it in form, and enough of the wood around the edge is removed to allow it to pass freely into the cask as a follower. The cask is then placed upright, and a hole is bored in one of the staves close to the lower head, into which is placed a faucet. This cask, which is to contain the sacks, may be placed high enough to allow the wine to run from the faucet directly into the bung of another cask to hold the wine. If the casks containing the lees are placed on a horse or platform, the latter may be run from the faucet-hole directly into the sacks, which may be fastened to the chime with small hooks, and be kept open with the hand or a small hoop. A dish should be placed under before withdrawing the spigot. Or, to avoid fouling the outside of the sack with the lees, they may first be run into a tub, and dipped into the sacks, the tub being provided with a sack-holder. As soon as a sack is sufficiently filled, it should be strongly tied with a bow-knot which can be easily untied, and laid in the cask provided; and a few small sticks should be placed over the inner end of the faucet so that it may not be stopped by a sack coming in contact with it. Sacks are placed in the cask till it is full. The faucet is left open, so that the wine, as fast as filtered, may run through a hose into a well washed and well sulphured cask, placed in position to receive it.

When the cask is full of sacks, the cover is placed on them and they are allowed to drain for several hours, weights being gradually placed upon the cover or follower. Further pressure is applied by means of a lever rigged for the purpose, one end made firm, and the other having weights attached.

It is best that the pressure be gradually applied, leaving the sacks to drain for several hours, then applying the lever, but loading it with weights several hours later, or the next day.

When the wine no longer runs, say twenty-four hours after loading the lever, the sacks are removed.

If the lees are not very thick, but little will be found in the sacks, and they may be refilled without removing it, and subjected to a second pressure. Then they must be thoroughly washed with water. Lye should not be used.

Where large quantities of lees are to be pressed, larger presses may be used, vats being employed instead of casks.

It is impossible to obtain all the wine by simple filtration without pressure, owing to the fact that the filters soon become foul, and the wine ceases to pass through.

If the first wine which runs off is turbid, it may be put by itself, and the clear wine caught separately. It is apt to run turbid when additional weight is applied.

Use of Dry Lees.—They have a certain value, and after being removed from the sacks they may be sold to the manufacturers of cream of tartar, if they are *virgin lees*. Lees from fined wines are of little value for this purpose. They may be dried on well-aired floors, or in the sun. They are also used for the production of pearlash by burning them. The ash produced is of a greenish gray color, and is crude pearlash. Good lees, perfectly dry, produce about 30 per cent. of this alkali.

Lees are also valuable as a fertilizer. Those from sweet wine contain considerable sugar, which may be utilized by fermenting and distilling the alcohol produced. This, however, will render them less valuable for making cream of tartar, a portion of which will be dissolved by washing.

MARC, OR POMACE—PIQUETTE.

Marc, or Pomace, is the residue remaining in the vat after the fermentation of red wine, or in the press, in making white wine.

After being pressed, it is used in many parts of France to make a weak wine called *piquette*, for the use of the laborers. For this purpose are utilized all the soluble principles remaining in the marc, by the following treatment:

1. The Unfermented Pomace of White or of Red Wine not Entirely Fermented, is well broken and crumbled up so as to finely divide it, and introduced into tuns, which are then completely filled with water, or into a fermenting vat, adding double its weight of water. After giving it a thorough stirring and mixing, the first piquette is drawn off. After a maceration of three of four days, renewing the water several times, the saccharine matter and soluble salts which the marc contains are completely removed. Piquette is fermented in casks and cared for like new wine. The weakest is first consumed.

Or the marc may be pressed and put into barrels, keeping it in as solid a mass as possible; the surface is then covered with sand and the casks closed air-tight. Piquette may then be made as needed, using the marc of one cask, washing with water till it is exhausted.

2. The Fermented Marc of Red Wine is treated as follows: After pressing, it is immediately put into a large vat. Double its weight of water is added, and after a complete stirring, it is allowed to macerate one or two days at most. The first piquette is then drained off, and water is put in several times till the soluble matters are removed.

Pressed marc is also used for forage, mixing it with half the quantity of hay.

As for making wine from marc by adding sweetened water, see *Watering and Sugaring Must*.

The following method of washing the marc is from an article on the Distillation of Marc, by J. Pezeyre, printed in *Le Parfait Vigneron, Almanach du Moniteur Vinicole*, 1881:

Six vats or barrels are set up side by side, each provided with a faucet, and a movable cover. The faucet is protected inside, as in the case of the ordinary fermenting vat.

To thoroughly exhaust the marc, it should be washed with six times its weight of water, or 100 lbs. of pomace require 72 gallons of water.

The vats being arranged, are charged with marc, which is pressed down till it fills the vat to within about ten inches of the top. The marc is kept submerged in the usual way, by a false, perforated head.

The first vat is filled with cold water, and left to rest for two hours. The liquid is then drawn off and filled into vat No. 2. No. 1 is then re-filled with fresh water. When the liquid in No. 2 has remained for two hours, it is drawn off and put into No. 3. No. 1 is then emptied into No. 2, and filled with water a third time. The maceration in No. 3 having continued for two hours, its liquid is drawn off and poured into No. 4; No. 3 is filled from No. 2, and this from No. 1, which is filled the fourth time with water. No. 5 is filled from No. 4, and each vat is filled from the preceding one, until No. 1 has received in water six times the weight of the marc contained in it.

The liquid from No. 5 is poured into No. 6, and after two hours is drawn from this last vat into the still.

When the wine has been drawn from the last vat, the marc in No. 1 having been washed six times with its weight of water, is exhausted of all its alcohol. It is then re-filled with marc, and becomes No. 6 of the series, and is filled with the liquid from No. 5. Each number is thereby carried around the circle, becoming successively No. 6.

In this way the pomace is, little by little, deprived of its alcohol, and the liquid coming from No. 6 is rich in spirit, and when delivered to the still is nearly equal in strength to the original wine.

When there is but little marc to operate upon, the liquid may be drawn off into buckets, and so filled into the vats; but time and labor may be saved by using a pump and hose.

CHAPTER XIX.

THE COMPOSITION OF WINE.

Generally.—Wine is not only composed of alcohol and water, which are the two most prominent ingredients, but a great number of other substances have been recognized, and others still are supposed to exist. Some substances which are found in one wine may not exist in another, or it may exist in a greater or less quantity. We know that alcohol, water, and acids exist in all wines, in varying quantities; that some are sweet, and contain sugar, and that others are dry, thoroughly fermented, and contain none. We also know that the alcohol in different wines may vary from 4 or 5 per cent. in piquette made by washing the pomace with water, to 20 or 25 per cent. in the more strongly fortified. And we know generally how a wine is modified as to its taste and effect on the system, by such substances as water, alcohol, sugar, and acid; but there are many substances whose effect is but little known, and others again only known by their effects. The science of chemistry has not yet been able to lay hold of them.

Substances Recognized.—The following table from Maumené indicates the different substances contained in different wines, the letter F indicating those produced by fermentation, the others existing in the juice of the grape. It will be observed that the amount of acid tartrate of potash (cream of tartar) mentioned is 5.5 grammes per litre at most, and this is the quantity contained in a new wine, old wines containing only one or two grammes per litre, and even less. This salt is contained in the grapes, and is soluble in water, but insoluble in alcohol, and, therefore, the greater part of it is precipitated as the alcohol increases by fermentation, and is deposited with the lees. The Report of the University of California, Department of Agriculture, referred to in the preface, shows the amount contained in different California wines and their lees.

COMPOSITION OF WINE.

			Grammes.
Water................................ 9 volumes,			900 to 891
Common Alcohol (Absolute or Pure), F. 1 volume,			80 to 79

Other Alcohols (Butyric, Amylic, etc.).........F.
Aldehydes (several ?) ....F.
Ethers (Acetic, Butyric, œnanthic, etc.), contributing principally to the bouquet...........F.
Essential Oils (several).......................
Grape Sugar (Dextrose and Levulose)..........
Mannite ....F.
Mucilage, Gum, and Dextrin ....
Pectin ....
Coloring Matters (œnocyanine) ....
Fatty Matters (and Wax ?) ....
Glycerin ....F.
Nitrogenous Matters (Albumin, Gliadin, etc.)
Ferments ....

Neutral Bodies.
  Salts.
    Vegetable.
      Acid Tartrate of Potash (5.5 grammes at most) ....
      Neutral Tartrate of Lime ....
      "   "   Ammonia.........
      Acid Tartrate of Alumina (simple, or with Potash.).......................
      Acid Tartrate of Iron (simple, or with Potash.).............................
      Racemates ....
      Acetates, Propionates, Butyrates, Lactates, etc..........................F.
    Mineral.
      Sulphates..
      Nitrates ...
      Phosphates.   With a base of Potash,
      Silicates ... Soda, Lime, Magnesia,
      Chlorides .. Alumina, Oxide of Iron,
      Bromides ..   Ammonia................
      Iodides ....
      Fluorides .

20—30

Free Acids.
  Carbonic (2.5 grammes at most) ....F.
  Tartaric and Racemic (Gluco-tartaric ?).........
  Malic...
  Citric..
  Tannic.......................................
  Metapectic ....F.
  Acetic......................................F.
  Lactic ....F.
  Succinic ....F.
  Butyric ....F.
  Valeric ? ....F.

1000—1000

COMPOSITION OF WINE. 187

A few of the more important ones will be briefly noticed.

Alcohol is considerably lighter than water, and from the specific gravity of any mixture of alcohol and pure water, the quantity of spirit contained in it can readily be ascertained. (See Table IV.)

To Ascertain the Alcoholic Strength of Wine, if it consisted of a mixture of water and alcohol alone, it would only be necessary to learn its specific gravity; but as all wines contain other substances which affect the weight of the liquid, it becomes necessary to separate the alcohol from the other matters by distillation; then by adding water enough to make up the original volume of the wine assayed, we will have simply a mixture of alcohol and water.

Small stills are sold in the market, with the necessary instruments accompanying them, with which to perform the operation. In the accompanying figure (43), which shows a French still, L is a spirit lamp, B a glass boiler with a perforated stopper, S a worm, contained in the cooler D, which is kept filled with cold water, as a condenser; t is a rubber tube connecting the boiler with the condenser, tightly fitted to the stopper of the former, and also to the end of the worm. E is a small hydrometer-jar, of glass, with a foot, for measuring the wine to be distilled, and for catching the distillate as it runs from the worm. It has three marks—the upper one, m, indicating the height to which it is to be filled with the wine, and also a ½ mark and a ⅓ mark. Sometimes it is provided with a groove along one side to carry the thermometer.

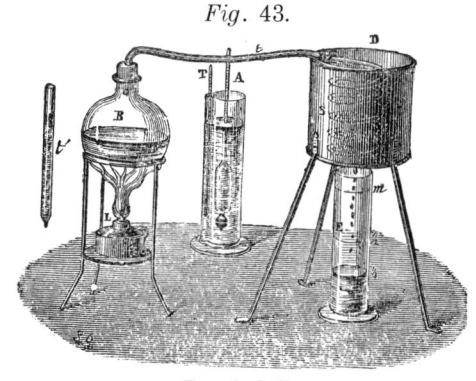

Fig. 43.

French Still.

COMPOSITION OF WINE.

A represents the hydrometer, or alcoholometer, being a spindle, usually of glass, similar in form to the saccharometer (*which see*), except that the zero mark to which the alcoholometer sinks in distilled water, is at the lower end of the stem, and the degrees are numbered from zero to the upper end, each figure representing one per cent. of alcohol. *T* is a thermometer, in its place in the jar with the hydrometer; *t'* is a small glass pipette to assist in filling the jar just to the mark.

To make use of the instruments, measure in the jar, *E*, the wine to be distilled, by filling it up exactly to the upper mark, *m*, using the pipette, *t'*, by which a little of the liquid can be sucked up, and let out, drop by drop, by increasing and diminishing the pressure of the finger applied to the upper opening. The wine so measured is poured into the boiler, *B*, draining out the last drop, or the little remaining may be rinsed out with a little water, which is poured into the boiler with the wine without affecting the result. The boiler is then placed over the lamp and connected with the condenser by means of the rubber tube, and the condenser filled with cold water. Light the lamp, and place the now empty jar under the lower end of the worm. The vapor of the alcohol first passing from the boiler through the rubber tube into the condenser, will there condense, and the liquid running from the worm into the test tube will be almost pure alcohol, but as the process goes on, more and more water comes out with the alcohol, till the spirit has all passed over. If the strength of the wine does not exceed 14 or 15 per cent., the alcohol will all have passed over when one-third of the wine has been distilled, as will be shown when the distillate reaches the $\frac{1}{3}$ mark on the glass. If the strength exceeds the above limit, one-half of the wine should be distilled. If, therefore, on testing the wine, it is found to contain 16 per cent. or more of spirit, and only one-third was distilled, another quantity should be distilled, and about one-half allowed to pass over. It is always safer, unless the wine is very weak, to distil over a little more than a third. If you are operating on a wine which foams to such an extent that a portion may pass through the tube into the condenser, which would spoil the effect of the operation, this may be prevented by putting into the boiler with the wine a pinch of tannic acid. In operating on a wine which contains an appreciable amount of acetic acid—is pricked—the acid ought to be neutralized before distillation, as it is volatile, and will go over with the alcohol and effect the result. This is easily done by adding to the wine caustic soda in drops, till it completely changes color, red wine becoming blue, and white wine, brown. These precautions, however, are generally omitted in analyses for commercial purposes.

When the distillation is complete, add to the distillate sufficient pure water (distilled water if possible), to make up the exact volume of wine measured. To do this, take the jar containing the distillate and hold it perpendicular, with the upper mark on a level with the eye, and carefully let in the water, drop by drop, by means of the pipette. The surface of the liquid will be seen to curve upward, owing to the attraction of the glass, and the tube should be filled till the bottom of the curve touches the mark; and the same precaution should be taken in measuring the wine in the first place.

Now we have a mixture corresponding in volume with the wine, and containing all the alcohol originally contained in the wine, and a certain amount of water, and nothing else.

As the density of the liquid also depends upon the temperature, it becomes necessary to have a fixed standard at which the test is made, and this is 60° F. in this country, and I believe in all countries except France, where it is 15° C., or 59° F. As the temperature affects the volume, it is better to adjust it by cooling the distillate before adding the last few drops of water, which may be done by dipping the jar into cold water, or if it is too cold, by warming it with the hand.

The hydrometer used will be adjusted to a temperature of 60° F., or 15° C., which is generally shown by directions accompanying the still, or will be marked on the instrument. Let the hydrometer be perfectly clean and dry, no moisture on the stem. Take the tip of the stem between the thumb and forefinger and lower it into the distillate till it floats, press it down with the finger very slightly, and let it come to equilibrium. Place the eye on a level with the surface of the liquid, and see where it cuts the stem, and the mark shows the percentage of alcohol contained in the wine. Remember that the mark to be taken is the one corresponding with the general surface of the liquid, not the top of the meniscus, or curve. With care, a result can be obtained sufficiently accurate for all commercial purposes.

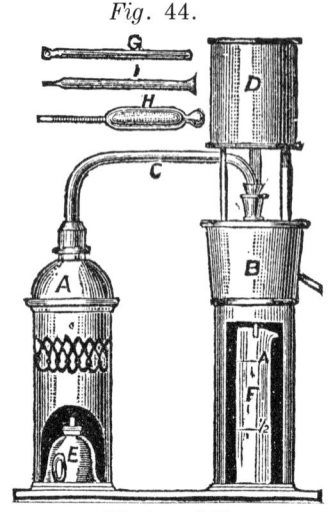

Fig. 44.

Monitor Still.

A table is usually sold with these stills, showing the corrections for different temperatures, so that by its use the reduction of the temperature to the standard may be avoided.

Fig. 44 represents a still made in New York, called the Monitor Still.

Ethers are formed by alcohol in presence of the different acids contained in the wine, and they take names corresponding to the acids, ocurring as compound ethers, the most common one being acetic ether. They have a powerful and characteristic odor, known as the etherous odor, which is somewhat disagreeable in the pure ether, but becomes agreeable and resembles the aroma of fruit and flowers when greatly diluted.

Among the important ethers contained in wine is *Oenanthic ether*, which is said to give to wine its characteristic vinous smell, which distinguishes it from any other fermented liquor.

Sugar is contained in many wines, especially sweet wines, and exercises an important influence upon the flavor.

To Estimate Sugar.—The quantity of sugar contained in a sweet wine may be estimated with sufficient accuracy, for commercial purposes, in the following manner. A certain quantity of wine is measured in the jar, and distilled in the same manner as in the estimation of alcohol (*which see*), or the wine may be placed in a shallow dish on a stove or over a lamp, and boiled slowly till the volume is reduced one-half, when the alcohol will be all evaporated; then the original volume should be restored by adding water. After it has rested for a day or so, the greater part of the salts will crystallize and be deposited, when the sugar strength can be ascertained by the use of the saccharometer, in the usual way (*see page* 8). One degree, however, should be deducted from the hydrometer reading.

Mannite, or the essential principle of *manna*, is produced in wine when sugar undergoes *viscous fermentation*. Its flavor is similar to that of sugar, and its composition is but little different from that of the same substance.

Mucilage.—The grand red wines of the Médoc, and of some other portions of the Gironde, and also the grand wines of Burgundy, says Boireau, preserve in aging a pronounced fruity taste, an unctuosity, a velvety mellowness, which, joined with their flavor and bouquet, make these wines in good years the delight of the *gourmets*. This velvety mellowness is found only in those seasons when the grapes ripen well. In poor years, when the grapes do not become completely ripe, the wines may have at times more or less distinctive flavor (*séve*), and sometimes even a little bouquet, but they are dry, and the mellowness is wanting.

Many ordinary wines possess while young, if they have been well made, and are produced in favorable years, a marked fruity flavor; but in the greater part of the wines of this kind, this mellowness does not last, and disappears gradually with age, while in the grand wines of good years, the unctuosity is more appreciable after the defecation of their lees than while they are new.

The substance which in a measure produces this quality is called *mucilage* by Maumené and some others. Others, again, have given it different names. Maumené says that it seems to be a sort of intermediary substance between *cellulose* and *dextrin*, and that its nature is not yet known, but that it is a near neighbor of sugar.

Mr. Boireau believes that the mellowness is produced by a modification of grape sugar, because, when not properly cared for, mellow wines undergo an insensible fermentation, especially if they are in their first and second years, and still contain ferments. Very often at the end of these secondary fermentations, the unctuosity has disappeared, and the wines have become dry. It seems, accordingly, that the substance is capable of undergoing the same transformations as sugar under the influence of ferments and heat.

Pectose is found in green grapes and other fruits, and by the acids is changed into *pectin*, which is the gelatinizing principle, is soluble in water, and may have some effect on the mellowness of wine. Alcohol precipitates it in the form of jelly.

Fatty Matters have been found in wine lees, which may be extracted from the seeds by long contact during fermentation, for it is known that the seeds yield such matters.

Glycerin is mentioned among fatty matters, but it is known to be produced by the fermentation of sugar, and is supposed to have its influence on the flavor of wine.

The Coloring Matter of red wine has received the name of *œnocyanine*. In its pure state it is blue, but is changed to red by acids. The yellow and brown color of some white wines is due to the oxidation of some of the matters contained in them. The change of color in red wines is also due to the oxidation of the tannic acid, thereby forming an insoluble compound, tannomelanic acid, which is precipitated, carrying down the œnocyanine, and the wine gradually becomes tawny.

Aldehydes are produced first in the transformation of alcohol into an acid by oxidation, acet-aldehyde occurring between alcohol and acetic acid, as mentioned in Acetic Fermentation. When a weak wine is exposed to the air it is gradually converted into vinegar, or acetic acid. If free access of air is permitted, it may be converted at once into acetic acid, but if the access of the air is very limited, or if the wine is rich and strong, oxidation stops at the first stage, and aldehyde is formed. It is a colorless liquid of a very suffocating smell, having an etherous odor, and is supposed to have an important influence on the flavor and bouquet of various wines. The strong wines of southern countries which are kept in casks in ullage, exposed to the action of the oxygen of the air, develop a certain amount of aldehyde in time, and it is supposed that sherry owes some of its qualities to this substance.

Acids.—We can only allude briefly to the acids which have been recognized in wines. The principal one is *tartaric acid*, found in considerable quantities in grapes, and is contained in the argols, or crude cream of tartar, *bitartrate of potash*, which is deposited on the inner walls of the casks in which the wine is kept. This substance principally gives the acid taste to wine.

Malic Acid, or the acid of apples, is found; and of *citric acid*, or the acid of lemons, traces have been recognized; also *pectic acid*, derived from the pectose.

Tannic Acid is a very important ingredient in wine, and is frequently mentioned in this work. (See *Fining, Tannin.*)

Carbonic Acid.—It has been shown in the chapter on Fermentation that carbon dioxide is the gas produced by fermentation. This gas, CO_2, was known to the old chemists as carbonic acid, or carbonic acid gas, and the latter terms are frequently used in this work in the sense of carbon dioxide, in accordance with common usage. But modern chemistry teaches us that carbon dioxide, CO_2, is not an acid at all, but in connection with water it takes up a molecule of the latter, and becomes $H_2 CO_3$, carbonic acid proper. The gas, however, as well as the acid, exists in all wines, and to the former, sparkling wines owe their effervescence. Its presence is important, exercising a preservative effect by preventing their oxidation, and also by keeping in dissolution substances which would otherwise cloud the wine. When the wine is first fermented it is saturated with carbon dioxide, and while it remains so, oxygen will not be absorbed, and hence its preservative effect. Mr. Maumené even recommends resort to artificial means to restore it, or to re-saturate the wine in case of its loss. If, however, the precautions heretofore indicated for keeping table wines are observed, the wine will be well preserved.

Acetic Acid is the result of oxidation, or *acetic fermentation* (*which see*), and *lactic acid* is derived from *lactic fermentation*, but is regarded as accidental in wine, probably not existing in the must, though it is found in some wines made from grapes which have been bruised and broken a long time before using.

Butyric Acid is the product of *butyric fermentation*.

Valeric Acid is supposed to exist in wine from the distinctive odor which is smelt in it under certain conditions.

Succinic Acid has been referred to as one of the products of alcoholic fermentation.

The Total Acids in wine vary a good deal, but four or five per mille is a fair average.

Space will not permit of more details on the various substances contained in wine, but those who desire further information are referred to the work of Maumené in French, and that of Thudichum and Dupré in English.

The Bouquet proper of wines is a perfume containing different odors, like that of a bouquet of flowers. It is very complex also in its origin, and the matters contained in the wine which give rise to it are but little known. It is variable, being different in different wines, and all the odorous matters doubtless contribute to its existence, such as œnanthic, and other ethers, the different alcohols, aldehydes, and perhaps even certain essential oils. The varieties of grapes, the season, and the soil, also have their effect, as well as the method of vinification. It is believed, however, that the bouquet is principally due to the ethers.

Artificial Bouquet.—In this connection, the experiments of

Mr. Maumené will be found interesting. He prepared one litre of a liquid similar to wine, but without a sensible odor, by adding distilled water to the distillate from a red wine of Bordeaux.

One drop of *aldehyde* produced no appreciable odor.

Six drops of *acetic ether* produced no sensible effect.

Nor did *crystallized acetic acid* change the result.

He then added 5 grs. 5 of *cream of tartar*, 0 gr. 18 of *succinic acid*, and 20 grs. of *glycerin*, without producing any odor in the liquid.

On adding certain ethers a remarkable change was produced.

By adding two small drops of *œnanthic ether* (obtained by distilling fresh wine lees), the liquid instantly gave an odor of wine.

Then he added, drop by drop, one cubic centimetre (1000th part by measure) of essence of pears, that is, the following mixture:

1 volume of valero-amylic ether.
6 volumes of alcohol of 36 per cent.

The first drops developed a bouquet which belongs to certain wines; but by adding the whole amount mentioned, a pear odor was developed, by which the liquid could be easily distinguished from wine. So he prepared another litre of the liquid containing the same substances, and added only two or three drops of essence of pears. He then added two drops of ordinary butyric ether, and the bouquet resembled in a remarkable degree that of a good Bouzy wine, and several persons took it for a decolored wine. By varying the experiment, the bouquet of wines can be imitated in a remarkable manner.

For those who are curious in such matters, I translate the following from Boireau:

Artificial bouquets are produced by aromatic substances, or essential oils, whose aroma is extracted or dissolved out by the help of alcohol. The aromatic principle may be extracted either by a simple alcoholic tincture, by digestion or distillation, by dissolving the oils themselves, etc., and the process varies with the substance used.

The aromatic substances most frequently employed to produce artificial bouquets in non-fortified wines, commencing with those which form the base and whose aromas are more dominant, are: iris, strawberry, gillyflower, the flower of the vine, mignonette, nutmeg, bitter almond, fruit pits, sassafras, etc. The latter are rarely employed alone, and play a secondary part by mixing with the two first, iris and strawberry, whose aromas are quite distinctive.

Iris.—There are two varieties of this. The roots only are employed; they are white, of an average diameter of 0 m. 02 (¾ in.), and of a very irregular form. They are sold in pieces about 0 m. 05 (2 in.) long, with the rootlets removed. They are largely employed in perfumery.

The root of the so-called Florence iris, which grows in Italy and the south of France, has a pronounced violet odor. Another variety, which grows in the north of France and in Germany, is sold under the name of German iris. An experienced person can distinguish the two.

The perfume of the iris is with difficulty and incompletely extracted by distillation; it is obtained by infusing the roots in alcohol, after first reducing them to a powder by means of a grater. The operation is long, but indispensable. The powder occurs in commerce, but in that form the roots lose their aroma, and it is moreover liable to be adulterated.

The tincture is prepared in the following proportions: old spirit of wine of 85 per cent., 10 litres (2½ gallons); Florence iris, 1 kilogramme (2⅛ lb.), reduced to powder.

Bung or cork the vessel containing it, stir it about for a few minutes, and then put it in a place of at least 68° F., but which does not go beyond 95°. Shake it occasionally during two weeks, and then press and filter it.

The tincture has a pronounced violet odor, and a harsh, bitter after-taste.

It may be employed alone, in a very small dose, rarely exceeding 5 centilitres per hectolitre (13½ fluidrams to 26½ gallons).

Oftener, however, a few drops of the essential oil of gillyflower, etc., are mixed with it.

Strawberry.—The preparation of an alcoholic infusion of strawberries is very simple. Take fully ripe berries, pick them over and hull them, and put them in a keg with a large bung. Ten kilogrammes of fruit to 12 litres of old spirits of wine of 85 per cent. (22 lbs. to $3\frac{1}{6}$ gals.) are used. After macerating for twenty-four hours, the liquor is drawn off and filtered. It is a rose-colored liquor of a very pleasant aroma. Then the fruit is crushed, and brandy of 50 per cent. is added, and the whole is allowed to macerate for a month, and then the marc is pressed. The second tincture has an odor and flavor inferior to the first, and has more color. It is filtered, or what is better, distilled in a water bath. In the latter way spirit of strawberry is obtained. It is preferable to employ the liquor of the first infusion. This aroma is generally used alone, and is much employed in the manufacture of sparkling wines. Sometimes a small quantity of other aromatic substances are added, allowing the strawberry to predominate. It is the best modifier of the aroma of young wines.

The dose varies according to the degree of the aroma, from 2 to 10 centilitres per hectolitre ($\frac{1}{6}$ to $\frac{5}{6}$ of a gill, or 5.4 to 27 fluidrams to 26.4 gals.)

Gillyflower, or Stockgilly.—The essential oil of this flower may be extracted by pressure, by maceration, or by distillation, and is found in commerce. To make the bouquet, the oil is used, or the concentrated essence, which is produced by the distillation of the bruised flowers with alcohol of 85 per cent., in the proportion of 300 grammes of the flowers to 5 litres of alcohol ($10\frac{1}{2}$ oz. to $5\frac{1}{4}$ quarts). In the absence of an alembic, the aroma may be extracted by infusion, as in the case of iris, by macerating 100 grammes of the bruised flowers to 1 litre of alcohol of 85 per cent. ($3\frac{1}{2}$ oz. to a quart) for eight days, and filtering. Gillyflower is rarely used alone; but by adding a very small quantity of it to iris, a good effect is produced, and the perfume becomes more intimately mixed with the wine, for the oil of gillyflower is heavier than water; but this aroma should never predominate, and is best for old wines without bouquet.

Vine Flowers are gathered and the petals infused in alcohol of 85 per cent., in the proportion of 100 grammes of flowers to 5 litres of alcohol (3½ oz. to 5¼ quarts). After macerating for eight days, it is distilled in a water bath. This aroma, which is very volatile, is used in the dose of 5 centilitres to a hectolitre (13.5 fluidrams to 26.4 gals.)

Mignonette.—The perfume of the mignonette, like that of many other flowers, is obtained by picking the flowers from their stems, bruising them, and placing them upon layers of cotton or pieces of linen impregnated with fresh oil, or other sweet fats; oil of ben is preferred. The flowers are renewed every four hours, till the cotton or the cloth is charged with perfume. The oil or fat is removed by pressure or otherwise, and the essential oil is dissolved out with alcohol of 85 per cent., which is afterwards separated from the fixed oil, and filtered. The extract of mignonette so obtained is employed in the proportion of 1 to 5 centilitres to a hectolitre (2.7 to 13.5 fluidrams to 26.4 gals.) but oftener it is mixed with other perfumes.

Nutmeg is employed in the form of spirit distilled from the nuts over the fire, 500 grammes of nuts to 10 litres of alcohol (1 lb. to 10½ quarts), or in the form of a tincture made with the same proportions of nuts and alcohol, or a small quantity of the essential oil is mixed with other aromatic substances. This preparation, particularly the tincture or the distilled spirit, has a good effect. Being heavier than water, it assists the mixture.

Bitter Almonds and Fruit Pits.—Their oil is found in commerce, and its aroma is due to the hydrocyanic (prussic) acid contained in it, which is poisonous, and therefore the oil should be employed in the smallest doses.

Sassafras.—The essential oil is extracted from the wood and bark by distillation, and can be purchased in the market. It is heavier than wine, and fixes the lighter perfumes. It is used only secondarily, and in very small quantities.

Other Aromas have been tried, but they can only be used as auxiliary to the three first named, iris, gillyflower, and strawberry, because their odors differ essentially from the natural bouquet of mellow wines.

Effects.—These preparations give wines a bouquet or aroma which partakes of the substances employed, but they do not give the distinctive flavor (*séve*) which characterizes fine wines, and the result only flatters the sense of smell. These perfumes are very volatile, and it does not require a very delicate or a much experienced palate to distinguish them from the natural bouquet of wine, and persons of delicate sensibilities are disturbed by them, if too pronounced.

When a wine has been artificially perfumed, it still preserves its taste and earthy flavor; it has simply changed its odor. Taste it without smelling, and its distinctive flavor will be recognized. Mr. Boireau says that, notwithstanding the contrary announcements of interested manufacturers, they are not preserved like the natural bouquets and flavors, but, little by little, they become enfeebled, and are volatilized with time.

He says that the trade is inundated with the announcements of pretended œnologists, chemists, etc., manufacturers of bouquets decorated with such pompous names as Médoc Flavoring (*Séve du Médoc*), Bouquet of Bordeaux, of Pomard, Bordeaux Extract, etc., and all these humbugs are advertised as giving the most ordinary wines the true Médoc flavor, etc., which, happily for the producers of Médoc, cannot be done.

It is better, as stated in the chapter on *Cutting Wines*, to improve wines by mixing them with those having expansible flavors and odors, rather than use these artificial bouquets.

CHAPTER XX.

GENERAL CHAPTER — MISCELLANEOUS.

The Proportion of Juice to Marc, as stated in Thudichum and Dupré's work, has been found in various grapes as follows:

White Chasselas, stems removed, gave by strong pressure, 97 per cent. of juice; marc of skins and seeds, 3 per cent.

Black Pinot grapes, stems removed, gave 94.8 per cent. of juice, and 5.2 per cent. of marc.

Black Pinot, pressed with the stems, gave 91.8 per cent. of juice, and 8.2 per cent. of marc, including stems.

Black Pinot, fermented with the stems and then pressed, gave 69.6 per cent. of wine, and 30.4 per cent. of marc.

In the latter case much wine is absorbed by the stems, which cannot be removed by pressure.

In the first three cases the pressure must have been such as to reduce the marc to near dryness to obtain so high a percentage of juice.

In the report of the work done in the Viticultural Laboratory of the University, referred to in the preface, the following figures are found, and are extracted from Table No. 1 of the report. Omitting the two extremes—Feher Szagos, 203.2, and Lenoir, 118—we obtain the average of 157 gallons of grape juice per ton of 2000 lbs. in twelve white wines, and 174.8 gallons per ton in twelve red wines; the word "red" being used in the table to designate the product obtained by fermenting white grapes with the skins and seeds, as well as to designate "red wine" proper.

The report says: "The red wines, of course, produce very much less pomace, which consists largely of skins and seeds only. The white pomace has much more of the pulp of the grape, and consequently a much larger amount of water. During the fermentation the internal structure of the grape is destroyed, the sugar is fermented out, and only the fibrous structure remains; even this is to a great extent broken up, and runs out with the wine when pressed."

MISCELLANEOUS.

NAME.	Color of Wine.	Weight in pounds of Grapes used.	Pomace, per cent.	Stems, per cent.	Air-dried Pomace, per cent.	Gallons of Must.	Gallons of Must per ton of Grapes— 2000 lbs.
Mission, just ripe.	Red	71.75	13.50	3.05	_ _ _	6.38	177.8
" fully "	White	106.50	18.30	3.75	_ _ _	9.20	172.6
" " "	Red	101.00	11.63	3.96	_ _ _	8.98	177.8
" _____	White	85.80	24.10	3.07	8.71	6.84	159.4
" _____	Red	73.92	12.20	2.91	5.26	6.30	170.5
Zinfandel _____	White	84.00	27.30	5.75	_ _ _	6.20	147.6
" _____	Red	126.00	13.40	5.55	_ _ _	11.00	174.6
" _____	White	87.78	29.07	4.51	7.31	6.32	144.0
" _____	Red	84.26	10.96	4.02	4.94	7.30	173.4
Malvoisie _____	White	116.00	18.10	2.58	_ _ _	9.90	170.6
" _____	Red	151.00	10.92	2.65	_ _ _	14.30	189.4
Charbono _____	White	97.00	30.92	6.18	_ _ _	7.00	144.2
Burger _____	White	74.00	22	.97	_ _ _	6.40	172.8
" _____	"Red"	95.00	12.10	7.36	_ _ _	8.25	173.6
Chasselas _____	White	103.84	31.35	2.96	5.93	7.47	143.8
" _____	"Red"	70.40	13.75	2.92	3.74	5.97	169.6
Golden Chasselas.	"Red"	139.70	12.28	4.56	3.15	12.90	184.6
Prolific _____	White	95.04	23.15	3.70	7.76	7.54	158.6
" _____	"Red"	86.24	11.73	3.57	4.24	7.30	169.2
Black Prince ____	White	108.24	25.60	5.18	9.01	8.13	150.2
" " ____	Red	103.40	15.74	4.46	5.21	8.54	165.2
Feher Szagos ____	White	92.40	25.95	2.14	4.89	7.47	161.8
" " ____	Red	77.99	9.01	2.28	2.55	7.93	203.2
Mataro _____	White	131.67	21.40	6.69	6.26	10.46	158.9
" _____	Red	90.20	12.19	5.60	5.02	7.76	172.0
Lenoir _____	Red	33.00	17.30	6.00	8.50	1.96	118.7

This table contradicts the opinion held by some wine makers, that the Mission grape yields a larger percentage of stems than other varieties. The five lots of Mission grapes analyzed give an average of nearly 3.35 per cent. of stems, which is less than the yield of every other variety mentioned, except Malvoisie, Chasselas, and Feher Szagos.

The Proportion of Wine to Grapes.—It is generally said that it takes about 12 lbs. of grapes to produce a gallon of wine; some give the number of pounds as low as 10; the product, however, is must, or new wine, for nothing is taken into consideration for loss by evaporation, etc., while aging. Some wine dealers here consider that it takes about 17 lbs. of grapes to produce a gallon of wine ready for consumption.

At a meeting of the St. Helena Vinicultural Club, Napa Valley, in this State, the following facts were stated, as reported in the newspapers. Mr. Krug said that he had always thought that 14 lbs. of grapes would give a gallon of good wine at the time of the second racking in March, April, or May. Mr. Scheffler said he had made last year 135.6 gallons of wine and 8 gallons of brandy to the ton of grapes. Counting each gallon of brandy as equal to 5 of wine, it was equal to about 176 gallons of wine. That was about the average of Riesling, Chasselas, Zinfandel, Malvoisie, etc. The general average was 136 gallons of wine and 8 of brandy, or 125 gallons of good wine and 10 of brandy. Mr. Heyman said he was glad to get 145 gallons of clear, marketable wine on the average. Mr. Pellet said that the very best grapes would make 150 gallons of wine at the first racking, and this is probably a fair average.

Wooden and Metal Utensils.—In European countries, and in all properly ordered wine cellars, wooden utensils are used wherever practicable; and it ought to be impressed upon the mind of every one who has anything to do with the handling of the liquid, that metal should never come in contact with wine, if it can be avoided, except it be a precious metal like silver. The reason is that wine, on account of the acids contained in it, has a powerful effect upon lead, copper, zinc, iron, etc. Whenever such a metal is exposed to the influence of the air, and of an acid liquor, the metal is readily oxidized, and the oxide combines with the acid to form a salt. Therefore, Mr. Maumené says that it is dangerous to keep wine for a few hours in vessels of copper or lead, on account of the poisonous effects of their compounds. It is bad even to leave it in iron, zinc, or tin. Among the acids contained in wine, that which is the most capable of causing oxidation of the metals is the tartaric acid and the crude tartar. So the principal salts formed by the wine in metallic vessels are the bi-tartrates of potash and the oxide of the metal. Iron wire wet with wine, in a few days becomes covered with a very dark, brown pellicle, the wine is reduced to a solution of tartrate of iron and potash, which is of that color. A piece of iron in the wine produces the same result. This salt, however, is not poisonous. But if the acid acts energetically on the iron, the water will be deprived of its oxygen, and the hydrogen thereby set free may seriously affect the wine, by combining with foreign bodies found in it, producing a detestable flavor and odor. A cask of wine may be completely ruined by a nail.

The salts of iron, therefore, are not to be feared on account of any deleterious effect upon the system, but rather on account of the ill effect which they may have upon the color, the flavor, and odor of the wine. On the other hand, the salts of copper and lead are highly poisonous, and should be carefully avoided.

Zinc and galvanized iron are also affected by wine, to the extent that when left in vessels made of either, it will cause serious indisposition to those who drink it.

Tin is also dissolved by wine, forming stannic oxide and stannic acid, which combine with the coloring matter and render it insoluble, making the wine cloudy at first, and finally rendering it nearly colorless. By long contact with tin the wine develops a fetid odor. Every wine maker knows how soon his tin vessels used about wine wear out, and the reason is apparent.

Cleanliness.—Whether wood or metal utensils are used, it is one of the essentials in making good, wholesome wine, that they should be kept scrupulously clean and neat. Stemmers, crushers, presses, buckets, funnels, and in fact everything that comes in contact with the liquid should be scrubbed and rinsed often enough to prevent their becoming sour, or contracting any disagreeable flavor or odor. If metal vessels *must be used*, by all means do not allow wine to stand in them. Run water through the hose and the pumps after using, and also before using again. For it is safe to assert that many of the bad odors and flavors met with in wines made by inexperienced persons are often due to want of care in these matters. The necessary care to be bestowed upon the casks has already been mentioned in the proper place.

Different Cellar Utensils which will be found convenient are represented in the following figures:

Fig. 45.   *Fig.* 46.   *Fig.* 47.

Tin Pitchers.   Wooden Pitcher.

Figures 45 and 46 are tin pitchers, and 47 is of wood.

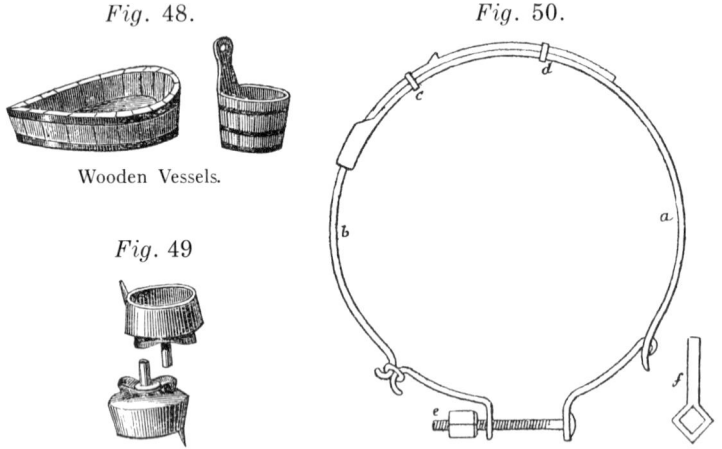

Fig. 48.   *Fig.* 50.

Wooden Vessels.

Fig. 49

Wooden Funnel.   Adjustable Hoop.

Figure 48 shows wooden vessels not necessary to describe.

Figure 49 is a wooden funnel for casks. Figure 50 is an adjustable hoop, useful in case of leakage in a cask caused by the breaking of hoops. It can be put around a cask and tightened with the screw till a new hoop is put in place. Where, however, casks are well hooped with iron, it is not likely to be needed.

Figure 51 are baskets for carrying bottles.

Every well ordered cellar should be provided with graduated measures (figs. 52 and 53) in which to measure the respective proportions to be taken of each kind of wine for cutting. They

MISCELLANEOUS.

can be had of any desired capacity, and graduated decimally, or otherwise, as needed.

Fig. 51.

Bottle Baskets.

Fig. 52.

Fig. 53.

Graduated Measures.

Figure 54, instruments of tin for drawing from the bungs of casks in tasting.

In the sherry districts, where the casks are not kept full, a narrow cup attached to a stick is used to dip out the wine through the bung. The practice of using a piece of hose for this purpose, by letting one end into the cask and sucking on the other with the mouth till the wine runs, as it is done in too many cellars in California, is not to be commended to the fastidious.

A pump in the form of figure 55 is sometimes useful for drawing wine from casks in certain positions.

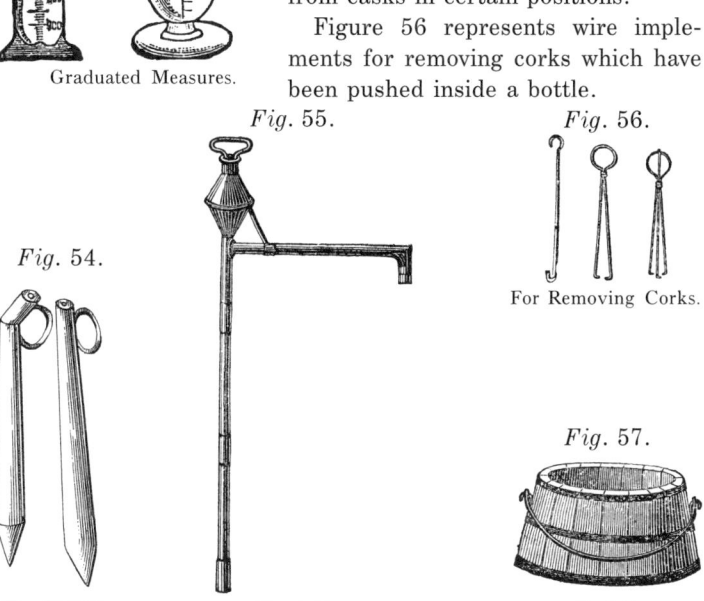

Figure 56 represents wire implements for removing corks which have been pushed inside a bottle.

Fig. 54.

Fig. 55.

Fig. 56.

For Removing Corks.

Fig. 57.

Tin Tasters.

Hand Pump.

Bucket

MISCELLANEOUS.

USEFUL RULES.

To Ascertain the Weight of a Given Number of Gallons of a Liquid, multiply 8.33 by the specific gravity of the liquid, and the product by the number of gallons. For instance, suppose we have 1000 gallons of a must which shows 22 per cent. sugar. From Table I we obtain the corresponding specific gravity, 1.0923 (the figure 1 is omitted except at the top of the column), which shows how much heavier it is than water, water being 1. Now, one gallon of water at 60° F. weighs 8.33 lbs., and the temperature of the must should be about the same. (See *Must— Testing for Sugar*.) 8.33 multiplied by 1.0923 = nearly 9.1, which is the weight in pounds of one gallon of the must. One thousand gallons would weigh nearly 9,100 lbs. If Beaumé's hydrometer is used, ascertain from Table II the specific gravity corresponding to the mark on the stem. This rule applies to all liquids whose specific gravity is known—syrup, wine, brandy, alcohol, etc.

The specific gravity of a wine of 12 per cent. is .9843, and by our rule, one gallon weighs about 8.2 lbs. a little less than a gallon of water.

Rule for Reducing Must from a higher to a lower percentage of sugar: Multiply the number of gallons of the must by its specific gravity, and the product by the difference between the given per cent. and the required per cent., and divide by the required per cent.

Suppose that we have 1000 gallons of a must of 27 per cent., how many gallons of water are required to reduce it to 23 per cent?

The specific gravity, by Table I, is 1.1154, and this multiplied by 1000 = 1115.4, which multiplied by 4, the difference between 27 and 23 = 4461.6, which divided by 23 gives 194 gallons, in round numbers.

Rule for Sugaring Must.—If crystallized sugar is used, dissolve it and make a strong syrup, or sugar water, and the proposition is: Given a must of a certain sugar per cent., and a syrup of a given per cent., how much of the syrup for each gallon of

MISCELLANEOUS. 207

must is required to produce a must of any required strength, between the two?

First—Multiply the required per cent. by the corresponding specific gravity.

Second—Multiply the per cent. of the must by its specific gravity.

Third—Multiply the per cent. of the syrup by its specific gravity.

Divide the difference between the first and second products by the difference between the first and third, and the quotient will be the fraction of a gallon required.

Suppose that we have a must of only 10 per cent. of sugar, and a syrup of 60 per cent.; how much of the second should be added to one gallon of the first to produce a must of 23 per cent.?

$$\frac{23 \times 1.0969 - 10 \times 1.0401}{60 \times 1.2899 - 23 \times 1.0969} = .284 \text{ of a gallon.}$$

Therefore, for every gallon of the must, we add 0.284 gallons of the syrup.

The same rule will apply to the mixing of a strong and a weak must.

Rules for Fortifying and Reducing Wines and Weak Liquors.—In mixing strong spirits, it is necessary to make an allowance for contraction, and tables are prepared for the purpose, but in mixing wines and weak spirits, it may be disregarded, and the following rules will be found sufficient.

To Reduce with Water.—Having a wine or a weak spirit of a certain per cent. of alcohol, how much water is required for each gallon to reduce it to any lower per cent.?

Divide the difference between the given per cent. and the required per cent., by the required per cent.

Suppose a wine or other alcoholic solution of 15 per cent. by volume, how much water is required for each gallon to produce one of 10 per cent.?

$$\frac{15-10}{10}=\tfrac{1}{2}$$

Therefore, add one-half gallon of water for each gallon of the wine or weak spirit.

To Reduce with Weaker Wine, or to Fortify with Stronger Wine or Alcohol.—Having two wines or other weak liquors whose percentages of alcohol are known, how much of the second is required for every gallon of the first, to produce a wine of any required strength between the two?

Divide the difference between the per cent. of the first, and the required per cent. by the difference between the per cent. of the second and the required per cent.

Having a wine, etc., of 18 per cent., and another of 8 per cent., how much of the second is required for every gallon of the first to produce one of 12 per cent.?

$$\frac{18-12}{12-8}=\frac{6}{4}=1\tfrac{1}{2}$$

Or one and one-half gallons of the second for every gallon of the first.

Or, suppose we have a wine of 15 per cent., how much brandy of 50 per cent. must be used for every gallon of the first to produce a wine of 20 per cent.?

$$\frac{20-15}{50-20}=\frac{5}{30}=\frac{1}{6}$$

Or one-sixth of a gallon of the brandy must be used for each gallon of the wine.

PLASTERING.

It is a Common Practice in Spain and in the southern part of France to plaster the wines, by adding more or less gypsum, or plaster of Paris. It is either thrown upon the grapes before or after crushing, or is added to the must. Gypsum is known to chemists, when pure, as calcium sulphate (sulphate of lime), but contains a certain amount of water of crystallization, and is generally found associated with other substances, such as rock salt, and calcium carbonate, or limestone. It is the commonest impurity found in spring water, and gives water its permanent hardness. Much has been written for and against the practice of plastering, and both sides of the question have strong advocates.

Objects.—There are many different reasons given for the practice, some of which are fanciful. It is claimed that it retards fermentation, and that red wines under its effects develop more color, because the marc can be left longer in the fermenting vat; that the froth of plastered wine is livelier and sooner disappears, which pleases the merchants; and that it has a preservative effect upon the wine. It is claimed by some that it renders the wine dryer and harsher, as it does, if used to excess, and by others, that it unites with a portion of the water of the juice, and renders the remaining juice richer in sugar. Again, it is added to neutralize a portion of the acid contained in the must.

Chemical Effects.—Maumené says that it transforms the potassium salts of the wine into insoluble lime salts and potassium sulphate, and this may have an important effect upon fermentation, for some chemists attribute to the acid potassium tartrate the property of holding ferments in solution, and that potassium sulphate, even with the freed tartaric acid, does not possess this power; that the carbonate of lime contained in the plaster, in neutralizing the acidity of the tartar, without doubt contributes to the precipitation of the ferment which this salt held in solution; and that during the neutralization, carbonic acid is disengaged, and the evaporation of the moisture carried up by the gas somewhat lowers the temperature. He supposes that all these causes combined retard the fermentation.

P. Carles (*J. Pharm. Chim.* [5], 6, 118-123), says that the calcium sulphate acts on the potassium bitartrate in the juice of the grape, forming calcium tartrate, tartaric acid, and potassium sulphate, a large proportion of the last two bodies remaining in the wine. That without plastering, wine contains about two grammes per litre of pure tartaric acid, whilst after plastering, it contains double or treble that amount, and even more, according to the quantity of potassium bitartrate decomposed.

In order to make clear what this chemist says, in ordinary language, we will say that the gypsum acts upon the cream of tartar in the grape juice, sets free a portion of the tartaric acid existing in combination in it, and also forms tartrate of lime and sulphate of potash.

At first sight, therefore, it would seem that the addition of gypsum, or plaster of Paris, actually increases the acid, and this would be true if the gypsum consisted of pure calcium sulphate, but it always contains more or less calcium carbonate, and this substance, which is but another name for chalk, limestone, or marble, precipitates the free tartaric acid, and the carbonate of lime does what is generally claimed for the gypsum—diminishes the acidity of the wine. But if the calcium carbonate does not exist in sufficient quantity in the gypsum to precipitate all the tartaric acid set free, the opposite effect would be produced. Why not add marble dust at once?

The experiments given in Thudichum and Dupré's work show that the amount of water withdrawn from must by the addition of even anhydrated plaster is so small as to be unworthy of notice, being only one-fourth the weight of the plaster used.

Effects on the Health.—This question was examined at Montpellier, in France, by a committee of chemists appointed by the court, and the results of their inquiries are frequently cited by those who are in favor of plastering:

1. That the plastered wine contains no new mineral substance.

2. That the quantity of plaster introduced into the wine may be considered null, because it is entirely changed into potassium sulphate, a slightly purgative salt, analogous in this respect to tartar.

Later, however, a commission was appointed by the *Conseil des Armées*, who reported as follows:

1. That by the taste, plastered wines could not be distinguished from the natural ones.

2. That plaster diminished the intensity of the color. (This, of course, refers to the direct effect.)

3. That the potassium bitartrate, one of the most useful principles contained in wine, is decomposed by plaster, and that potassium sulphate is formed, which remains in solution, and calcium tartrate, which is precipitated.

4. That potassium phosphate, also one of the salts naturally contained in wine, is equally decomposed by plaster.

5. That plastering profoundly modifies the nature of wines, by substituting for the potassium bitartrate a purgative salt in the proportion of from 3 to more than 7 grammes per litre.

And they demand the exclusion of all wine containing more than 4 grammes of the sulphate per litre.

And Mr. Carles, above quoted, concludes that, owing to the purgative effect of this salt, potassium sulphate, the quantity present should not exceed 2 grammes per litre, or half as much as the army commission allow.

Still later, we have the instructions of the Minister of Justice of France to the *procureurs Généraux*, issued in 1880, as follows:

After several judicial decisions relative to the sale of plastered wines, one of my predecessors expressed to the Minister of Agriculture and Commerce the desire that new experiments should be made in order to establish, if in the present state of science the immunity accorded to plastered wines by the circular of July 21, 1858, should be maintained.

Having examined the question, the consultation committee of public hygiene issued the following notice:

1. That the absolute immunity which plastered wines enjoy on account of the circular of the Minister of Justice dated July 21, 1858, ought no longer to be officially allowed.

2. That the presence of potassium sulphate in the wines of commerce, which results from plastering the must, from the mixture of plaster or sulphuric acid with the wine, or from cutting with plastered wines, should only be tolerated to the maximum limit of 2 grammes per litre (about 117 grains per gallon).

In calling my attention to this notice, my colleague of agriculture and commerce informs me that he completely concurs.

He, therefore, instructs the officers to prosecute, under the laws against adulterations, the dealers who shall sell wine containing more than the quantity indicated of potassium sulphate, as dangerous to the health of the consumers.

Plastering Sherry—Quantity Used.—Mr. Vizitelli says that during his stay at Jeres, he paid particular attention to the plastering question, saw the gypsum applied in almost a hundred instances, and questioned the overseers in scores of vineyards. He states that within his own knowledge gypsum is by no means invariably used in the vinification of sherry, as already stated under the head of *Sherry*. And although applied in the majority of cases, but a few pounds per butt are used, say 6 lbs. at most in a dry season, and a little more than double that quantity in years when great dampness prevails. And he argues from the Montpellier experiment, already mentioned, where the committee added 40 grammes of gypsum to a litre of wine, and found only 1.240 grammes of sulphate of potash per litre where pure calcium sulphate was used, and 1.828 grammes where ordinary plaster was employed, that when the Spaniards add the amount which they do to the must in sherry making, no injury to the wine can occur. It may be proper to suggest, however, for the benefit of future inquirers, that wine, after insensible fermentation, contains but a small proportion of the potassium bitartrate which was contained in the grape, the greater part of it having been deposited with the lees and the marc. Wines do not contain tartar enough to furnish 2 grammes per litre of potassium sulphate, nor enough to act upon 1 gramme of pure gypsum. But it is far otherwise with grape juice. Now 6 lbs. of gypsum to one butt of wine of 108 Imperial gallons would be the same as about 5.5 grammes per litre, and if pure, ought to produce, on being fully satisfied with the acid potassium tartrate, as much as 8 grammes per litre of potassium sulphate, and Mr. Carles, above quoted, says that it does amount to from 4 to 7.5 grammes per litre in plastered wines.

Supposing the following to be the correct reaction, 1 gramme of pure gypsum ought to produce, with 2.6 grammes of cream of tartar, 1.477 grammes of sulphate of potash; and to produce the 2 grammes per litre of the latter would only require 1.353 of the former; and but a little more than 1 lb. of pure gypsum could safely be added to 100 gallons of must:

$$Ca\ SO_4 + 2\ C_4\ H_5\ KO_6 = C_4\ H_4\ Ca\ O_6 + C_4\ H_6\ O_6 + K_2\ SO_4$$

As the gypsum is usually added to the pomace itself, or to the grapes before crushing, it is unsafe to argue from the effects produced by adding it to wine.

By Adding Water to must, the effects of plastering may be produced, if the water is hard by reason of the gypsum contained in it.

SHERRY FLAVOR.

In many California wines a flavor called the "sherry flavor" is often observed; and in the red wines may frequently be tasted what would with equal propriety be called a "port flavor;" and the "sherry flavor" would by some be called a "Madeira flavor."

Mr. Pohndorff stated at the State Viticultural Convention of 1882, that he was of the opinion that this flavor was due to the oxidation of the wine. If this is so, the remedy would be to use greater care in its management, and avoid exposing it to the air, in fact, observe just the treatment indicated in this book for all but sweet and fortified wines.

Without attempting to say anything authoritative on the subject, the author would suggest that in addition to the above cause, these flavors are largely due, *first*, to our hot climate; *second*, to over-maturity of the grapes; and *third*, to aging the wine in too high a temperature; for these conditions all exist in southern countries, whose wines are apt to have a peculiar flavor, called by some writers the "cooked flavor," which is unobjectionable in a sweet wine. The first is not always within the control of the producer, but the two last can always be controlled by the grape grower and the cellar-man.

APPENDIX.

TABLE I.

Balling's degrees (per cent. of sugar), corresponding degrees Baumé, and specific gravity at $63\frac{1}{2}°$ F.—Chas. Stammer.

Balling or per cent. sugar	Baumé	Specific Gravity	Balling or per cent. sugar	Baumé	Specific Gravity	Balling or per cent. sugar	Baumé	Specific Gravity	Balling or per cent. sugar	Baumé	Specific Gravity
1	.56	1.0039	26	14.35	.1107	51	27.71	1.2383	76	40.36	1.3894
2	1.11	.0078	27	14.90	.1154	52	28.24	.2439	77	40.84	.3959
3	1.67	.0117	28	15.44	.1201	53	28.75	.2495	78	41.33	.4025
4	2.23	.0157	29	15.99	.1249	54	29.27	.2552	79	41.81	.4092
5	2.78	.0197	30	16.53	.1297	55	29.79	.2609	80	42.29	.4159
6	3.34	.0234	31	17.07	.1345	56	30.31	.2666	81	42.78	.4226
7	3.89	.0278	32	17.61	.1393	57	30.82	.2724	82	43.25	.4293
8	4.45	.0319	33	18.15	.1442	58	31.34	.2782	83	43.73	.4361
9	5.00	.0360	34	18.69	.1491	59	31.85	.2840	84	44.21	.4430
10	5.56	.0401	35	19.23	.1541	60	32.36	.2899	85	44.68	.4499
11	6.11	.0443	36	19.77	.1591	61	32.87	.2958	86	45.15	.4568
12	6.66	.0485	37	20.30	.1641	62	33.38	.3018	87	45.62	.4638
13	7.22	.0528	38	20.84	.1692	63	33.89	.3078	88	46.09	.4708
14	7.77	.0570	39	21.37	.1743	64	34.40	.3138	89	46.56	.4778
15	8.32	.0613	40	21.91	.1794	65	34.90	.3199	90	47.02	.4849
16	8.87	.0657	41	22.44	.1846	66	35.40	.3260	91	47.48	.4920
17	9.42	.0700	42	22.97	.1898	67	35.90	.3322	92	47.95	.4992
18	9.97	.0744	43	23.50	.1950	68	36.41	.3384	93	48.40	.5064
19	10.52	.0787	44	24.03	.2003	69	36.91	.3446	94	48.86	.5136
20	11.07	.0833	45	24.56	.2056	70	37.40	.3509	95	49.32	.5209
21	11.62	.0878	46	25.09	.2110	71	37.90	.3572	96	49.77	.5281
22	12.17	.0923	47	25.62	.2164	72	38.39	.3636	97	50.22	.5355
23	12.72	.0969	48	26.14	.2218	73	38.89	.3700	98	50.67	.5429
24	13.26	.1015	49	26.67	.2273	74	39.38	.3764	99	51.12	.5504
25	13.81	.1061	50	27.19	.2328	75	39.87	.3829	100	51.56	.5578

OECHSLE'S MUST SCALE indicates specific gravity to three decimal places. When two figures are shown on the scale, a cipher before them must be understood. For instance: 83 means 1.083, or 20 per cent., Balling; and 106 means 1.106, or 25 per cent., Balling.

TABLE II.

Baumé's degrees, corresponding degrees, Balling (per cent. sugar,) and specific gravity at $93\frac{1}{2}°$ F.

Baumé	Balling or per cent. sugar	Specific Gravity	Baumé	Balling or per cent. sugar	Specific Gravity	Baumé	Balling or per cent. sugar	Specific Gravity	Baumé	Balling or per cent. sugar	Specific Gravity
0.0	0.00	1.0000	13	23.52	1.0992	26	47.73	1.2203	39	73.23	1.3714
0.5	0.90	.0035	13.5	24.43	.1034	26.5	48.68	.2255	39.5	74.25	.3780
1	1.80	.0070	14	25.35	.1077	27	49.63	.2308	40	75.27	.3846
1.5	2.69	.0105	14.5	26.27	.1120	27.5	50.59	.2361	40.5	76.29	.3913
2	3.59	.0141	15	27.19	.1163	28	51.55	.2414	41	77.32	.3981
2.5	4.49	.0177	15.5	28.10	.1206	28.5	52.51	.2468	41.5	78.35	.4049
3	5.39	.0213	16	29.03	.1250	29	53.47	.2522	42	79.39	.4118
3.5	6.29	.0249	16.5	29.95	.1294	29.5	54.44	.2576	42.5	80.43	.4187
4	7.19	.0286	17	30.87	.1339	30	55.47	.2632	43	81.47	.4267
4.5	8.09	.0323	17.5	31.79	.1383	30.5	56.37	.2687	43.5	82.51	.4328
5	9.00	.0360	18	32.72	.1429	31	57.34	.2743	44	83.56	.4400
5.5	9.90	.0397	18.5	33.65	.1474	31.5	58.32	.2800	44.5	84.62	.4472
6	10.80	.0435	19	34.58	.1520	32	59.29	.2857	45	85.68	.4545
6.5	11.70	.0473	19.5	35.50	.1566	32.5	60.27	.2915	45.5	86.74	.4619
7	12.61	.0511	20	36.44	.1613	33	61.25	.2973	46	87.81	.4694
7.5	13.51	.0549	20.5	37.37	.1660	33.5	62.23	.3032	46.5	88.88	.4769
8	14.42	.0588	21	38.30	.1707	34	63.22	.3091	47	89.96	.4845
8.5	15.32	.0627	21.5	39.24	.1755	34.5	64.21	.3151	47.5	91.03	.4922
9	16.23	.0667	22	40.17	.1803	35	65.20	.3211	48	92.12	.5000
9.5	17.14	.0706	22.5	41.11	.1852	35.5	66.19	.3272	48.5	93.21	.5079
10	18.05	.0746	23	42.05	.1901	36	67.19	.3333	49	94.30	.5158
10.5	18.96	.0787	23.5	42.99	.1950	36.5	68.19	.3395	49.5	95.40	.5238
11	19.87	.0827	24	43.94	.2000	37	69.19	.3458	50	96.51	.5319
11.5	20.78	.0868	24.5	44.88	.2050	37.5	70.20	.3521	50.5	97.62	.5401
12	21.69	.0909	25	45.83	.2101	38	71.20	.3585	51	98.73	.5484
12.5	22.60	.0951	25.5	46.78	.2152	38.5	72.22	.3649	51.5	99.85	.5568

TABLE III.

Baumé's degrees and corresponding per cent. of sugar at 60° F.

Baumé degrees	Sugar per cent.	Baumé degrees	Sugar per cent.	Baumé degrees	Sugar per cent.	Baumé degrees	Sugar per cent.
1	1.72	11	19.88	21	38.29	31	57.31
2	3.50	12	21.71	22	40.17	32	59.27
3	5.30	13	23.54	23	42.03	33	61.23
4	7.09	14	25.34	24	43.92	34	63.18
5	8.90	15	27.25	25	45.79	35	65.19
6	10.71	16	29.06	26	47.70	36	67.19
7	12.52	17	30.89	27	49.60	37	69.19
8	14.38	18	32.75	28	51.50	38	71.22
9	16.20	19	34.60	29	53.42	39	73.28
10	18.04	20	36.40	30	55.36	40	75.35

TABLE IV.

Showing the specific gravities of mixtures of alcohol and water, containing from 0.1 to 30 per cent. by volume, of absolute alcohol, and corresponding per cent. by weight, for every 0.1 per cent. by volume, compared with water at 60°F.
The specific gravity of absolute alcohol according to U. S. standard being .7939, referred to water at its greatest density as unity, or .79461, referred to water at 60° F.

Per cent. by volume	Per cent. by weight	Specific Gravity	Per cent. by volume	Per cent. by weight	Specific Gravity	Per cent. by volume	Per cent. by weight	Specific Gravity	Per cent. by volume	Per cent. by weight	Specific Gravity
0.1	0.08	.99986	3.8	3.04	.99460	7.5	6.02	.98974	11.2	9.03	.98530
0.2	0.16	.99972	3.9	3.12	.99445	7.6	6.10	.98961	11.3	9.11	.98519
0.3	0.24	.99957	4.0	3.20	.99431	7.7	6.18	.98949	11.4	9.20	.98508
0.4	0.32	.99943	4.1	3.28	.99417	7.8	6.26	.98936	11.5	9.28	.98497
0.5	0.40	.99929	4.2	3.36	.99403	7.9	6.35	.98924	11.6	9.36	.98486
0.6	0.48	.99915	4.3	3.44	.99388	8.0	6.43	.98911	11.7	9.44	.98475
0.7	0.56	.99901	4.4	3.52	.99374	8.1	6.51	.98899	11.8	9.52	.98463
0.8	0.64	.99886	4.5	3.60	.99360	8.2	6.59	.98886	11.9	9.60	.98452
0.9	0.72	.99872	4.6	3.68	.99346	8.3	6.67	.98874	12.0	9.69	.98441
1.0	0.80	.99858	4.7	3.76	.99332	8.4	6.75	.98861	12.1	9.77	.98430
1.1	0.88	.99844	4.8	3.84	.99317	8.5	6.83	.98849	12.2	9.85	.98419
1.2	0.96	.99830	4.9	3.92	.99303	8.6	6.91	.98837	12.3	9.93	.98408
1.3	1.04	.99815	5.0	4.00	.99289	8.7	7.00	.98824	12.4	10.01	.98397
1.4	1.12	.99801	5.1	4.08	.99276	8.8	7.08	.98812	12.5	10.10	.98386
1.5	1.20	.99787	5.2	4.16	.99263	8.9	7.16	.98799	12.6	10.18	.98375
1.6	1.28	.99773	5.3	4.24	.99250	9.0	7.24	.98787	12.7	10.26	.98364
1.7	1.36	.99759	5.4	4.32	.99237	9.1	7.32	.98775	12.8	10.34	.98352
1.8	1.44	.99744	5.5	4.40	.99224	9.2	7.40	.98762	12.9	10.42	.98341
1.9	1.52	.99730	5.6	4.49	.99211	9.3	7.48	.98750	13.0	10.51	.98330
2.0	1.60	.99716	5.7	4.57	.99198	9.4	7.57	.98737	13.1	10.59	.98319
2.1	1.68	.99702	5.8	4.65	.99186	9.5	7.65	.98725	13.2	10.67	.98308
2.2	1.76	.99688	5.9	4.73	.99173	9.6	7.73	.98713	13.3	10.75	.98297
2.3	1.84	.99673	6.0	4.81	.99160	9.7	7.81	.98700	13.4	10.83	.98286
2.4	1.92	.99659	6.1	4.89	.99148	9.8	7.89	.98688	13.5	10.92	.98275
2.5	2.00	.99645	6.2	4.97	.99135	9.9	7.97	.98675	13.6	10.10	.98264
2.6	2.08	.99631	6.3	5.05	.99123	10.0	8.05	.98663	13.7	11.08	.98253
2.7	2.16	.99617	6.4	5.13	.99110	10.1	8.14	.98652	13.8	11.16	.98242
2.8	2.24	.99602	6.5	5.21	.99098	10.2	8.22	.98641	13.9	11.24	.98231
2.9	2.32	.99588	6.6	5.29	.99086	10.3	8.30	.98630	14.0	11.33	.98220
3.0	2.40	.99574	6.7	5.37	.99073	10.4	8.38	.98619	14.1	11.41	.98209
3.1	2.48	.99560	6.8	5.45	.99061	10.5	8.46	.98608	14.2	11.49	.98199
3.2	2.56	.99546	6.9	5.54	.99048	10.6	8.54	.98597	14.3	11.57	.98188
3.3	2.64	.99531	7.0	5.62	.99036	10.7	8.62	.98586	14.4	11.65	.98178
3.4	2.72	.99517	7.1	5.70	.99024	10.8	8.71	.98574	14.5	11.74	.98167
3.5	2.79	.99503	7.2	5.78	.99011	10.9	8.79	.98563	14.6	11.82	.98156
3.6	2.88	.99488	7.3	5.86	.98999	11.0	8.87	.98552	14.7	11.90	.98146
3.7	2.96	.99474	7.4	5.94	.98986	11.1	8.95	.98541	14.8	11.98	.98135

TABLE IV.—Continued.

Per cent. by volume	Per cent. by weight	Specific Gravity	Per cent. by volume	Per cent. by weight	Specific Gravity	Per cent. by volume	Per cent. by weight	Specific Gravity	Per cent. by volume	Per cent. by weight	Specific Gravity
14.9	12.07	.98125	18.7	15.21	.97733	22.5	18.37	.97344	26.3	21.55	.96950
15.0	12.15	.98114	18.8	15.29	.97722	22.6	18.45	.97334	26.4	21.64	.96939
15.1	12.23	.98104	18.9	15.37	.97712	22.7	18.53	.97323	26.5	21.72	.96928
15.2	12.32	.98094	19.0	15.46	.97702	22.8	18.62	.97313	26.6	21.81	.96917
15.3	12.40	.98083	19.1	15.54	.97692	22.9	18.70	.97302	26.7	21.89	.96906
15.4	12.49	.98073	19.2	15.62	.97682	23.0	18.78	.97292	26.8	21.98	.96896
15.5	12.57	.98063	19.3	15.70	.97671	23.1	18.87	.97282	26.9	22.06	.96885
15.6	12.65	.98053	19.4	15.78	.97661	23.2	18.95	.97272	27.0	22.15	.96874
15.7	12.73	.98042	19.5	15.87	.97651	23.3	19.04	.97261	27.1	22.23	.96863
15.8	12.82	.98032	19.6	15.95	.97641	23.4	19.12	.96251	27.2	22.32	.96853
15.9	12.90	.98021	19.7	16.04	.97631	23.5	19.20	.97241	27.3	22.40	.96842
16.0	12.98	.98011	19.8	16.12	.97620	23.6	19.29	.97231	27.4	22.48	.96832
16.1	13.06	.98001	19.9	16.20	.97610	23.7	19.37	.97221	27.5	22.57	.96821
16.2	13.14	.97990	20.0	16.29	.97600	23.8	19.45	.97210	27.6	22.65	.96810
16.3	13.22	.97980	20.1	16.37	.97590	23.9	19.54	.97200	27.7	22.74	.96799
16.4	13.31	.97969	20.2	16.45	.97580	24.0	19.62	.97190	27.8	22.82	.96789
16.5	13.39	.97959	20.3	16.54	.97569	24.1	19.71	.97180	27.9	22.91	.96778
16.6	13.47	.97949	20.4	16.62	.97559	24.2	19.79	.97170	28.0	22.99	.96767
16.7	13.55	.97938	20.5	16.70	.97549	24.3	19.87	.97159	28.1	23.07	.96756
16.8	13.63	.97928	20.6	16.79	.97539	24.4	19.96	.97149	28.2	23.16	.96745
16.9	13.71	.97917	20.7	16.87	.97529	24.5	20.04	.97139	28.3	23.24	.96733
17.0	13.80	.97907	20.8	16.95	.97518	24.6	20.13	.97129	28.4	23.33	.96722
17.1	13.88	.97897	20.9	17.03	.97508	24.7	20.21	.97118	28.5	23.41	.96711
17.2	13.96	.97887	21.0	17.12	.97498	24.8	20.29	.97108	28.6	23.50	.96700
17.3	14.05	.97876	21.1	17.20	.97488	24.9	20.38	.97097	28.7	23.58	.96689
17.4	14.13	.97866	21.2	17.28	.97478	25.0	20.46	.97087	28.8	23.67	.96677
17.5	14.21	.97856	21.3	17.37	.97467	25.1	20.55	.97076	28.9	23.75	.96666
17.6	14.29	.97846	21.4	17.45	.97457	25.2	20.63	.97066	29.0	23.84	.96655
17.7	14.38	.97835	21.5	17.53	.97447	25.3	20.71	.97055	29.1	23.93	.96644
17.8	14.46	.97825	21.6	17.62	.97437	25.4	20.80	.97045	29.2	24.01	.96632
17.9	14.54	.97814	21.7	17.70	.97427	25.5	20.88	.97034	29.3	24.10	.96621
18.0	14.62	.97804	21.8	17.78	.97416	25.6	20.97	97023	29.4	24.18	.96609
18.1	14.71	.97794	21.9	17.87	.97406	25.7	21.05	.97013	29.5	24.27	.96598
18.2	14.79	.97784	22.0	17.95	.97396	25.8	21.13	.97002	29.6	24.35	.96587
18.3	14.87	.97773	22.1	18.03	.97386	25.9	21.22	.96992	29.7	24.44	.96575
18.4	14.96	.97763	22.2	18.12	.97375	26.0	21.30	.96981	29.8	24.52	.96564
18.5	15.04	.97753	22.3	18.20	.97365	26.1	21.39	.96970	29.9	24.61	.96552
18.6	15.12	.97743	22.4	18.28	.97354	26.2	21.47	.96960	30.0	24.69	.96541

The basis of the foregoing table is Table III of the U. S. Manual for Inspectors of spirits, giving the respective volumes of absolute alcohol and water in 100 volumes of spirits of different strengths, for every 0.5 per cent. by volume, and the specific gravities, referred to water at 60° F.

TABLE V.

Variety of Wine.	Name of Contributor.	Locality.	Vintage.	Color of Wine.	Alcohol, vol. per ct.	Acid as tartaric.
Mission, just ripe	Dr. J. Strentzel	Martinez	1880	White	10.0	.5370
" " "	"	"	"	Red	8.5	.5400
" fully "	"	"	"	White	12.8	.3490
" " "	"	"	"	Red	13.3	.3300
"	George West	Stockton	1881	White	11.9	.6690
"	"	"	"	Red	12.6	.5590
"	Prof. G. Husman	Napa ?	1880	White	13.0	.4297
"	I. De Turk	Santa Rosa	1881	"	11.9	.3900
"	"	"	"	"	13.1	.4500
"	Chas. Lefranc	San Jose	1873	Red	12.0	.4245
"	J. DeBarth Shorb	San Gabriel	1881	White	15.2	.7395
"	"	"	1878	"	12.4	.4897
"	I. De Turk	Santa Rosa	1881	"	12.0	.5347
"	George West	Stockton	"	"	14.9	.7020
Black Prince	"	"	1880	Red	15.2	.6450
"	Chas. Krug	St. Helena	"	White	16.7	.4270
Malvoisie (Malvasia?)	"	"	"	Red	14.5	.2460
"	R. Hasty	Clayton	1881	White	13.8	
"	G. Husman	Napa ?	"	Red	14.0	.4635
"	"	Napa ?	1878	White	13.5	.5430
"	T. F. Eisen	Fresno	1880	"	13.7	.6622
Zinfandel	"	"	"	"	17.2	.5197
"	Chas. Krug	St. Helena	"	Red	12.6	.6000
"	Geo. West	Stockton	1881	White	12.9	.3900
"	"	"	"	Red	14.1	.4200
"	Gundlach & Co	Sacramento		"	14.3	.4370
"	I. De Turk	Santa Rosa	1879	"	11.9	.6750
"	"	"	1881	"	13.4	.6495
"	G. Husman	Napa ?	"	"	13.2	.6750
"	I. De Turk	Santa Rosa	1880	"	13.2	.4777
"	"	"	"	"	12.7	.6900

Variety of Wine.	Name of Contributor.	Locality.	Vintage.	Color of Wine.	Alcohol, vol. per ct.	Acid as tartaric.
Zinfandel	B. Dreyfus & Co			Red	12.4	.7170
Charbono	General Naglee	San Jose	1880	White	8.1	.4750
"	"	"	"	Red	6.5	.4420
"	J. T. Doyle	Santa Clara Co. ?		"	12.5	.4320
Mataro	Chas. Lefranc	San Jose	1880	White	14.1	.4245
"	"	"	"	"	12.4	.5250
Grenache	"	"	1876	Red	11.6	.7920
"	"	"	1881	"	12.5	.3450
California Burgundy	"	"	"	"	10.8	.7500
Lenoir	H. W. Crabb	Oakville	1881	"	11.1	.8070
"	"	"	"	"	11.9	.5145
Chasselas	J. Gundlach	Sonoma	"	White	13.5	.6337
"	"	"	"	with skins	11.7	.6495
"	"	"	"	White	13.5	.3375
Rose Chasselas	Dresel & Co		1881	"	13.0	.3720
Golden Chasselas	G. Husman	Napa ?	"	with skins	12.4	.5925
Riesling	Chas. Krug	St. Helena		White	12.5	.6180
"	Dresel & Co	Sonoma		"	12.9	.6750
"	B. Dreyfus & Co		1880	"	13.6	.8325
"	J. De Barth Shorb	San Gabriel	"	"	12.6	.7522
"	Kramp & Bro	Diamond Springs		"	13.1	.6825
Blanc Elba (Elbling?)	J. De Barth Shorb	San Gabriel	1881	"	10.6	.5625
Feher Szagos	G. Eisen	Fresno	"	with skins	10.2	.5250
"	"	"	"	White	14.5	.6750
Prolific	Geo. West	Stockton	"	with skins	15.6	.5347
"	"	Stockton	"	White	13.3	.6187
Sauvigon Vert	Chas. Lefranc	San Jose	1875	"	9.0	.5620
Burger	Chas. Krug	St. Helena	1880	with skins	9.2	.5250
"	"	"	"	White	11.5	
Elvira	R. Hasty	Clayton		"	11.9	.5145
"	H. W. Crabb	Oakville	1881	"	14.1	.5475
"	Kramp & Bro	Diamond Springs	1880			

APPENDIX. 221

Variety of Wine.	Name of Contributor.	Locality.	Vintage.	Color of Wine	Alcohol vol. per ct.	Acid as tartaric.
Malaga	T. F. Eisen	Fresno	1877	White	14.6	.6525
"	"	"	1881	"	17.9	.2175
Madeira	B. Dreyfus & Co			"	18.2	....
Muscat	I. De Turk	Santa Rosa	1876	"	11.5	.5775
"	T. F. Eisen	Fresno	1881	"	16.7	.5325
"	"	"		"	17.2	.2250
Port, Zinfandel	"	"	1878	Red	18.4	.3450
"	"	"	1875	"	21.0	.4957
Port	J. De Barth Shorb	San Gabriel	1881	"	22.1	.3525
"	"	"		"	22.9	.2048
Port, Tenturier	T. F. Eisen	Fresno	1875	"	18.8	.3975
Angelica	J. De Barth Shorb	San Gabriel	1881	White	18.3	.3825
"	"	"		"	21.8	.1448
Sherry (Feher Szagos)	T. F. Eisen	Fresno	1877	"	18.8	.3600
" dry	"	"	1878	"	16.1	.5550

Where the name of the locality is followed by (?), it was omitted from the report.

Averages.—In thirteen Mission wines: Alcohol—maximum, 15.2; minimum, 8.5; average, 12.2. Acid—maximum, .7395; minimum, .3300; average, .4955.

In seven Malvoisie wines: Alcohol—maximum, 17.2; minimum, 13.5; average, 14.77. Acid in six—maximum, .6622; minimum, .2460; average, .4769.

In ten Zinfandel wines: Alcohol—maximum, 14.3; minimum, 11.9; average, 13.07. Acid—maximum, .7170; minimum, .3900; average, .5731.

In four Riesling wines: Alcohol—maximum, 13.6; minimum, 12.5; average, 12.6. Acid—maximum, .8325; minimum, .6180; average, .71.94.

In four Port wines, including two Zinfandel: Alcohol—maximum, 22.9; minimum, 18.4; average, 21.1. Acid—maximum, .4057; minimum, .2048; average, .3270.

INDEX.

	Page.
Acetic acid	194
fermentation	30
Acid in California wines.	x, 220
in European wines	xii
increased by stems	20
in wine	x, xi, xii, 193, 220

see acetic, carbonic, citric, tartaric, malic, pectic, tannic, salicylic, lactic, valeric, succinic and plastering.

Acidity, disease, see sourness.
  in casks..................... 65
Acquired defects and diseases...... 137
Acrity......................... 149
  in bottles.................... 167
Adjustable hoop, see utensils.
Aerating must 23
  stirring pomace 42
  see treading, air, influence of.
  port wine..................... 112
Age, effect on wine 51, 52
Aging wine—effect of various influences...................... 76
  general considerations........ 76
  requisite to make agreeable and healthful 76
  care to age and preserve...... 76
  new wine..................... 76
  different wines require different periods 76
  development of bouquet and flavor 76

	Page.
Aging wine, old wine, characteristics of	76
color, aroma and flavor	77
influences which develop, also destroy	77
influences on weak wine and strong wine	77
influence of the air, see aerating.	77
variations of temperature	78
influence of heat	78
aging by heat	79
preserving by heat	80
influence of cold and frozen wines	81
influence of light	82
aging by sunlight, insolation	82
effect of motion and voyages	82–84
wines suitable for shipment	82
aging by fining	84
generally	84
fine before aging	84
what wines gain the most by the processes	85
heating Maderia	113

see casks, size of
Air, influence of 77
  see port, aerating
Albumen, see fining.
Alcohol in California wines.. ix, x, 220
  in European wines............ xii
  relation to sugar 11, 28, 34
  required in dry wine.......... 11
  to keep wine sweet.58, 59, 106, 107
  in aging by heat 80

INDEX.

	Page.
Alcohol required in aging by sunlight	82
for shipping wines	82
by weight and by volume	33
burning to arrest fermentation	74
lost by evaporation	112
natural in sweet wines	105
adding in fining	102
to sweet wines	105, 106, 107
to port	111, 112
to sherry	117, 123
to Madeira	114
see rules.	
amount in port	112
in Madeira	115
in sherry	123
estimation of	187
limits by fermentation	36
Alcoholic weakness	133
fermentation, see fermentation.	
Aldehyde	30
Almonds, bitter, see bouquet, artificial	
Analysis of dry lees	176
Areometer	7
Aroma, see bouquet.	
Arresting fermentation	72
see sulphuring, sulphurous acid..	
by burning alcohol	74
aqueous sulphurous acid	74
bisulphite of lime	74
salicylic acid	75
Arrope	119
Artificial must	14
Balling's saccharometer	7, 8, 9
Barrels, see casks.	
Barrel flavor	145
Basket, decanting	169
bottle	205
Bastardo grape, see port.	
Basto, see sherry.	

	Page.
Baumé's saccharometer	7, 8
Bins for bottles	164
Bisulphite of lime	74
Bitartrate of potash, see cream of tartar	
Bitter almonds, see bouquet, artificial.	
Bitterness	131, 149
in bottles	167
Blending, see cutting.	
sherry	122
Blood, see fining.	
Blotting paper, see fining.	
Bluish wines	134
Boiling must	106
Borers of casks	66
Bottles, wine in, bottling, etc., see wine in bottles.	
washer, drainers	156
piling	163
racks and bins	164
baskets	205
Bouquet, short vatting promotes	44
development of, by age	76, 77
how lost	77
generally	194
artificial	194
substances used	196
iris	196
strawberry	197
gillyflower, stock gilly	197
vine flowers	198
mignonette	198
nutmeg	198
bitter almonds and fruit pits	198
sassafras	198
other aromas	199
effects	199
Brandy, shipments of California	vi
casks, empty	66
casks for	66
Bung turned to one side	51, 53
screw	158

INDEX.

	Page.
Butyric fermentation	29
California, prices of grapes	vi
exports of wine and brandy	vi
product of wine	vi
wines, alcohol and acid in	ix, x, 220
wines compared	ix, x, 220
musts	viii
Capsules and capsuling	162
Carbonic acid produced by fermentation	34
in wine	193
Carbon dioxide, see carbonic acid.	
Casks	61
redwood	61
oak, different kinds, principles contained in	61
temper with new wine	61
storing	61
sulphured before storing	62
new, preparing, washing	62
old, washing	63
to remove lees, rinsing chain	63
to examine inside, visitor	63
wash empty ones at once	64
do not leave in the sun	64
examine to ascertain condition	64
leaky, to expel bad air	64
flatness in, acidity in, mouldy	65
rottenness	66
brandy, do not sulphur	66
for brandy	66
oil casks	66
which have contained aromatic liquors	66
borers	66
size of	67
see different wines.	
large, preferable	67
why sulphured	69
how sulphured	70
caution in sulphuring	71

	Page.
Casks, filling from vats	45
of new wine loosely closed	48
must be kept full	48
bung to one side, old wine	51, 53
for white wine	55
small for sweet, large for dry	55
filling during fermentation of white	55
see froth, racking.	
flavor	145
how long wine to remain in	154
supporting and arranging	89
implements for tipping	95
Cellars	87
temperature	87
dampness, floors	88
ventilation, evaporation	88
other precautions	89
supporting and arranging casks	89
for port	112
for sherry	118
utensils	204
Cement for corks, see wax.	
Centres, see white wine.	
Chain for washing casks	63
Charcoal to remove sulphur flavor	74
deprives wine of color and carbonic acid	74
Citric acid	193
Clarification, clarifying powders, see fining.	
Cleanliness about wine making	94, 203
Climate of sherry districts	115
Coal, see charcoal.	
Cold, influence of on wine	81
Color, increased by long vatting	44
dark, not necessary to fine wines	44
precipitated by sulphur	71
by blood	101
removed by charcoal	74
changed by age	77

INDEX.

	Page.
Color affected by light	82
heat and motion	83
weakened by fining	99
want of	134
dull, bluish, lead-colored wines	134
see port, tawny.	
wine, see sherry.	
Coloring matter in red wine	39
Composition of wine	185
cream of tartar	185
not composed of alcohol and water alone	185
alcohol, acid, and sugar generally	185
table of substances recognized	186
alcohol and estimation of	187
stills for and operation	187
monitor still	190
ethers	190
sugar and estimation	190
mannite	191
mucilage and mellowness	191
pectose, pectin	192
Composition of wine	185
fatty matters	192
glycerin	192
coloring matter, œnocyanine	192
aldehydes	192
acids	193
tartaric	193
malic	193
citric	193
pectic	193
tannic	193
carbonic	193
acetic	194
lactic	194
butyric	194
valeric	194
succinic	194
total	194

	Page.
Composition of wine, bouquet, natural and artificial	194
Copper affected by wine	202
Corks	158
preparation of	160
sealing for	161
utensils to remove, see utensils.	
Corking machines, corking	159, 160
Corkscrews	169
Cream of tartar, see plastering, lees, composition of wine, fining.	
Crushing and methods of	22
aerating must by	23
Crushing and stemming, rapidity	24
special practice in the Médoc,	24
effect of	24
dry grapes	108
Crushers	23
Cutting wines	171
most French wines mixed	171
when necessary, effect	171
tithe wines, singular case	171
no precise rules	171
mix wines of same nature	173
fine wines	173
ordinary wines	174
time must be allowed	174
quantity to mix	174
mixing new and old wines	174
green wine	174
white and red wine	175
diseased wines	125, 126, 175
mixing grapes	175
precaution	175
Dampness, see cellars.	
Decanting wine from bottles	188
basket	169
instrument	169
Decomposition of wine, see diseases.	

INDEX.

	Page
Defects and diseases	125
division, general considerations	125
better avoided than cured	125
not always cured by mixing	126
doses in treating	126
natural defects	126
earthy flavor and causes	126
how prevented, treatment	127
wild taste, grassy flavor	128
greenness and causes	128
how prevented, treatment	129
roughness	130
not a fault, disappears in time	130
to avoid excess of tannin	130
how removed	131
bitterness and causes in new wine	131
how prevented, treatment	131
stem flavor	131
sourness and causes	132
how prevented, treatment	132
alcoholic weakness	133
how avoided, treatment	133
want of color and causes	134
how guarded against, treatment	134
dull, bluish, lead-colored wine, flavor of lees, and causes	134
how avoided, treatment	135
putrid decomposition and causes	136
how avoided, treatment	137
several natural defects combined	137
acquired defects and diseases	137
flat wines, flowers, and causes	137
prevention	138
treatment	139
sourness, acidity, pricked wine and causes	140
what wines liable to	140
how prevented, treatment	141

	Page.
Defects and diseases, pricked wine, experiments with substances in treating	142
Machard's treatment	144
other methods	144
cask flavor, barrel flavor, and causes	145
treatment	146
mouldy flavor	147
prevention, treatment	147
foreign flavors	147
ropiness, causes and treatment	148
in bottled wines	148, 167
other treatment	148
acrity and treatment	149
in bottles	167
bitterness	149
treatment	150
according to Maumené	150
in bottles	167
fermentation, taste of the lees, yeasty flavor	151
how prevented, treatment	152
in bottles	165
degeneration, putrid fermentation	87, 152
in bottles	167
duration of different wines	152
treatment	153
deposits and turbidity in bottles	166
Degeneration of wines	87, 152
see diseases.	
Density of sweet wines	107
musts, see musts, different wines, sugar.	
Deposits, see diseases, lees, wine in bottles.	
Diseases and defects	125
Drainers for bottles	156
Drawing off, see racking.	
from vats	43, 44, 45

228   INDEX.

	Page.
Dry grapes, crushing	108
wines, see white, red, treatment casks for	55
Dull-colored wine	134
Duration of different wines	152
of fermentation, see fermentation, different wines.	
Earthy flavor	126
Echaud	151
Effervescent wines not to be sulphured	71
Eggs, see fining.	
Empty casks, see casks.	
Estufa, see Madeira, heating house.	
Ethers	190
European wines, alcohol and acid in	xii
Evaporation of wine in cellars	88
weakens wine	112
see casks, size of.	
Event, éventé, see flatness.	
Exports of California Wine and brandy	vi
Exportation, see shipping.	
Fatty matters in wine	192
Ferments, origin of	31
destroyed by heat	81
see yeast, *saccharomyces*.	
Fermentation, its causes	25
kinds of	25
alcoholic generally	25
yeast plant, *saccharomyces cerevisiæ*	25
functions of yeast	26
normal conditions of the life of	26
surface and sedimentary	26
physical conditions, temperature	27

	Page.
Fermentation, chemical conditions	27
action of various chemical and physical agents	28
viscous or mannitic	29
lactic	29
butyric and putrefactive	29, 136, 152, 167
acetic, aldehyde	30
mycoderma aceti, mother of vinegar	30
mycoderma vini, flowers of wine.	31
origin of ferments	31
alcoholic, in wine making	32
sugar, cane, grape or glucose	32
alcohol by weight and by volume	33
its products, per cent. sugar to per cent. alcohol	34
different authors	34
limits of sugar and spirit	36
temperature	37
surrounding vats with straw	37
fermenting houses	38
duration of in red wine	44
in white wine	93
insensible	47, 48
arresting, see sulphuring, arresting.	
by burning alcohol	74
aqueous solution of sulphurous acid	74
bisulphite of lime	74
salicylic acid	75
increased by stems	20
by open vats	40
slow in closed vats	40
under pressure and not so complete	42
disease	151, 165
in bottles	165
see white wine, filling casks, different wines, plastering, effects of.	

INDEX. 229

	Page.
Fermenting houses	38, 109
tanks or vats	39, 41, 108
material, size, number, arrangement of	39
surrounding with straw	37
filling	39, 40, 108
open, closed	40
best practice	41
hermetically sealed, cooled with condenser	42
practice in the Médoc	42
stirring pomace in	42, 108
drawing from	43, 44
Filling vats	39, 40
casks from vats	45
during fermentation of white wine	55
see froth, ulling.	
Filtering, see fining.	
Fining	99
when necessary, objects of	99
best avoided unless necessary	91, 99
caution	99
substances employed	99
which act mechanically, blotting paper, fine sand, powdered stone	99
filtration	99
substances which act chemically and mechanically	99
gelatinous substances	99
gelatine proper	100
its preparation	100
isinglass, fish glue, ichthyocol	100
its preparation	100
adding cream of tartar for white wine	100
albuminous substances	101
blood, milk	101
white of eggs	101
the fining for red wine	101

	Page.
Fining, clarifying powders	102
gum arabic	102
addition of salt	102
addition of alcohol	102
addition of tannin	102
method of operation	103
implements for stirring	103
time necessary for	103
new wines	50
sweet wines	106
sherry	124
to age wine	84
before aging	84
wines extracted from lees	179, 180
Finings, see fining.	
leaving wine on	91, 104
Fino, see sherry.	
Fish Glue, see fining.	
Flatness, influence of air	78
in casks	65
Flat wine	137
Flavor developed by aging	76, 77
how lost	77
causes of change of	77
sulphur, causes and removal	73
foreign	147
barrel, cask	145
sherry, madeira, port	213
fruity, see fruity flavor.	
Flowers on wine	31, 77, 118, 137
Fortified wines, see sweet wines.	
Fortifying, see alchol.	
rule for	208
Foul casks	64
French wines generally mixed	171
alchol and acid in	xii
Froth in filling a cask	104
Frozen wine	81
Fruity flavor, how lost	50, 52, 99
preferred by *gourmets*	84
Fruit pits, see bouquet, artificial.	

230 INDEX.

Funnels, see utensils.
Furmint wine 107

Gallons of must per ton of grapes
.... 200, 201
 of wine per ton of grapes 201
 of liquid, weight of 206
Galvanized iron affected by wine.. 203
Gas in empty casks.............. 64
Gathering grapes, maturity, utensils 1
 number of pickers............ 1, 12
 when to commence 1
 time of, successive gathering.... 2
 before complete maturity....... 4
 after complete maturity........ 5
Gelatine, see fining.
General treatment of table wines.. 86
 sweet wines 105
 see different wines
Gillyflower, see bouquet, artificial.
Glass, materials in 157
Gleucometer, gleuco-oenometer.... 8
Glucose, must 6
 for a gallon of wine........... 16
 cost of glucose wine........... 16
 effect on Burgundy............ 14
 experiment................... 17
 use condemned 17
 name of user published 18
 grape sugar, generally.......... 32
Glue, fish, see fining
Glycerine, produced by fermentation 34
 in wine................. 186, 192
Gourmets, wine preferred by...... 84
Gout d'évent, see flatness.
 de travail 151
Graduated measures, see utensils.
Grand wines should not be aged
 artificially................... 84
 see different practices and treatment, red wine, white wine.

Grapes, prices in California v
 Mission..................... v
 picking..................... 1
 see gathering, maturity.
 sorting 3
 tons stemmed and crushed in a
 day 24
 gallons of wine per ton of...... 201
 juice, see must.
 per cent. of stems in different... 201
 sugar....................... 6, 32
Grassy flavor................... 128
Green wine, mixing 174
Greenness 128
Gum arabic, see fining.
Gypsum, see plastering.

Head wines, see white wines.
Heat, influence on wine......... 78
 aging by.................... 79
 preserving by................ 80
 destroys ferment germs 81
 see fermentation.
Heating Madeira................ 113
Hoop, adjustable, see utensils.
Houses, fermenting 38, 109
Hydrometer................. 7, 8, 9
 tables, see appendix.
Hygienic effects of red and white
 wine........................ 54

Ichthyocol, see fining.
Implements, see utensils.
Influences, effect of various on wine 76
 which develop, also destroy..... 77
Ingredients in wine, see composition.
Insensible fermentation 47
 when finished................ 48
Insolation, see sunlight.
Iris, see bouquet, artificial.
Iron affected by wine........ 202, 203
Isinglass, see fining.

INDEX. 231

	Page.
Juice, grape, proportion to marc	200
see must.	
Lactic fermentation	29
acid	186, 194
see milk, fining.	
Lagar, see port, sherry.	
Lead affected by wine	202
Lead-colored wine	134
Leaky casks, see casks.	
Lees, marc, piquette	176
residues often put in the still	176
wine	176
should not be neglected	176
quantity of wine contained in	176
contents of dry parts, analysis	176
composition varies	176
treatment of	177
wine should not be left long in contact with	178, 180
except sweet	106
casks for, barreling	177
sulphuring, storing, ulling	177
how often to draw wine from	178
from diseased wine, put by themselves	178
extracting wine from with siphon	178
extracting wine from with faucet	179
fining wine extracted from	179
wines from lack color, difficult to clarify	180
red wine from, to fine	180
white wine from, to fine	180
pressing thick sediment	180
sacks for	181
press for	181
applying pressure	182
to remove from casks	63
use of dry	182

	Page.
Lees, flavor of	134, 151, 165
see racking, fining, etc.	
marc or pomace, piquette	182
unfermented and partly fermented pomace	183
fermented marc	183
Pezeyre's method of washing	183
deposits	86, 166
Light, influence on wine	82
port	112
aging by	82
Liqueur wines, see sweet wines.	
Liquid, to ascertain weight of	206
Lime, bisulphite	74
see diseases.	
Loss by evaporation, see cellars, casks, size of.	
Madeira	113
making, casks, treatment	113
adding alcohol	113
heating, heating houses	113
general treatment	114
solera system, ullage	114
alcoholic strength	115
flavor	213
Malic acid	186, 193
Mannite	186, 191
Mannitic fermentation	29
Marc of sweet wine, use of	107
passing wine over	139
proportion of juice to	200
see lees, marc, piquette.	
Matches, sulphur	70
Matters in wine, see composition.	
Maturity of grapes	3
signs of	4
gathering before complete	4
gathering after complete	5
according to required strength	5
for port	108

	Page.
Maturity for sherry	115
of wine, see white, red wine, aging.	
Maumené's sulphurer	69
Mellowness, how lost	52, 84
cause of	191
see white, red wine.	
Measures, graduated, see utensils.	
Metal utensils, wood preferable	202
affected by wine	202
Middle wines, see white wines, *centres*	
Mignonette, see bouquet, artificial.	
Milk, see fining.	
Miscellaneous chapter	200
Mission grape	v
Mixing pressings	45, 47
see red, white, port.	
wines, see cutting.	
Monté, vin	151
Mother of vinegar	30
Motion, effect of, aging	82, 84
shipping	83
Mouldy casks	65
flavor	147
Mucilage	186, 191
Muscat, sweet	107
Must, composition of	6
grape sugar, glucose	6
scale, saccharometer	7, 8
testing for sugar	8
proper amount of sugar	11, 12
sugaring	13
nothing gained by	15
artificial	14
cost of	16
glucose, experiment with	17
condemned	17
watering	18
when allowable	16
aerating	23, 43
rule for reducing	206

	Page.
Must, why sulphured	69
unfermented, sulphuring	72
clarifying, care of	72
prepared in two ways	72
proportion of to marc	200
shipping	83
of sweet wine	57, 58, 105
of dry white wine, density	56
of mellow wine	57, 58
of port	108
boiling	101
per ton of grapes	201
California	viii
Musty, see mouldy.	
Mute wine	72
Mycoderma aceti	30
Mycoderma vini	31
see flowers.	
Natural defects	126
New red wine, treatment of	47
summary of rules	50
white wine	58, 60
wine differs from old	76
influence of heat	78, 79
shipping	83
see racking, fining.	
Nutmeg, see bouquet, artificial.	
Oakwood, see casks, vats.	
Oechsle's must scale	7, 8, 9, 10
Oenocyanine	192
Old red wine, treatment	51
characteristics	52, 76, 77
wine. influence of heat	78, 79
see racking, albuminous substances, fining.	
Oloroso, see sherry.	
Passing wine over marc	139
Pedro Jimenes grape	119

INDEX. 233

	Page.
Pectic acid	193
Pectin	192
Pectose	192
Pèse sirop, pèse mout	7
Picking grapes	1
see gathering.	
Piling bottles	163
Piquette, see lees, marc, piquette.	
Pitchers, see utensils.	
Plastering	208
common in Spain and South of France	208
objects	209
chemical effects	209
effects on health	210
report of committee at Montpellier	210
of *conseil des armées*	211
instructions of French Minister of justice	211
sherry and quantity added	115, 212
chemical reaction	213
by adding water	213
Pomace, per cent. in different grapes	200, 201
see lees, marc, piquette.	
stirring in vat	42
Port wine	108
must, fermentation, maturity of grapes	108
filling lagar, stirring, drawing off, sorting grapes	108
treading	109
Vizitelli's description	109
adding alcohol	111, 112
storing, racking	111
storehouses	112
mixing	112
loses color in wood	112
alcoholic strength of	112
becomes weaker by evaporation	112

	Page.
Port wine, flavor	213
Pousse	151
Powdered stone, see fining.	
Powders, clarifying, see fining.	
Preserving by heat	80
Pressing and press wine, red	47
white wine	56
sweet wine	107
sediment	180
see different wines.	
Pressings, mixing, different	46, 47
Presses, wine	46
for lees	181
Prices of grapes in California	v
Pricked wine	140
Proportion of juice to marc	200
wine to grapes	201
Pumps	97, 98
hand, see utensils.	
Putrefaction, putrid fermentation, decomposition	29, 87, 136, 152, 167
Queues, see white wine.	
Racking, objects of	91
first time	91, 92
leaving wine on finings	91
rules for	91, 92
new red wines	50, 92
before shipping	50
old red wine	51, 53, 93
new white wine	93
subsequent rackings	60, 93
care to be observed, other precautions	94
lees must not be disturbed	94
different methods	95
by bucket and funnel	95
implements for tipping cask	95
without contact with air	97
pumps and siphons	97
see different wines.	

INDEX.

Racks for bottles 164
Rancio flavor caused by heat 80
    in bottles 167
Red wine...................... 39
    coloring matter 39
    fermenting tanks, or vats, filling same...................... 39
    open vats, closed vats 40
    best practice 41
    hermetically sealed vats........ 42
    practice in the Médoc.......... 42
    stirring pomace in vat......... 42
    souring of the crust 43
    when to draw from vats........ 43
    duration of fermentation 44
    objections to long vatting, fine wines 44
    how to know when to draw from vats....................... 45
    method of drawing from vats, filling casks 45
    wine presses.................. 46
    pressing and press wine........ 47
    practice for fine wines 47
    treatment of new.............. 47
        insensible fermentation 47
        storing new 48
        tasting, filling up or ulling... 48
        summary of rules for treatment of...................... 50
    of old 51
    characteristics of age 51, 52
    grand and common characteristics 52
    how soon bright 52
    summary of rules for 53
    hygienic effects of............. 54
    how differs from white 54
    should be sparingly sulphured... 71
    fining, see gelatine............100
        see blood, milk, white of eggs.101
        red wine extracted from lees..180

Red wine put in colored bottles...157
    with earthy flavor.............128
    see racking, fining, etc.
Reducing must and wine, see rules.
Redwood, see casks, vats.
Rinsing chain for casks.......... 63
Ripeness, signs of............... 4
    see maturity.
Ropiness, viscous fermentation 29, 148. 167
Ropy wines should not be sulphured 71
Rotten casks 66
Roughness.....................130
    improved by aging............ 85
Rules to ascertain weight of liquid.206
    for reducing must.............206
    for sugaring must.............206
    for fortifying and reducing wine.207
        to reduce with water........207
        weaker wine 208
        to fortify with stronger wine or alcohol...............208

Saccharometer................. 7, 8
Saccharomyces cerevisiæ.......... 25
    conditions of life.............. 26
    action of chemical and physical agents..................... 28
    destroyed by heat and alcohol .. 81
Sacks for pressing lees...........181
Salt in clarifying, see fining.
Salicylic acid................... 75
Sand, see fining.
Sassafras, see bouquet artificial.
Sealing wax for casks...........161
    to remove 162
Sea voyage, effect of, see aging.
Seeds should not be broken in crushing.................... 23

INDEX. 235

	Page.
Seeds, tannin from	103
yield fatty matters	192
Settling and skimming must for white wine	75
Sherry	115
climate, vintage, crushing gypsum	115
pressing	116
stemming, fermenting, racking	117
fortifying	117, 123
casks in ullage and open	117
a nearly dry wine	118
bodegas or storehouses	118
seasoned casks alone used	118
changes in the wine	118
fino, oloroso, basto	118
flowers	118
vino dulce, or sweet wine, and preparation	119
vino de color, or color wine, and preparation, *arrope*	119
mature wine	120
solera system	120
establishing a solera	120
standard soleras	121
drawing the wine	122
blending for shipment	122
formulas, fining	123
influence of air	78
flavor	213
Shipments of wine and brandy from California	vi
Shipping, rack before	50, 106
wine suitable for	12, 82
new wine or must	83
Shot, do not clean bottles with	156
Siphons	97
of glass	178
to clean	95
Skimming and settling must (white wine)	55

	Page.
Smoothness increased by pressure	42
Solera, see sherry.	
Sorting grapes	3, 108
for grand white wines	57
Sour casks	65
Sourness	132, 140
Spirit, see alcohol, see tables in appendix.	
Stems, effect on fermentation	20
how to remove	22
when to ferment with	20, 21
increase tannin	20, 21
when to remove	20, 21
effect of too long contact	21
flavor	, ...21, 44, 131
per cent. in different grapes	201
Stemmers	21
Stemming, diversity of opinion	20
effect of	20
proper practice	20
see sherry	117
and crushing	20
rapidity of operation	24
special practice	24
Stills, assay	187, 190
Stirring implements, fining	103
pomace, see aerating, treading, vats, port.	
Stockgilly, see bouquet, artificial.	
Stone, powdered, see fining.	
Storing casks	61
wine, see different wines, cellars.	
casks for	67
Straw wines	108
Strawberry, see bouquet artificial.	
Substances in wine, see composition.	
Succinic acid	34, 194
Sugar, grape	6
testing for in must	8
in wine	190
correction for temperature	10

236   INDEX.

	Page.
Sugar and alcohol	11, 34
in must of dry wines	11, 12, 56
sweet wines	57, 105
weight of for a pound of alcohol.	16
for a gallon of wine	16
crystalized, purity of	16
and glucose generally	32
limits of in fermentation	36
necessary to growth of yeast	27
not all converted by first fermentation	45
to increase in grapes	105
in must, to reduce, rules	206
see must, tables in appendix.	
Sugaring and watering must	13
carried too far	13
effect on burgundy	14
artificial must	14
nothing gained by sugaring	15
cost of glucose wine	16
experiment with glucose	17
glucose condemned	17
rule for sugaring	206
watering	18
rule for	207
Sulphur matches or bands, how made	70
flavor, how caused	73
how removed	74
Sulphurer or sulphur burner	69
Sulphuring casks	62, 69, 70
caution	71
partly empty	73
wine	69, 71
when to avoid	71
from lees	177
must	69, 72
white wine to arrest fermentation	69, 72
Sulphurous acid	69
arrests fermentation in two ways	69

	Page.
Sulphurous acid, aqueous solution of	74
see acetic fermentation	31
Sunlight, influence on wine	82
aging by	82
Sweet, fortified, liqueur wines	105
defined	105
sweetness of must for	57, 105
natural alcohol in	105
increasing sugar in grapes	105
without fermentation	105
care required	105
alcohol necessary to keep	105
fining, rack before shipping	106
boiling must	106
to be kept on lees	106
sweet muscat	107
pressing	107
marc, use of	107
alcohol, amount to add	107
density of	107
Furmint wine	107
straw wines	108
should not be sulphured	71
influence of heat, aging	79, 80
of sunlight	82
casks for	55
see air, influence of, heat, influence of, red wine, white wine, port, Madeira, sherry.	
Table wines, see treatment.	
of substances in wine	186
of sugar, density, alcohol, hydrometers, see appendix.	
Tail wines, see white wines.	
Tanks, see fermenting tanks.	
Tannin increased by stems	20, 21
how to know if sufficient	21
excess of, how avoided	130
how removed	100, 131

INDEX.

	Page.
Tannin, when added in fining	102
tannic acid	102, 193
use and proportions	102
from the vine preferred	103
how prepared from seeds	103
from stems	103
tannified wine	103
soaking seeds in wine	103
Taré, vin	151
Tartaric acid	193
see wine, California, European, acid in.	
Tasters, see utensils.	
Tawny color by age	77
see old wine.	
flavor by heat	80
in bottles	167
Temperature, correction for in sugar testing	10
effect on yeast	27, 81
in fermentation	37
variation of, aging	78
see heat, cellars, hydrometers.	
Testing for sugar in must	8
in wine	190
Têtes, see white wines.	
Tin, affected by wine	203
Tipping casks, implements for	95
Tithe wines, see cutting.	
Tourné, vin	151
Travail, goût de	151
Treading in vat	42, 109
crushing	22, 109, 113, 116
aerating must	23, 43
Treatment, general, of table wines	86
sweet wines	105
deposits, lees	86
degeneration	86
of Madeira	113
of wine in bottles	165
see different wines, cellars, racking, fining, aging, etc.	

	Page.
Tubes to clean	95
Tuns, see casks, cellars.	
Turbidity in bottles	166
see lees, deposits, etc.	
Ulling the casks	48
utensils for	49
Unfermented must	72
clarifying, care of	73
Unfortified wines, see treatment.	
Utensils, wooden or metal	202
effect of wine on metals	202
cleanliness necessary	203
different cellar	204, 205
pitchers of tin and wood	204
wooden vessels	204
wooden funnels	204
adjustable hoop	204
bottle baskets	205
graduated measures	205
tin tasters	205
hand pump	205
for removing corks	205
for stirring, fining	103
for ulling	49
bung screw	158
bottle washer	156
bottle drainers	156
reservoir for filling bottles	157
corking machines, needles	159, 160
to remove wax	162
capsuler	162
bottle racks and bins	164
decanting basket	169
instrument	169
corkscrews	169
presses, wine	46
lees	181
sacks for pressing lees	181
for tipping a cask	95
rinsing chain	63

238 INDEX.

	Page.
Utensils, visitor to examine casks	63
crushers	23
for racking	95, 96, 97
for picking grapes	1
Variations of temperature, aging	78
Valeric acid	194
Vats, see fermenting vats.	
Vatting, long, effects of	44
Ventilation, see cellars	88
Vessels, see utensils.	
Vine flowers, see bouquet, artificial.	
Vin de liqueur, see sweet wines.	
monté, taré, tourné	151
dulce, see sherry.	
Vinegar, mother of	30
see acetic acid, acetic fermentation.	
Vineyards, acreage of in California	vi
Vinification, essentials the same everywhere	vii
Vinous fermentation, see alcoholic fermentation.	
Viscous fermentation	29
Visitor to examine casks	63
Voyage, effect on wine, see aging.	
Water, necessary to growth of yeast	27
Watering must	18
when allowable	19
rule for	206
wine, rule for	207
Wax for sealing corks	161
how removed	162
Weakness in alcohol	133
Weight of a liquid, to ascertain	206
Whip for stirring	103
White of eggs, see fining.	
White wine	54
from red and white grapes	54
how differs from red	54

	Page
White wine, hygienic effects	54
process of making	55
settling and skimming	55
to keep sweet	55
to make dry	55
barrels for	55
filling barrels during fermentation	55
pressing and filling casks	56
different kinds of	56
dry white wines	56
mellow white wines	56
sweet white wines	57
see sweet wines.	
grand white wines	57
ripening the grapes, *pourris*	57
têtes, centres, queues, head, middle, tail	57
treatment of	58
density of must to keep sweet	58
dry wines	59
mellow wines	59
summary of rules, racking	60
sulphured to keep from turning yellow	69, 71
bleached with sulphur	71
with blood, milk	101
fermentation arrested by sulphuring	72
fining, see gelatine	100
isinglass	100
white of eggs, blood, milk	101
extracted from lees	180
with earthy flavor	128
matures earlier than red	155
mixing with red	175
in transparent bottles	157
Wild taste	128
Wine, California, shipments	vi
product	vi
alcohol and acid in	ix, x, 220
European, alcohol and acid in	xii

INDEX. 239

	Page.
Wine making, essentials everywhere the same	vii
plastering	208
grand and common, characteristics	52, 84
red, maturity of	52
new, treatment of	47
old, treatment of	51, 53
see red wine.	
why sulphured	69
how sulphured	71
when to be sulphured	71
effect of heat	78, 79, 80
varies in different casks	67
dry strength of	11
constantly undergoing changes	76
influence of heat	78
preserving by heat	80
weak, see influence of air.	
heat, sunlight, see aging.	
suitable for shipment	82
shipping new	83
kinds preferred by *gourmets*	84
which gain most by aging processes	85
diseased, see defects and diseases.	
what liable to sour	140
duration of	152
lees, see lees.	
from lees, see lees.	
composition of	185
proportion of to grapes	201
rules for reducing and fortifying	207
mixing, see cutting.	
bad, often due to want of cleanliness	203
should not be left on the lees and finings	178, 180
unless sweet	106
presses	46

	Page.
Wine, tannified	103
see aging, white wine, red wine, sweet, fortified, new wine, old wine, grand wine, general treatment, frozen wine, the different kinds.	
Wine in bottles, bottling	154
when ready for bottling	154
how long to remain in wood	154
how prepared for bottling	155
most favorable time for	155
bottles, washing, bottle washer, etc	156
shot must not be used	156
draining, drainers	156
rinsing with wine	156
sorting	157
different kinds	157
materials in glass	157
filling, adjusting casks, etc	157
reservoirs for	157
corks	158
corking machines, needles	159, 160
preparing the corks	160
how far inserted	160
sealing corks	161
sealing wax for, how made, how applied	161
coloring the wax	161
capsules and capsuling	162
pincers for removing wax	162
capsuler	162
piling bottles	162
bottle racks and bins	164
treatment of wine in bottles	165
fermentation in the bottles	165
deposits, turbidity	166
bitterness, acrity, ropiness	167
degeneration and putridity	167
decantation	168
corkscrews, baskets	169

	Page.
Wine in bottles, operation of decanting	169
decanting instrument	169
Wood, wine, how long to remain in	154
Wooden utensils preferable	202
Yeast plant	25
functions of	26
surface and sedimentary	26
conditions of life, physical and chemical	26
temperature	27

	Page.
Yeast plant, action of chemical and physical agents	28
water, sugar, oxygen, etc., necessary	27
origin of ferments	31
Yeasty flavor, see lees, flavor of.	
Yellows, see white wine, sulphuring.	
Yield of juice by different grapes	200
wine per ton of grapes	201
Zinc affected by wine	202, 203

AFTERWORD

The Robert Mondavi Institute for Wine and Food Science offers this 125th-anniversary edition of E.H. Rixford's *The Wine Press and the Cellar* with pride and pleasure. We hope that its practical advice and simple charm will inspire a new generation of wine lovers, and might even be helpful to some modern winemakers.

I am particularly pleased and honored that this book will debut in 2008—the centennial of the University of California, Davis—during the opening celebrations for the Robert Mondavi Institute. The Rixford book inaugurates a series of books that will be produced on an occasional basis, made possible by the generous philanthropic support of an anonymous donor.

The goal of this edition has been to reproduce *The Wine Press and the Cellar* with beauty and exactitude, and its form is the result of a series of careful decisions. For example, we found original bindings of Rixford's book in a variety of colors, from which we have chosen green. The cover artwork is taken from a particularly fine copy at UC Davis—the only one with the handsome endpapers that we have reproduced here. The type has been reset to match the original as closely as possible. Page, paragraph and line breaks—as well as typographical errors—have been preserved.

The illustrations presented a real challenge. Our first idea was to reproduce them directly from the 1883 edition of *The Wine Press and the Cellar*, in all their rough charm. But during our research we discovered that nearly all of the illustrations came from books in Rixford's personal library: Raimond Boireau's *Culture de la Vigne*, M.W. Maigne's *Nouveau Manuel Complet* and Henry Vizetelly's *Facts About Sherry*. Today, these very books—a gift to UC Davis from Rixford's son, Halsey (1888-1964)—are at UC Davis' Peter J. Shields Library. This circumstance presented us with the compelling possibility of reproducing the originals from the originals! We could not resist taking advantage of this serendipitous opportunity.

As a result, we were able to reproduce forty-nine of Rixford's fifty-seven "figures" directly from his own source material, with two exceptions. The illustrations from his Boireau had been meticulously removed and pasted back into place. But his source for figure 32 appears to have been damaged when Rixford had his copy of Boireau rebound. Figure 39 (from Vizetelly) had been removed but never replaced. For these, we have used the best copies of Boireau and Vizetelly available. The only illustration requiring any modification was figure 20, from Rixford's copy of Boireau. Here, we have deleted the French branding that appears on the Boireau original, just as Rixford did 125 years ago. The sources for the rest of Rixford's illustrations (including figures 1, 2, 4, 5, 6, 44, 52 and 53) remain a mystery. We have reproduced these from the 1883 edition of *The Wine Press and the Cellar*.

We are deeply grateful to Paul Draper for his insightful foreword. We are indebted to the indefatigable Daryl Morrison, John Skarstad and Axel E. Borg at the Peter J. Shields Library, UC Davis, for their expertise. We also wish to acknowledge Susan Snyder, The Bancroft Library, University of California, Berkeley; David Burkhart; Charles L. Sullivan; Bob Mullen, Woodside Vineyards; Robert Zerkowitz, the Wine Institute, San Francisco; the San Francisco History Center, San Francisco Public Library; and the California History Room, California State Library, Sacramento.

This special edition was produced by Will Suckow, Will Suckow Illustration & Design, Sacramento.

Clare M. Hasler
Executive Director
Robert Mondavi Institute for Wine and Food Science
College of Agricultural and Environmental Sciences
University of California, Davis
August 2008

E. H. Rixford, 1880,

—Inscription from Rixford's personal copy of Maigne's *Nouveau Manuel Complet*